The Complete ECAA Guide

The Complete ECAA Guide

For the New 2020 ECAA Specification

By

Dipanshu Gandhi, Aryan Jain and Rishi Shah

Great Britain, 2020

First Paperback Edition July 2020.

ISBN: 9798658865225

Independently published

Website: sapienteducation.co.uk

Email: contact@sapienteducation.co.uk

Table of Contents

About the ECAA

The Economics Admission Assessment (ECAA) is an examination taken by applicants for Economics at the University of Cambridge. This test is at the end of October/early November, prior to your interview.

The ECAA specification was updated on the 22nd of June 2020, the new specification focuses solely on mathematics and your economics essay writing ability. What Cambridge is looking to identify is your analytical and mathematical rigour in thinking, this is especially true in the essay where each college marks your essay. They want to understand how you approach and breakdown the question. If a candidate's method of thinking is strong, they are very teachable which is what any university is looking for, your teachability rather than your current level of knowledge. The ECAA is designed to cause even the best of students with impeccable academic records to trip up, they need to differentiate the strong candidates and the candidates which will end up at Cambridge and the ECAA is their first port of call, followed by an interview.

What has changed within the new specification?

The new ECAA altogether removes the problem-solving aspect, and it has also removed logic from the mathematical requirements for the test. The revised ECAA moves towards a heavier emphasis on mathematic rigour and essay writing, with increased lengths for these sections. A strong foundation in mathematics is deemed crucial for an undergraduate degree in Economics and these changes further cement this statement, therefore it is essential to develop a comfort within mathematics.

Format

Section 1 (60 minutes):

40 multiple-choice mathematics questions split into two parts.

i.	Part A Mathematics	(20 questions)
ii.	Part B Advanced Mathematics	(20 questions)

The University recommends you split your time evenly between both sections. One important consideration is results for each part will be reported separately. Answers for this section will be marked on a separate answer sheet, this will be a machine-readable bubble answer sheet. There is no allowance for a calculator or a dictionary here, and answers must be filled out using an HB pencil.

Section 2 (60 minutes):

A passage of 1-2 pages in length will be presented, and you will be asked to write an essay in relation to the question, drawing on material in the passage and any other ideas that they consider relevant. There is no allowance for a calculator or a dictionary here, and answers must be filled out using a black pen, we recommend going with a biro or a smudge-resistant pen to keep your work legible.

Where do I sit the ECAA?

The ECAA can only be taken at a Cambridge authorised test centre, for most candidates this will be their school, however, we recommend checking with the staff in your current school in advance to prevent issues. Authorised test centres can be found on the Cambridge Assessment Admissions Testing's website.

How do I register for the ECAA?

The test centre at which you have decided to take your exam will have to register you as a candidate, the deadline for registration is 15th October in your final year of school, this is the same day as the deadline to submit UCAS for Oxbridge and medical science subjects. The ECAA is not an examination that has an associated entry cost.

When will I receive my scores?

Cambridge Assessment Admissions Testing nor the University of Cambridge will notify you of your score until the entire admissions process has been completed, and your confirmation of application status provided. However, ECAA scores can be provided as part of your application's feedback process. Note, this does vary by college and the system may change every year, hence we recommend that you further consult the University of Cambridge Admissions Office.

What scoring system does the ECAA use?

Each section mark is allocated a grade on the scale of 1.0-9.0, the test marks are allocated along this scale using a modified Rasch distribution such that 4.0 is the average mark achieved by candidates. While there is no good score, as Freedom of Information data has shown candidates on either end of the spectrum can be rejected or accepted, a higher score is always deemed better.

What is the significance of the ECAA?

Economics at Cambridge is one of the most respected courses in the UK, and the world, therefore it draws heavy competition. Of the students that apply, the vast majority have been predicted or have achieved a majority of A* grades at A-Level or equivalent, the ECAA is used as a tool to help the Admissions Tutors ascertain who are the best students. You should see the ECAA as another method to quantifiably show the University of Cambridge, Admissions Tutors, and College Director of Studies' that you are the most suited candidate for the course.

When is the correct time to begin preparation for the ECAA?

We recommend to start preparing for the ECAA around June/July time, you should focus on familiarising yourself with all of the mathematical concepts we mention in this book, and ensure your A-Level/IB or equivalent mathematical knowledge is complete. Our guidance would be to polish your knowledge of these topics by the end of August, such that you begin using this textbook for practice for the ECAA exam you will sit at the end of October/early November.

How should I use this book?

We recommend solidifying your mathematical foundations by the start of September on all of the topics included in the specification, and then working through this book once, making note of any questions you solved incorrectly, noting down the reasoning for your mistake (this is outlined in our Mathematics Questions Study Tips). After you have completed the book once, go through it once again this time solely focussing on questions you incorrectly answered initially, or you marked as tough. If you have the time, going through the book in its entirety for a third time is also highly recommended, as the more comfortable you are with the content, the more natural the ECAA exam will feel.

ECAA Key Tips

Before the Exam

- It is best to start revising early, in the summer before Year 13. This will ensure you have enough time to learn all the topics in the specification, build up your speed in answering and practise as much as you can
- Read through the ECAA specification, on the Cambridge website, to ensure that you have thoroughly prepared for every examinable topic.
- Speed is particularly important in the ECAA, therefore, practise on becoming faster and faster at maths, such as by learning tips, tricks, and shortcuts to increase your speed. Secondly, mental maths is key, therefore, practise doing long calculations in your head, even if it is simply adding up a list of numbers or multiplying two-digit numbers together.
- Practice makes perfect, therefore, gain exposure to a wide range of questions, and the fact that you are reading this book means you have made the correct first step! In addition to attempting all the questions in this book, here is a list of a range of other sources that provide multiple-choice maths questions:
  1. The "Mathematics" section from the Cambridge engineering entrance exam (ENGAA)
  2. The "Mathematics" section from the Cambridge Natural science entrance exam (NSAA)
  3. Section 1 of the MAT test paper
  4. Paper 1 and Paper 2 of the TMUA Cambridge entrance exam
  5. Finally, the actual ECAA past papers that are found on the Cambridge Admissions testing website.
- Practise the above questions under time conditions, to build up speed and accuracy. Some of the sources provide questions harder than you will find in the ECAA, so do not be disheartened if they seem challenging, and equally, note that some of the sources provide questions easier than in the ECAA
- The ECAA is designed to test your mathematical and essay-writing skills under time pressure, such that the admissions team can gauge "how you think". It is important to remember, however, that the ECAA is just one component of the full picture, with the interview, personal statement and teacher reference among other things being crucial aspects.

Multiple-choice questions study tips

1. If there are x options, remember $x - 1$ of them are wrong, eliminate these options to ensure your answer is correct.
2. Always understand your mistakes, this is essential to see changes in your quality of performance. Mistakes usually can be classed in the following four categories; we recommend you categorise your mistakes as you mark them to fully benefit.
   a. Content Weakness
   b. Timing Issues
   c. Understanding of the question
   d. Careless Mistake
3. Read the entire question carefully, often in multiple-choice small changes are added to the question to trip up candidates.
4. Always look back at answers in the context of the question.
5. Eliminate answers you know to be wrong; this is not always possible but often will help.
6. Use the process of elimination to increase the probability of correctly answering a question, particularly in time crunches.
7. Read every option carefully, there will be subtle differences designed to only catch the eye of the most attentive candidate.
8. When you come across "All of the above" and "None of the above" answer choices, do not select "All of the above" if you are confident any one of the answers provided is incorrect. The same applies for "None of the above" if you are confident that at least one of the answer choices is true.
9. When two or more answers are correct in a multiple-choice and an 'All of the above' option is available, then remember to choose it.
10. When practising questions, specifically graph-based questions envision the graph and draw it out, use online graphing tools to check your technique.
11. Entrance exams do not negatively mark, it is always better to make an educated guess than to leave an answer blank.
12. If a question has you perplexed, do not waste precious time, instead move on and return, often your thinking would have reset and now the answer will become clear.

13. Watch for qualifiers; these are words that make an absolute statement. They tend to make an answer false. Be wary of words such as always, never, none, and every, which may indicate a false response.

During the exam

- If a question is too long or complex, then do not spend too long on it and move on. But circle the question or make a note to return to it after you have finished. Spending too long on one question may prevent you from finishing the paper. Each correct answer has equal mark weighting, therefore, there is no use in getting bogged down into one question
- Use the fact that all questions are multiple-choice to your advantage! Before solving the question, try and eliminate a few options. If you cannot solve a question, then first eliminate any answers you know to be wrong, and this will increase your probability of guessing correctly
- It is best to pace yourself steadily throughout the exam and finish the last question at the end of the time limit. Spend an equal length of time on all questions, and if you cannot solve one in the allotted time, move on!

After the exam

The test is meant to be challenging! Do not be disheartened if you struggled in the paper, that just means the ECAA functioned as it was designed to. It is meant to differentiate between students who are remarkably similar in all aspects, such as top GCSE grades, therefore you should not expect to find it simple.

The following section is a detailed revision guide for the Mathematics (M) and the Advanced Mathematics (AM) parts of the specification. We have gone line-by-line in the specification, with the numbered bullet point writing out what the specification states, and then underneath each point, we have written in detail all the necessary content.

In areas which are more straightforward and basic, we have not included excessive detail as we assume it is standard knowledge, but for the more complex topics, we have given a lot of detail, to best prepare you for the ECAA.

The Maths Section

ECAA Maths Guide

300 Maths Questions

300 Fully Worked Solutions

Mathematics Content

M1 Units

1. Standard and compound units
   - Mass is commonly measured in kilograms
   - Length is commonly measured in millimetres, centimetres $(10mm)$, metres $(100cm)$ or kilometres $(1000m)$
   - Time is commonly measured in seconds
   - Money is commonly measured in pounds, but questions can use exchange rates, which represent how many pounds are exchanged to get one unit of a foreign currency
   - Speed is commonly measured in meters per second (ms^{-1})
   - Rates of pay could include ideas such as the national minimum wage which is $£ \, x \, per \, hour$
   - Density is commonly measured in kilogram per cubic metre
   - Pressure is commonly measured in pascals, which is $\frac{N}{m^3}$

2. Converting between units in numerical and algebraic contexts
   - You can convert between standard and compound units, by applying the correct maths operation to a given value.

M2 Number

1. Ordering real numbers and understanding basic symbols
   - Understand the symbols: $=, \neq, <, >, \leq, \geq$. Respectively, these are "equal, not equal, strictly less than, strictly greater than, less than or equal to and greater than or equal to".

2. Applying the four operations to real numbers in any form and using place value
   - Place value can be used to form more complex questions. The order is:
     - "hundreds, tens, units, tenths, hundredths, thousandths"
   - Any number can be written as the sum of individual place values parts. For the three-digit number abc, such as 756, where $a = 7, b = 5 \, and \, c = 6$, this can be written as $100a + 10b + c$, where it is broken up into its place value parts.

3. Range of concepts relating to factors
   - **Prime Numbers**: a number that is only divisible by itself and one
   - **Factors**: a number, that when multiplied by another number produces a given expression. E.g. 5 is a factor of 15
   - **Multiples**: a number that can be divided by another number, to produce a given expression without a remainder
   - **Common factors**: factors which are common between any two given numbers
   - **Highest common factor**: the highest number that can be divided into each of two or more numbers
   - **Lowest common multiple**: the lowest number that is a multiple of two or more numbers
   - **Prime factorisation**: breaking down a number into a list of prime numbers that multiply to form that number, commonly derived using a prime factor tree

4. Relations between operations, using cancellations to simplify working and BODMAS
   - A common factor that is present in all terms of the numerator and denominator of a fraction can be cancelled out.
   - When applying operations in a calculation, start by expanding or simplifying any brackets first. Then deal with orders (indices, powers, roots, and reciprocals), followed by division, multiplication, addition and finally subtraction.

5. Systematic listing strategies
   - If there are a ways of completing task 1 and b ways of completing task 2, then there are ab ways of completing both tasks

6. Root notation
   - Square is x^2, where you multiply a number by itself
   - Square root is $\sqrt{x}$, which reverts a square number to its square root
   - Cube is x^3, where you multiply a number by itself twice
   - Cube root is $\sqrt[3]{x}$, which reverts a cube number to its cube root
   - A square root gives two answers, one positive and one negative, such as $\sqrt{4} = \pm 2$. The positive value is called the positive square root, and the negative value is called the negative square root

7. Index laws
   - For any given number, written in index form, to be a square number it must have an even power and to be a cubic number it must have powers all divisible by 3
   - $a^m \times a^n = a^{m+n}$
   - $a^m \div a^n = a^{m-n}$
   - $(a^m)^n = a^{mn}$
   - $a^{-m} = \frac{1}{a^m}$
   - $(\sqrt[n]{a})^m = a^{\frac{m}{n}}$

8. Standard index form
   - Standard form is written as $a \times 10^n$, where a is always between $1 \leq a < 10$, a single-digit number, and n can be any integer (can be positive or negative)
   - To add or subtract in standard form, you can convert to ordinary decimal numbers and perform the operation. Alternatively, adjust "a" in one of the numbers (multiplying or dividing it by 10), such that both numbers are written with the same power of ten, and then add or subtract the decimals.
   - To multiply and divide in standard form, you respectively multiply or divide the "a" value from each number, and then add or subtract the indices "n", to find the power of 10.
     - $(a \times 10^n)(b \times 10^m) = ab \times 10^{n+m}$
     - $\frac{(a \times 10^n)}{(b \times 10^m)} = \frac{a}{b} \times 10^{n-m}$

9. Converting between terminating or recurring decimals, percentages and fractions
   - A percentage can be converted to a fraction by multiplying by 100, as a percentage is just the number given divided by 100.
   - A terminating decimal can be converted into a fraction, as any number right of the decimal point is simply a fraction with a denominator of 10, 100, 1000 or 10000 and so on, depending on the number of digits.
   - A recurring decimal can be converted into a fraction in two ways, as shown below.

Method 1:

- Firstly, you can let $x =$ the recurring decimal
- Then depending on the order of the recurrence, you find a second expression. If it recurs on an order of 1, such as $5.1111 \dots$, then find the expression for $10x$, in this case, $51.111 \dots$ If it recurs on an order of 2, such as $5.1212 \dots$, then find the expression for $100x$, in this case, $512.1212 \dots$
- Then, you subtract the first expression $x =$, away from the second expression $10x$ or $100x =$. As the recurring decimals occur identically in both the expression, the recurring values are removed.
- Rearrange for x and this will derive the fraction that is equal to the recurring decimal.

Method 2:

- Any recurring decimal is the sum of an infinite geometric series of fractions. You can find the sum to infinity of this convergent geometric series, $\frac{a}{1-r}$, to give the fraction.
- For example, $5.232323 = 5 + 0.23 + 0.0023 + 0.000023 = 5 + (0.23 + 0.0023 + 0.0023 \dots)$

- The expression in the brackets is an infinite convergent geometric series, with the values $a = 0.23$ and $r = \frac{1}{100}$.
- The expression $\frac{a}{1-r} = \frac{0.23}{1-\frac{1}{100}} = \frac{23}{99}$

10. Using fractions (including equivalent), decimals and percentages
    - It is useful to know the key conversions between fractions, decimals and percentages. For example, 3.962×2.322 is roughly equal to 4×2.3333, which is $4 \times \frac{7}{3} = \frac{28}{3} = 9.33$.
    - For many percentage problems, you can start at the value 100 and work through the changes from there to get to a final value

11. Calculating and simplifying with fractions, surds, and multiples of π
    - Surds are irrational numbers and multiple rules can be used with surds:
        - $\sqrt{ab} = \sqrt{a} \times \sqrt{b}$
        - $\sqrt{\frac{a}{b}} = \frac{\sqrt{a}}{\sqrt{b}}$
        - Rationalising the denominator: $\frac{1}{\sqrt{a}} \times \frac{\sqrt{a}}{\sqrt{a}}$ $\qquad \frac{1}{a+\sqrt{b}} \times \frac{a-\sqrt{b}}{a-\sqrt{b}}$ $\qquad \frac{1}{a-\sqrt{b}} \times \frac{a+\sqrt{b}}{a+\sqrt{b}}$

12. Using upper and lower bounds
    - Upper bound: the highest value that would round down to give a given value
    - Lower bound: the lowest value that would round up to give a given value
    - For example, for the number 5, the bounds are $4.5 \leq x < 5.5$.
    - For a fraction, the largest positive value is when the numerator is the largest possible positive bound and the denominator is the smallest possible positive bound. The smallest value of a fraction is when the numerator is the smallest possible positive bound and the denominator is the largest possible positive bound.

13. Rounding numbers to an appropriate degree of accuracy
    - You can round a number to cover a range of possible values.
    - Significant figures can be used, such that, they are the number of digits in a value contributing to the degree of accuracy. It begins at the first non-zero digit.
    - If there are zeros after the decimal point before non-zero numbers, then they are not significant. Any non-zero number is always significant. Zeros after non-zero numbers are significant
        - 5300 has 2 significant figures
        - 3021.20 has 6 significant figures
        - 0.024 has 2 significant figures

14. Using approximations in calculations (in those involving surds or π)
    - $\sqrt{2} \sim 1.4$ $\quad \sqrt{3} \sim 1.7$ $\quad \sqrt{5} \sim 2.2$, which is useful to know as there is no calculator in the ECAA
    - If you want to know what is bigger a surd or an integer, you can square both sides: If we wanted to compare the value $3\sqrt{3}$ to 4: $3\sqrt{3} > 4$ as $27 > 16$.
    - If you have to find what is largest from a set of numbers, assume one is larger than another, then prove the inequality. If it works then it is larger if not, then it is smaller.
    - In approximations, you always attempt to keep the numbers as close to the true values as possible, which is especially important if the multiple-choice options are very similar

M3 Ratio and proportion

1. Scale factors, scale diagrams and maps
   - The square root of the area scale factor is the length scale factor and the length scale factor cubed is the volume scale factor
   - Scale diagrams and maps, take the measurements of a real-size area and scale it down to draw it in a smaller area. Carefully read the units and the scale factor applied to convert between a scale drawing and the real-size area.

2. Express a quantity as a fraction of another
   - This can give you a fraction less than 1 or greater than 1, depending on the relative sizes of each value.

3. Ratio notation
   - A colon is used to represent a ratio, where the ratio of a to b is shown as $a:b$. The total size is $a+b$, where a takes up the fraction $\frac{a}{a+b}$ and b takes up the fraction $\frac{b}{a+b}$

4. Divide a given quantity into a ratio
   - To divide a quantity into a ratio of two or more parts, you divide the quantity by the overall sum of the number of parts, and to get the quantity associated with 1 unit in the ratio. Then multiply to find the sizes of each part.
   - For example, to divide 360 in the ratio $1:2:3$, first you find the total number of parts, which is $1+2+3=6$. Then you divide 360, by this value, to get 60 which represents one unit. This gives a ratio: $60:120:180$

5. Apply ratios to real-life contexts
   - Ratios are used in questions involving conversion, comparison, scaling, mixing and concentrations. Apply the basic principles of ratios to solve any question.

6. Proportion and relate ratios to fractions and linear functions
   - Proportion is essentially a fraction of the total value.
   - Ratios can be linked-to fractions, for example, if the ratio $a:b=1:2$, then $\frac{a}{b}=\frac{1}{2}$
   - Ratios can be linked-to linear functions, for example, if $y=2x$, the ratio $x:y=1:2$

7. Work with fractions in ratio problems
   - A common method to solve ratio problems. Is to convert the ratio into a fraction. Hence, you can apply standard algebraic operations to solve the fraction for any unknown values, before reverting to ratios to give your answer. Recall that if the ratio $a:b=1:2$, then $\frac{a}{b}=\frac{1}{2}$

8. Percentages, including percentage change, interest calculations and comparing quantities
   - A percentage is simply the number of parts per hundred, such that 5% is 5 parts per 100. Percentage changes are values that are used to multiply value A by, to reach value B. If value B is 5% greater than value A, then to reach value B you multiply A by 1.05.
   - You can use the multiplier to find the original value after a percentage increase or decrease, by dividing the new value by the multiplier.
   - Simple interest formula: final value = initial balance × (1 + rate × time) = $P(1+rt)$. To find the final value you multiply the initial balance by (one plus the interest rate times the number of years). This is because the interest rate is equal to the initial value, multiplied by the number of years, multiplied by the initial rate ($I=Prt$). As the final value is the sum of the initial balance and the interest earned, it becomes final value = $P+Prt=P(1+rt)$
   - If value A has a higher percentage, relative of a given value, than a second value B, then we know that value A is bigger than value B. For example, 10% of 50 is greater than 5% of 50, hence percentages can be used to compare quantities. If the given value changes between two quantities, work out each value and then compare: 5% of 360 is bigger than 10% of 10.

9. Direct and inverse proportion
   - Direct proportion means that as the first variable increases, the second variable also increases. $y \propto x$, hence $y = kx$, where k is a constant for proportionality.
   - The graph for direct proportion is any straight line with a positive gradient through the origin.
   - Inverse proportion means that as the first variable increases, the second variable decreases. $y \propto \frac{1}{x}$, or $y = \frac{k}{x}$, where k is a constant for proportionality.
   - The graph for inverse proportion is the same as the reciprocal graph $y = \frac{1}{x}$ where there are asymptotes at both axes, as you change the constant of proportionality, the graph moves further out.

10. Length, areas, and volumes in ratio notations (similar shapes and scale factors)
    - This will require you to apply your knowledge of ratios to geometry. Recall that the length scale factor squared is the area scale factor, and the length scale factor cubed is the volume scale factor. An example of ratios in geometry is trigonometric ratios, which represent the ratio of different side lengths in a triangle.
      - $sin(x) = \frac{O}{H}$ $cos(x) = \frac{A}{H}$ $tan(x) = \frac{O}{A}$

11. Growth and decay problems (compound interest) and iteration
    - Compound interest is calculated using the formula:
      - $final = initial \times interest\ rate^{time}$
    - This is where the interest rate is written as a multiplier (5% interest written as 1.05).
    - If there is decay, this can be adapted, such that the interest rate multiplier is less than 1 (5% decay gives a 0.95 multiplier)

M4 Algebra

1. Using algebraic notation
   - These are the basic principles of notation:
     $$nm = n \times m$$
     $$5x = x + x + x + x + x$$
     $$x^3 = x \times x \times x$$

2. Index laws in algebra
   - $a^m \times a^n = a^{m+n}$
   - $a^m \div a^n = a^{m-n}$
   - $(a^m)^n = a^{mn}$
   - $a^{-m} = \frac{1}{a^m}$
   - $(\sqrt[n]{a})^m = a^{\frac{m}{n}}$

3. Formulae and inequalities terms
   - **Expressions**: a set of terms with different operations between them (no equals sign involved)
   - **Equation**: two expressions equated using an equal's sign
   - **Formulae**: a mathematical rule showing the relationship between variables
   - **Identities**: an equation that is true for all values in a range of validity
   - **Inequalities**: comparing the size of two expressions
   - **Terms**: a single number or variable
   - **Factors**: a number, that when multiplied by another number produces a given expression. E.g. 5 is a factor of 15

4. Collect like terms, factorising and expanding
   - Expanding binomials uses the FOIL method, e.g. $(x + 1)(x - 3) = x^2 - 3x + x - 3 = x^2 - 2x - 3$.
   - If there is a common factor in all terms of an expression, it can be factorised outside:
   - $2x^2 + 4x + 8x^2y = 2x(x + 2 + 4xy)$
   - Look for patterns if you want to factorise complex expressions. For example, for the following cubic: $x^3 + 6x^2y + 12xy^2 + 8y^3 = (x + 2y)^3$.

10

5. Factorising quadratics and the difference of two squares
   - Use the standard method to factorise quadratics such as $x^2 + bx + c$ or $ax^2 + bx + c$
   - One possible method is splitting up the x terms into two parts (part one and part two) and then factorising.
     - The product of the parts one and two in the quadratic $ax^2 + bx + c$, is ac and the sum of the part one and two is b.
     - $x^2 + x - 6$: the sum of part one and part two is 1 and their product is -6. By considering the factors of 6, we can find that part one is 3 and part two is -2. $x^2 + x - 6 = x^2 - 2x + 3x - 6$. Then factorise both halves: $x^2 - 2x + 3x - 6 = x(x - 2) + 3(x - 2) = (x - 2)(x + 3)$
   - The difference of two squares rule: $x^2 - y^2 = (x + y)(x - y)$
     - $x - 64x^3 = -x(64x^2 - 1) = -x(8x - 1)(8x + 1)$.

6. Simplifying expressions
   - To simplify any expression, you can factorise, cancel terms, apply laws of indices and a range of other methods.
   - If you have to find the number of solutions to a challenging expression, apply logic to try and solve it before using algebra. Such as for $(x^2 - 1)^{10} = -1 - (x - 1)^2$, notice the LHS is always positive and the RHS is always negative so there are no solutions.

7. Rearranging the subject of the formula
   - This is changing what is the subject of the formula. Apply each operation step by step to try and get a certain variable on its own. You may need to factorise multiple terms if they all have the variable.

8. Equations and identities
   - An equation is true only for certain values of the variable (which you can solve for), whereas an identity is true for all values of the variable.
   - An equation uses an equal sign, $=$, for example, $5x = 10$, which is only true when $x = 2$
   - An identity uses a "three-line" sign, $\equiv$, for example, $2(2x) \equiv 4x$ or $(x + y)^2 \equiv x^2 + 2xy + y^2$, which are both always true

9. Coordinates in all four quadrants
   - The four quadrants are:
     - Q1: 0 to 90 degrees where x and y are both positive
     - Q2: 90 to 180 degrees where x is negative and y is positive
     - Q2: 180 to 270 degrees where x and y are both negative
     - Q4: 270 to 360 degrees where x is positive and y is negative

10. Gradients and intercepts of linear functions ($y = mx + c$), parallel and perpendicular lines. Equation of a line through two points, or one point with a gradient
    - Straight Line Graph: the equation of a line is $y = mx + c$ where m is gradient and c is the y-intercept. For points with coordinates: (x_a, y_a) and (x_b, y_b)
    - The gradient of a line through both points, $m = \frac{y_b - y_a}{x_b - x_a}$
    - The length of this line is: $\sqrt{(y_b - y_a)^2 + (x_b - x_a)^2}$
    - The midpoint the line is: $\frac{x_a + x_b}{2}, \frac{y_a + y_b}{2}$
    - The equation of a line with gradient m that passes through a point (x_a, y_a) is:
    - $y - y_a = m(x - x_a)$, input y_a and x_a and then, you rearrange for y
    - The product of the gradients of two perpendicular lines is -1, such that the gradients are negative reciprocals of each other. If the lines are parallel, then the gradients are the same.
    - If you are given two coordinates, to find the equation use: $\left(\frac{y - y_a}{y_b - y_a} = \frac{x - x_a}{x_b - x_a}\right)$, rearrange for y.

11. Roots, intercepts and turning points of quadratic functions graphically and algebraically
- If $f(x) = ax^2 + bx + c$, to sketch the quadratic:
  - Find $y - $ intercept when $x = 0$
  - Find the minimum or maximum point by completing the square: $if\ f(x) = a(x + p)^2 + q$, then the turning point is $(-p, q)$. To complete the square, use the idea that: $x^2 + bx = \left(x + \frac{b}{2}\right)^2 - \left(\frac{b}{2}\right)^2$
  - Find the two roots when $y = 0$
  - If x^2 coefficient positive, then U-shaped parabola. If the x^2 the coefficient negative, then ∩-shaped parabola

12. Sketch linear, quadratic, cubic, reciprocal, exponential and trigonometric graphs
- A linear graph is any graph that is in the form of $y = mx + c$ and has a constant gradient
- A quadratic graph has a ∪ or ∩ shape, and the exact manner in which to sketch and identify a quadratic graph has been explained in the section above.

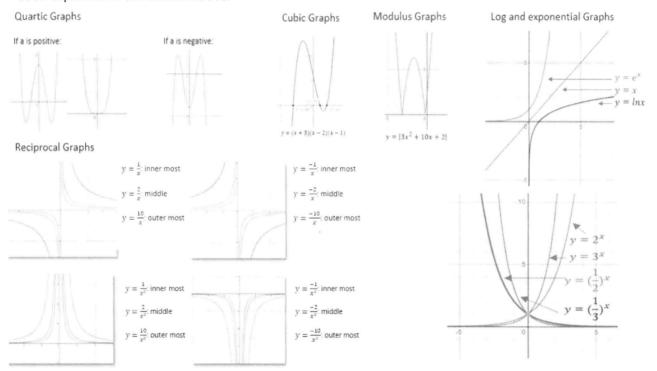

- Graphs of the Sine, Cosine and tangent (Sin, Cos, and Tan): periodic graphs that repeat after a certain interval
  - $y = \sin\theta$ repeats every 360 degrees and crosses the x-axis at $-180, 0, 180, 360$. It has a maximum of 1 and a minimum of -1.
  - $y = \cos\theta$ repeats every 360 degrees and crosses the x-axis at $-90, 90, 270, 450$.
  - $y = \tan\theta$ repeats every 180 degrees and crosses the x-axis at $-180, 0, 180\ 360$. It has no maximum or minimum, instead vertical asymptotes reaching $\pm\infty$, and tan is undefined at $x = -90, 90, 270 \dots$

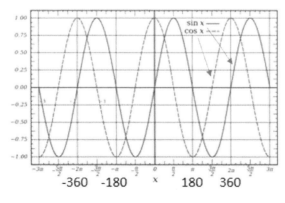

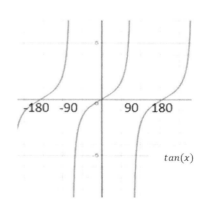

13. Interpret graphs in context (including speed, distance, and acceleration)
14. Find the gradient and areas under graphs (and interpret the results)
   - Graphs can be applied in context, for example, a reciprocal graph to model decay, an exponential graph to model growth rate. Then you have different relations between speed, distance, and time.
   - Displacement time graphs, with "s" on the vertical axis and time on the horizontal
   - Velocity time graphs, with "v" on the vertical axis and time on the horizontal
   - Velocity: the rate of change of displacement, or speed in a given direction. On a displacement time graph, the gradient is velocity. If it is a straight line, then there is constant velocity. To find the fastest speed, compare the gradients of the displacement time graph segments.
   - Acceleration is the rate of change of velocity; therefore, it is the gradient of a velocity-time graph. If it is a straight line on a velocity-time graph, then there is a constant velocity with no acceleration. The area between the velocity-time graph and the horizontal axis is the distance travelled.
   - To find the gradient of a graph, you can differentiate it and then plug in a value of x, to find the gradient of the tangent at that point.
   - To find the area under a curve, either integrate it or split it into different shapes and find the area of each shape, before adding up the smaller areas to find the overall area.

15. Form and solve simple (simultaneous) equations to find solutions
   - Simultaneous equations:
      i. A linear simultaneous equation is solved by elimination and substitution.
      ii. For one linear and one quadratic simultaneous equation, they have up to two pairs of solutions. To solve, you substitute the linear equation into the quadratic equation, rearrange to get 0 on one side and solve the quadratic. After substituting, use the discriminant of the resulting quadratic equation ($ax^2 + bx + c = 0$) to determine the number of solutions:
      iii. Alternatively, the solution to a pair of simultaneous equations is the points of intersection of their graphs.

16. Solve quadratic equations by factorising, completing the square and the quadratic formula
   - Quadratics: they are in the form $ax^2 + bx + c = 0$. To solve a quadratic equation, use either:
      o The quadratic formula which is $\frac{-b \pm \sqrt{b^2 - 4ac}}{2a}$
      o Complete the square: $x^2 + bx = (x + \frac{b}{2})^2 - (\frac{b}{2})^2$
      o You can find approximate roots of a quadratic, by using the method outlined previously to sketch the quadratic. The points at which the graph cuts the x-axis are the roots of the equation.

17. Solve linear inequalities and represent the solution
   - Rearrange the inequality to have the variable on one side, on its own, and this gives the range of acceptable values. If you multiply or divide both sides of an inequality by a negative number, then the direction that the inequality points should flip.
   - You can represent the range of values that inequality can take, either in words ("x is strictly greater than 5"), on a number line or a graph.

18. Generate terms of a sequence using term-to-term or position-to-term rules
   - Term-to-term: $a_{(n+1)} = 5a_n$, where to find the next term in a sequence, you multiply the previous term by 5.
   - Position-to-term: n^{th} term $2n + 6$, where to find the term, you have to use a function of the term position

19. Calculate the nth term of linear or quadratic sequences
   - Linear sequence: the nth term of a linear sequence involves finding the common difference between each term. The nth term of a linear sequence is in the form: $an + b$, where a is the common difference and the first term is $a + b$.
      o For 2,4,6,8: the common difference is $a = 2$ and the first term is also 2, hence, $b = 0$. n^{th} term is $2n$
   - Quadratic sequence: the nth term is in the form $an^2 + bn + c$, where c is the 0th term and a is half of the 2nd (common) difference. Find a and c, and then substitute this into the expression when $n = 1$ and solve to find b.

M5 Geometry

1. Conventional terms and notation
   - **Points**: a single coordinate or location, shown as a dot
   - **Lines**: a straight one-dimensional figure with no thickness, extending infinitely
   - **Line segments**: a specific part of a line, that connects two points
   - **Vertices**: a point where two or more lines or edges meet, to form the corner of a polygon
   - **Edges**: a line segment joining two vertices in a polygon (the side of a shape)
   - **Planes**: a flat two-dimensional surface that extends infinitely
   - **Parallel lines**: two lines with the same gradient, hence they do not meet or intersect at any point
   - **Perpendicular lines**: two lines that meet at 90 degrees, and their gradients are negative reciprocals (the product of the gradients is -1)
   - **Right angle**: 90 degrees
   - **Subtended angles**: the angle between the arc of a curve, or between two lines, as seen from a specific viewpoint
   - **Polygons**: a plane contained within a finite number of straight lines
   - **Regular polygons**: a polygon where all angles are equal, and all sides have the same length
   - **Rotational symmetry**: a polygon can be rotated and still look the same
   - **Reflectional symmetry**: you can fold the shape along a certain line and both halves of the shape will match exactly

2. Angle rules
   - The sum of all exterior angles of a polygon is always 360 degrees
   - To find the total size of interior angles in a regular polygon, the formula is $(n-2)180$, where n is the number of sides.
   - The angle around a point is 360 degrees
   - The angle between perpendicular lines is a right angle (90 degrees)
   - The angles on a straight line add up to 180 degrees
   - Vertically opposite angles at a vertex are equal in size when two lines intersect
   - Between two parallel lines, corresponding (F) angles are equal in size
   - Between two parallel lines, alternate (Z) angles are equal in size
   - Supplementary angles add up to 180 degrees

3. Properties of quadrilaterals and triangles
   - **Rhombus**: all sides are equal in length, there are 2 pairs of parallel lines and opposite angles are equal. If you have two similar rhombi, then the ratio of their angles is 1.
   - **Parallelogram**: opposite sides are equal in length and there are 2 pairs of parallel lines
   - **Kite**: adjacent sides are equal and there are two equal angles opposite each other.
   - **Square**: all four sides and angles are equal in size
   - **Trapezium**: one pair of parallel side, the diagonals of a trapezium bisect each other
   - **Rectangle**: diagonals that bisect each other, opposite sides are parallel and equal in length to each other and each interior angle is equal to 90 degrees
   - **Isosceles triangle**: a triangle with two equal sides, hence two angles of the triangle are equal
   - **Scalene triangle**: a triangle with no sides equal in length, hence three different angles
   - **Equilateral triangle**: a triangle with three equal side lengths, hence all angles are 60 degrees

4. Congruence criteria (SSS, SAS, ASA, RHS)
   - If the any of the below conditions are true for two triangles, then they are both congruent
     - **SSS**: all three sides are equal in length
     - **ASA**: two angles are the same and a corresponding side (the side opposite one of the two equal angles) is equal in both triangles
     - **SAS**: two sides are equal and the angle in between both these sides is also equal
     - **RHS**: a right angle, the hypotenuse and a corresponding side are equal

5. Using angle rules, properties of shapes and congruence
   - The difference between triangle congruence and similarity is that if two triangles are congruent this means that all three sides and all three angles are equal, whereas, if two triangles are similar, then it only means that all three angles are equal.
   - The angle rules, congruency rules and similarity rule can all be used together to solve complex geometry

6. Construct congruent and similar shapes with various transformations
   - **Rotation**: rotating the shape about a set point and by a set angle and direction (such as 90 degrees anti-clockwise about the origin). If there is a 180-degree turn, then it does not matter whether it is clockwise or anticlockwise.
   - **Reflection**: reflecting every point across the line and then join the points up
   - **Translation**: shifting a shape by a given vector, where you translate every point by the given vector and then join the dots. For $\frac{a}{b}$, if a is positive then it is a rightward shift, if a is negative then it is a leftward shift. If b is positive then it is an upward shift, if b is negative then it is a downward shift.
   - Different transformations can be combined.

7. Pythagoras' theorem
   - $a^2 + b^2 = c^2$, this is used in a right-angled triangle, and it can be applied in two and three dimensions.

8. Conventional circle terms
   - **Centre**: point inside the circle that is of equal distance from every point on the circumference of the circle
   - **Radius**: a straight line from the centre of the circle to the circumference (any point), half the length of the diameter
   - **Chord**: a line segment joining two points on a circle
   - **Diameter**: a straight-line connecting two opposite points on a circle that passes through the centre of the circle and is twice the length of the radius
   - **Circumference**: the boundary enclosing a circle, going all the way around it
   - **Tangent**: a straight line that touches (not intersecting) a circle at one point only, and meets the radius to that point at 90 degrees
   - **Arc**: a portion of the circumference of a circle
   - **Sector**: the part of a circle enclosed by two radii, the smaller area between the two radii being the minor sector and the larger area between the two radii being the major sector
   - **Segment**: a region in a circle that is between the arc of the circle, and a chord connecting the endpoints of the arc

9. Circle theorems
   - Circles: the equation of a circle is $(x - a)^2 + (y - b)^2 = r^2$, where r is the radius and (a, b) is the centre. You complete the square to find the equation of the circle, the centre and the radius.
   - Opposite angles in a cyclic quadrilateral add to 180 degrees
   - The tangent is perpendicular to the radius at the point of intersection.
   - A chord is the line segment that joins 2 points on the circumference of the circle. The perpendicular bisector of a chord will go through the centre of the circle. To find the centre of a circle, find the perpendicular bisectors of 2 chords and the coordinates of their intersection is the centre.
   - The angle in a semicircle is always a right angle
   - The angle subtended by the arc at the centre of the circle is double the size of the angle subtended by the arc on the circumference
   - Angles in the same segment are equal
   - When a tangent meets a chord the alternate segment theorem applies, where angles in alternate segments are equal in size

10. Solving geometric problems
    - These problems will require you to use all the above rules for circle, angles and any other shape, to find missing angles or sides

11. Key terminology
   - **Faces** or surfaces: the surface of a three-dimensional shape
   - **Edges**: a line segment joining two vertices in a shape
   - **Vertices**: the corner of a shape where the edges meet
   - Common 3-D shapes include: cubes, cuboids, prisms, cylinders, pyramids, cones, spheres and hemispheres

12. Interpreting plans and elevations of 3D shapes
   - The plan of a shape is a 2-D version of what each side of a 3-D shape looks like from the top
   - The elevation of a shape is a 2-D version of what each side of a 3-D shape looks like from the front and sides (front elevation and side elevation)

13. Use maps, scale drawings and bearings
   - Bearings are always measured clockwise from the north and given with three figures (therefore, if the bearing is less than 100 degrees, then add zeros on the front such as 060 degrees for a 60-degree bearing). You can use all the angle rules learnt previously to find bearings of different points.
   - The bearing of each point is measured clockwise, therefore, the bearing of A from B is not the same as the bearing of B from A. Hence, always read the question carefully to see what point the bearing is relative to.

14. Finding the area of triangles, parallelograms and trapezia and the volume of prisms
15. Circle, cylinder and sphere formulae

2D shapes area	3D shapes surface area	3D shapes volume
Circle: πr^2	Cube: $6a^2$	a^3
Parallelogram: $base \times vertical\ h$	Cylinder $2\pi r^2 + 2\pi rl$	$\pi r^2 h$
Trapezium: $\frac{1}{2} \times h \times (a+b)$	Cone: $\pi r^2 + \pi rl$	$\frac{1}{3}\pi r^2 h$
Triangle: $\frac{1}{2} \times b \times h$	Sphere: $4\pi r^2$	$\frac{4}{3}\pi r^3$

   - The volume of a cuboid is the area of the cross-section face, multiplied by the length of the cuboid. The circumference (perimeter) of a circle is πd
   - The area or surface area of a composite shape is the sum of the areas or surface areas respectively of the shapes it is made up of.

16. Arc lengths, angles, and areas of sectors of circles
   - The area of a sector of a circle is: $\frac{x}{360} \times \pi r^2$
   - The arc length of a sector of a circle is: $\frac{x}{360} \times \pi d$

17. Using congruence and similarity
   - You can use the idea of congruence and similarity to work out the lengths, areas and volumes of two shapes given information about one of the shapes. Use the idea that the ratio between the lengths of the similar shapes is the length scale factor (which is 1 for congruent shapes). The length scale factor squared is the area scale factor and the length scale factor cubed is the volume scale factor.

18. Trigonometric ratios and exact values

x	$\sin x$	$\cos x$	$\tan x$
$0°$	$\dfrac{\sqrt{0}}{2} = 0$	$\dfrac{\sqrt{4}}{2} = 1$	$\dfrac{0}{1} = 0$
$30°$	$\dfrac{\sqrt{1}}{2} = \dfrac{1}{2}$	$\dfrac{\sqrt{3}}{2}$	$\dfrac{\frac{1}{2}}{\frac{\sqrt{3}}{2}} = \dfrac{1}{\sqrt{3}}$
$45°$	$\dfrac{\sqrt{2}}{2}$	$\dfrac{\sqrt{2}}{2}$	1
$60°$	$\dfrac{\sqrt{3}}{2}$	$\dfrac{\sqrt{1}}{2} = \dfrac{1}{2}$	$\sqrt{3}$
$90°$	$\dfrac{\sqrt{4}}{2} = 1$	$\dfrac{\sqrt{0}}{2} = 0$	$\dfrac{1}{0} = undefined$

- $sin(x) = \dfrac{opposite}{hypotenuse}$ $cos(x) = \dfrac{adjacent}{hypotenuse}$ $tan(x) = \dfrac{opposite}{adjacent}$
- These ratios apply in right-angled triangles, where the side opposite the right angle is called the hypotenuse. Relative to the angle x, the side opposite the angle x is the "opposite" side and the side next to the angle x is called the "adjacent" side.
- The range of $\sin x$ is $-1 \rightarrow 1$ and the range for $\sin^2 x$ and $\cos^2 x$ is between 0 and 1.
- If you have to maximise a trigonometric function, begin with the simple form and see what the maximum and minimum possible answers are. For example: $(3\sin^2(10x - 11) - 7)^2$.
  - $\sin(10x - 11)$ is between -1 and 1 as this is the standard linear bracket sin expression
  - When square the expression, $(\sin(10x - 11))^2$, the range is between 0 and 1 as you square the previous range of -1 and 1.
  - When the expression is multiplied by 3, then it becomes $3(\sin(10x - 11))^2$, the range is between 0 and 3 as you multiply the previous range 0 and 1 by 3
  - When you subtract 7, the expression $3(\sin(10x - 11))^2 - 7$, the range is between -7 and -4 as you subtract 7 from the previous range 0 and 3
  - When you squared this, the expression is $(3(\sin(10x - 11))^2 - 7)^2$, and the range is 16 and 49 as you square the previous range -7 to -4.
  - Therefore, the overall maximum of the expression $(3(\sin(10x - 11))^2 - 7)^2$ is 49 and the minimum is 16.

19. Vector calculations and representation
- When you add two column vectors, they must have the same dimensions, and you add the respective components across both vectors.
- When you subtract two column vectors, they must have the same dimensions, and you subtract the respective values across both vectors.
- If you multiply a vector by a scalar, you need to multiply all the values in the vector by that scalar.
- Vectors can be drawn diagrammatically, where you can show their magnitude and direction.
- You can use two vectors to construct geometric arguments and proofs

M6 Statistics

1. Tables, charts, and diagrams
   - Categorical Data:
     - Two-way tables have two categories to display the information, for example:

	Maths	English	Total
Girls	11	12	23
Boys	23	12	35
Total	34	24	58

   - Frequency tables represent the frequency of data points for each category of data.
   - Bar charts represent the numerical values of each category as the height of the rectangle, each with an equal width.
   - The pie chart represents the data in a circle which is divided into sectors that each represent a proportion of the whole quantity (360 degrees is divided up in sectors of a circle proportional to the size of the quantity relative to the whole).
   - Pictograms are graphs where for each category there is a symbol representing the frequency
   - For ungrouped discrete numerical data, you can use a vertical line chart.
   - For time-series data you can use tables and lines graphs, where you can plot the rolling average across a period.

2. Discrete and continuous data representations
   - Discrete data is where the data can only take specific values within a given range and continuous data is where it can take any value in the given range
   - For grouped discrete data or continuous data, you can use a histogram with equal or unequal class widths or a cumulative frequency graph.
   - Drawing cumulative frequency diagrams: Find cumulative frequencies and plot the upper bounds of the class width. Then you can calculate the median and IQR. In a grouped table, you do not have exact values, use cumulative frequency to find quartiles, percentiles or the median.
   - Histograms: gives a picture of the distribution and spread of data. Without frequency density, the bars aren't representative of the class width and frequency together. In a histogram, the area of a bar is proportional to the frequency in each class. Therefore, they can be used even with unequal class intervals. The y-axis always starts at 0. The height of the bar is frequency density; the width of the bar is the class width and the area of the bar is the frequency of the data group.
     - area of bar $= k \times$ frequency. If $k = 1$ then frequency density $= \frac{\text{frequency}}{\text{class width}}$.
     - Find the total area of all bars, if it is not equal to total frequency, then k is not one. Divide the area by frequency to find k. Joining the top of each polygon at the midpoint of the class width forms a frequency polygon.

3. Averages for ungrouped and grouped data used to compare populations and data sets
   - A population is all the values of data in a group, whereas a sample is a selected subset of the group. A population can be described using statistics such as the mean, mode, median and the range.

- Each of the median, mode, mean and range can be found graphically depending on the representations, such as on a box plot. The distance between the whiskers is the range, the lines show Q1, Q2 and Q3. In a frequency graph, the highest line represents the mode.

	Median	Quartiles (1/4), Deciles (1/10) and Percentiles (1/100)
List/ Discrete data	$\frac{n}{2}$ If integer choose the next half number up. If half number choose the next integer up.	$\frac{n}{2}$ or $\frac{3n}{4}$ or $\frac{n}{10}$ If integer choose the next half number up. If non-integer rounds up to next integer.
Frequency table	$\frac{n}{2}$ As above	$\frac{n}{2}$ or $\frac{3n}{4}$ or $\frac{n}{10}$ As above
Grouped Frequency	$\frac{n}{2}$ Change nothing and use interpolation to find value	$\frac{n}{2}$ or $\frac{3n}{4}$ or $\frac{n}{10}$ Change nothing and use interpolation to find value

- List data
  - **Median**: use the table above
    - Benefits: does not use all the values of data and therefore it is unaffected by extreme values or outliers
    - Negative: does not use all the values, so if there are no outliers, then the mean is better.
  - **Mean**: Find the sum of all values and divide this by the number of values.
    $$\frac{\text{the sum of all sample values}}{\text{number of data items in the sample}} \quad \bar{x} = \frac{\sum x}{n}$$
    - Benefits: uses all the data points, hence accurate if there are no outliers.
    - Negative: it is inaccurate and negatively affected if there are large outliers
  - **Mode**: the number that occurs with the highest frequency
  - **Range**: the highest number minus the smallest number. It shows the spread of data as it is the difference between the largest and smallest values but it is very prone to be negatively affected by outliers.
- Frequency Table
  - **Mode**: the value with the highest frequency is the mode.
  - **Median**: See the table above for the formula to use. This gives the median value and then go along the table to find the group that the value is found in cumulatively.
  - **Mean**: Find the sum of all values by finding the total of xf and dividing by f. Therefore: $\frac{\sum fx}{\sum f}$
- Grouped Frequency Table
  - **Mode**: find the modal group, which is the group with the highest frequency.
  - **Mean**: Find the sum of all the grouped values by finding the total of xf and dividing by f. Therefore: $\frac{\sum fx}{\sum f}$. Use the midpoint of the data to find x value for the formula, as we are assuming all the data in a group is found at the midpoint, it is an estimate and not fully accurate.
  - **Median**: grouped continuous data cannot be turned into a list. Find the sum of all frequencies and use the formula: $\frac{n}{2}$. This is the median value and goes along the table to find a group. Use interpolation to find far along the group it is, by assuming all data is equally spread among the group. As we are assuming the data is equally spaced, the median is only an estimate and not fully accurate.
    - The formula for median interpolation is:
    $$\text{lower class bound} + \left(\frac{\text{median}^{\text{th}} \text{ value} - \text{previous total cumulative frequency}}{\text{class frequency}} \times \text{class width} \right)$$

- Two data sets can also be compared using statistics, by comparing the mean, median, mode or range between both sets. When comparing data comment on measures of location and spread. For example, "On average class A did better than class B in Maths, shown by higher median/ mean. Class B is more consistent in marks with a lower spread. This is shown by lower IQR/ range.

4. Scatter graphs for bivariate data, correlation, causation, interpolation and extrapolation
   - Bivariate data: data with pairs of values for 2 variables show on scatter diagram.
   - Correlation describes the nature of a linear relationship between 2 variables (how close to a straight-line).
   - Two variables have a causal relationship if a change in one variable causes a change in other. Correlation does not imply causation, look at the context and apply common sense to see if it is causal.
     - Strong/ Weak describes how close points are to a line. Positive/ Negative describes the gradient of the line.
   - Linear regression: a line of best fit is drawn on a scatter diagram, and it approximates the relationship between variables.
   - For interpolation, only use it to find the dependent/ Y variable. If you know the value of the independent variable from bivariate data, then use the line of best fit to estimate the dependent variable.
   - Extrapolation is less reliable, therefore, only use the line of best fit to make predictions for values of the dependent variable within the range of the data.

M7 Probability

1. Using tables and frequency trees
   - You can analyse the frequency of outcomes from probability experiments using tables and frequency trees. They show you the event that occurs and the frequency with which it occurs

2. Using randomness, fairness, and equally likely events to find expected outcomes
   - **Experiment**: a repeatable process that leads to one or more outcomes
   - **Event**: a collection of one or more outcomes
   - If events are equally likely, then their probability of occurrence is the same. For example, the probability of getting any number between 1 to 6 when rolling dice has an equal probability of $\frac{1}{6}$.
   - If an experiment is repeated, the outcome may be different (for example, every time you throw a dart, the probability of hitting bullseye changes as you improve at the game).

3. Expected frequencies and theoretical probabilities
   - Theoretical probability is the likelihood that something will occur, which is calculated by dividing the number of "successful or favourable" outcomes by the total number of possible outcomes.
   - The relative expected frequency is the count of an individual kind of outcome divided by the count of all kinds of outcomes.
   - The probability scale is from 0 to 1, and a probability can take any number within this range.

4. Probabilities of an exhaustive set and for mutually exclusive events sum to one
   - Mutually exclusive events: events with no outcomes in common, hence the expression is $P(A \cup B) = P(A) + P(B)$ as there is no intersection.
   - Non-Mutually Exclusive: $P(A \cup B) = P(A) + P(B) - P(A \cap B)$
   - For an exhaustive set of all potential outcomes, the probabilities of all the outcomes will always add up to one.
   - The probability for any mutually exclusive events will also sum to one.

5. Venn and tree diagrams
   - Venn diagrams are used to represent events graphically with probabilities placed inside for simultaneous events. The notation for Venn diagrams is shown below:
     - $\in$: universal set $\emptyset$ null set (no outcomes) A, B, C are events.
   - $P(A') = 1 - P(A)$, A complement, not A.
   - $A \cap B$ intersection of A and B (outcomes in both).
   - $A \cup B$ union of A and B (outcomes in A or B or both).
   - $n(A)$ number of outcomes whereas $P(A)$ is the probability of A.
   - The number of regions in a Venn diagram is equal to $2^{\text{number the sets}}$
     - For example, $P(A) = 0.25, P(B) = 0.4, P(C) = 0.45$ and $P(A \cap B \cap C) = 0.1$. A and B independent and B and C independent. $P(A) \times P(B) = 0.1$. Therefore, as the intersection of all three sets is 0.1, the area A and B only is the empty set. B and C has a product of 0.18, hence B and C only is 0.08.

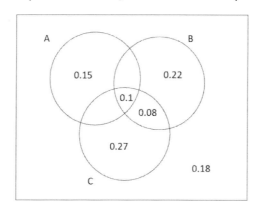

21

- Tree Diagrams: used to show outcomes of two or more events happening in succession. Multiply along the branches and add downwards. This is shown in the example tree diagram below.

	Pick 1	Pick 2	Outcome	Probability
		$\frac{6}{10}$ A	AA	$\frac{36}{100}$
	A $\frac{6}{10}$	$\frac{4}{10}$ B	AB	$\frac{24}{100}$
	B $\frac{4}{10}$	$\frac{6}{10}$ A	BA	$\frac{24}{100}$
		$\frac{4}{10}$ B	BB	$\frac{16}{100}$

6. Theoretical possibility spaces for single and combined experiments
   - A sample space is a theoretical probability space showing all outcomes.
   - Theoretical possibility space for a single experiment with equally likely outcomes, for example, rolling a dice:
     - You can get 1, 2, 3, 4, 5 or 6
   - Theoretical possibility space for a combined experiment with equally likely outcomes, for example, rolling two dice and finding the sum of the scores:

Dice A/Dice B	1	2	3	4	5	6
1	2	3	4	5	6	7
2	3	4	5	6	7	8
3	4	5	6	7	8	9
4	5	6	7	8	9	10
5	6	7	8	9	10	11
6	7	8	9	10	11	12

   - From this you can find the probability of achieving a certain number, for example, probability of rolling two dice and achieving a sum of 12 is $\frac{1}{36}$

7. Conditional probabilities (two-way tables, tree diagrams and Venn diagrams) and independent and dependent probabilities
   - For probability trees, multiply along the branches and add then totals of the branches.
   - For tree diagrams, if the events are independent of the previous outcome, then the second round's probabilities will not depend on the outcome in the first round.
   - If the events are dependent, then depending on the first-round outcome, the probability for the second round is affected.
   - For example, if you play two games of tennis, the probability of winning the first match and then losing the second may not be the same as the probability of losing the first match and then winning the second match. This is because after winning the first match your confidence may be very high, increasing the chance of winning again. If you lose the first match, your confidence may be very low, increasing the change of losing again.

- Two-way table: If students are asked about viewing habits. 56 watch sport (S), 77 watch dramas (D) and of those that watch drama 18 watch sport. To draw a two-way table, two columns on the top are sport and not sport and side are drama and not drama.

	D	D'
S	18	38
S'	59	5

- Conditional Probability: the probability of an event changes depending on the outcome of a previous event, which is modelled using conditional probability. The vertical line means "given that" such that the probability that B occurs given that A has already occurred is written as $P(B|A)$.
    - For events A and B, $P(A|B) = \frac{P(A \cap B)}{P(B)}$ and $P(B|A) = \frac{P(A \cap B)}{P(A)}$
- There is a link between tree diagrams and Venn diagrams, as shown in the image below:

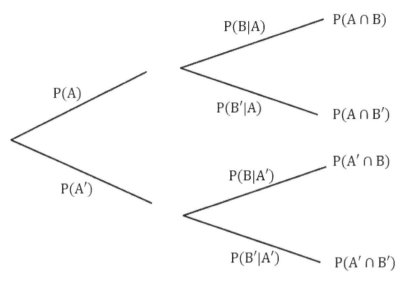 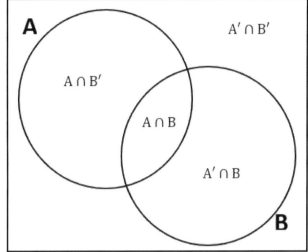

- If events are sequential then use a tree diagram and if they are simultaneous a Venn diagram.
- If A and B are independent, then the probability of A does not depend on the outcome of B and vice versa. For independent events, A and B:
    - $P(A \cap B) = P(A) \times P(B)$ $P(A|B) = P(A|B') = P(A)$ $P(B|A) = P(B|A') = P(B)$
        - If the above rules are not true, then A and B are dependent.

23

Advanced Mathematics Content

AM1 Algebra and functions

1. Laws for indices
   - $a^m \times a^n = a^{m+n}$
   - $a^m \div a^n = a^{m-n}$
   - $(a^m)^n = a^{mn}$
   - $a^{-m} = \frac{1}{a^m}$
   - $(\sqrt[n]{a})^m = a^{\frac{m}{n}}$

2. Manipulation of surds
   - Surds are irrational numbers and multiple rules can be used with surds:
   - $\sqrt{ab} = \sqrt{a} \times \sqrt{b}$
   - $\sqrt{\frac{a}{b}} = \frac{\sqrt{a}}{\sqrt{b}}$
   - Rationalising the denominator: $\frac{1}{\sqrt{a}} \times \frac{\sqrt{a}}{\sqrt{a}}$ $\qquad$ $\frac{1}{a+\sqrt{b}} \times \frac{a-\sqrt{b}}{a-\sqrt{b}}$ $\qquad$ $\frac{1}{a-\sqrt{b}} \times \frac{a+\sqrt{b}}{a+\sqrt{b}}$

3. Quadratic functions and their graphs (the discriminants, completing the square and solving)
   - For a quadratic polynomial in the form $ax^2 + bx + c$, with roots α and β:
     - $\alpha + \beta = \frac{-b}{a}$ and $\alpha\beta = \frac{c}{a}$.
   - Discriminant: for quadratics in the form $f(x) = ax^2 + bx + c$, $b^2 - 4ac$ is the discriminant, and it shows the number of roots for $f(x)$, such that:
     - If $b^2 - 4ac > 0$ then two distinct different roots
     - If $b^2 - 4ac < 0$ then no roots
     - If $b^2 - 4ac = 0$ then one repeated root, the curve turns on the x −axis
- $f(x) = ax^2 + bx + c$
   - When sketching graphs:
     - i. Find y − intercept when $x = 0$
     - ii. Find minimum or maximum point by completing the square: if $f(x) = a(x + p)^2 + q$, then the turning point is $(-p, q)$. To complete the square, use the formula: $x^2 + bx = \left(x + \frac{b}{2}\right)^2 - \left(\frac{b}{2}\right)^2$
     - iii. Find the two roots when $y = 0$
     - iv. If x^2 coefficient positive, then U-shaped parabola. If x^2 coefficient negative, then ∩-shaped parabola
   - When solving for roots, $f(x) = 0$:
     - The quadratic formula which is $\frac{-b \pm \sqrt{b^2 - 4ac}}{2a}$
     - Complete the square: $x^2 + bx = \left(x + \frac{b}{2}\right)^2 - \left(\frac{b}{2}\right)^2$
     - You can find approximate roots of a quadratic, by using the method outlined previously to sketch the quadratic. The points at which the graph cuts the x −axis is the roots of the equation.

4. Simultaneous equations
   - A linear simultaneous equation is solved by elimination and substitution. This is where you rearrange the formula to make a certain variable the subject of the formula, for example, x. Then you substitute this expression for x into the second simultaneous equation, wherever there is a "x". Then you are left with an equation in terms of only one variable, which you can solve.
   - For one linear and one quadratic simultaneous equation, they have up to two pairs of solutions. The solution to a pair of simultaneous equations is the points of intersection of their graphs. To solve, you substitute the linear equation into the quadratic equation. After substituting, use the discriminant of the resulting quadratic equation $(ax^2 + bx + c = 0)$ to determine the number of solutions:

5. Inequalities (linear and quadratic)
   - Rearrange the inequality to have the variable on one side, on its own, and this gives the range of acceptable values. If you multiply or divide both sides of an inequality by a negative number, then the direction that the inequality points should flip.
   - You can represent the range of values that inequality can take, either in words ("x is strictly greater than 5"), on a number line or a graph.
   - Quadratic inequalities: to solve a quadratic inequality: rearrange it so the right-hand side of the inequality is 0. Then pretend it is an equation with an equal sign and solve it to find the critical values. Then sketch the graph of a quadratic function to find the required set of values when you use the correct inequality sign.

6. Algebraic manipulation of polynomials (expanding brackets, factorisation, Factor and Remainder theorem)
   - Expanding binomials uses the FOIL method, e.g. $(x + 1)(x - 3) = x^2 - 3x + x - 3 = x^2 - 2x - 3$. If there is a common factor in all terms of expression, it can be factorised outside:
     - $2x^2 + 4x + 8x^2y = 2x(x + 2 + 4xy)$
   - Polynomial long division: $\frac{F(x)}{divisor}$(improper fraction)$= Q(x) + \frac{remainder}{divisor}$
   - Factor Theorem: given that $f(x)$ is a polynomial then if f(p) $= 0$, then $(x - p)$ is a factor of $f(x)$
   - Remainder Theorem: when a polynomial, $f(x)$, is divided by a linear polynomial, which is in the form $(x - p)$, the remainder of that division will be equivalent to $f(p)$.
   - To find the remainder when a polynomial is divided, use long division, or substitute the number into the polynomial and the solution is the remainder. E.g. divide $x^3 + 3x^2 - 3x - 14$, by $(2x + 1)$, when $x = \frac{-1}{2}$ the solution (remainder) is $\frac{-95}{8}$.
   - For a cubic polynomial in the form $ax^3 + bx^2 + cx + d$, with roots α, β and γ then $\alpha + \beta + \gamma = -\frac{b}{a}$ and $\alpha\beta + \alpha\gamma + \beta\gamma = \frac{c}{a}$ and $\alpha\beta\gamma = \frac{-d}{a}$

7. Functions can be a many-to-one or one-to-one mapping
   - Domain: the set of possible inputs for a function and Range: set of possible outputs for a function
   - The roots of a function are when $f(x) = 0$
   - One to One: each input (domain) will map to its output (range): $f(x) = x^3$
   - Many to One: multiple possible inputs (domains) lead to one same output (range) such as $f(x) = x^2$.
   - One to Many is not allowed and it is a function where one domain (input) has more than one range (output) such as $f(x) = \sqrt{x}$.
   - For one to many functions, we can limit the domain or range. For example, when dealing with $f(x) = \sqrt{x}$, we state that the positive root is always taken, which limits it to a one-to-one function.
   - For $f(x) = |x|$, this takes the modulus or positive value of x. A positive number into a modulus function stays the same. A negative number into a modulus function multiplies by a negative. E. g. $(x - 4)$: if positive stays $x - 4$ and if negative $4 - x$. If $x > 0$ then $|x| = x$ and if $x < 0$ then $|x| = -x$.
   - Functions $f(x)$ and $f^{-1}(x)$ are inverses of each other and $ff^{-1}(x) = f^{-1}f(x) = x$. The graphs of both $f(x)$ and $f^{-1}(x)$ are reflections of each other in the line $y = x$.

AM2 Sequences and series

1. Recurrence relations
   - A recurrence relation has the form $x_{n+1} = f(x_n)$
   - If you have an unknown expression or nth term which gives a sequence, then find the first few terms to see if a pattern emerges.
   - If a sequence repeats every 6 terms going 1,2,3,4,5,6,1,2,3,4,5,6, to find the 2017th term you do 2017 divided by 6, which has a remainder of 1. Hence, it is the first term in the sequence which is 1.

2. Arithmetic series
   - An arithmetic sequence has an nth term $a + (n-1)r$, where a is the first value and r is the common difference and n is the term number
   - The sum of an arithmetic series is $\frac{n}{2}$(first term + last term) or $\frac{n}{2}[2a + (n-1)d]$, where a is the first value and r is the common difference and n is the number of terms

3. Sum of a finite and infinite (convergent) geometric series
   - A geometric sequence has an nth term ar^{n-1}, where a is the first value and r is the common difference and n is the term number
   - The sum of a convergent geometric series to infinity, where $|r| < 1 = \frac{a}{1-r}$, and the general sum to n is $\frac{a(1-r^n)}{1-r}$, where a is the first value and r is the common difference and n is the number of terms

4. Binomial expansion
   - The binomial expansion: the general term is given by: $(a + b)^n = \binom{n}{r} a^{(n-r)} b^r$

   $$(a + b)^n = a^n + \binom{n}{1} a^{n-1}b + \binom{n}{2} a^{n-2}b^2 + \ldots + \binom{n}{r} a^{n-r}b^r + \ldots + b^n$$

   $$\text{where } \binom{n}{r} = {}^n C_r = \frac{n!}{r!(n-r)!}$$

   - $(1 + x)^n = 1 + nx + \frac{n(n-1)}{2!}x^2 + \frac{n(n-1)(n-2)}{3!}x^3 \ldots \frac{n(n-1)\ldots(n-r+1)}{r!}x^r$.
   - Factorial notation: a quick way to find coefficients.
     - $0! = 1$ $3! = 3 \times 2 \times 1$ $n! = n \times (n-1) \times (n-2) \ldots$ or $\qquad n! = n \times (n-1)!$
   - To choose r items in a group n: ${}^n C_r$ or $\binom{n}{r}$. This equal to: $\frac{n!}{r! \times (n-r)!}$
   - The rth entry in n^{th} row of Pascal's triangle is ${}^n C_r$ or $\binom{n}{r}$, where the first row of the triangle is 0th row.
   - You can simplify factorials such as $\frac{(n-1)!}{(n-2)!} = \frac{(n-1) \times (n-2)!}{(n-2)!} = n - 1$

AM3 Coordinate geometry

1. Equation of a straight line
   - Straight Line Graph: the equation of a line is $y = mx + c$ where m is gradient and c is $y-$intercept. For points with coordinates: (x_a, y_a) and (x_b, y_b)
   - The gradient of a line through both points, $m = \frac{y_b - y_a}{x_b - x_a}$
   - The length of this line is: $\sqrt{(y_b - y_a)^2 + (x_b - x_a)^2}$
   - The midpoint the line is: $\left(\frac{x_a + x_b}{2}, \frac{y_a + y_b}{2}\right)$
   - The equation of a line with gradient m that passes through a point (x_a, y_a) is:
     - $y - y_a = m(x - x_a)$, input y_a and x_a and then rearrange for y.
   - If you are given 2 coordinates (x_a, y_a) and (x_b, y_b), to find the equation of a line, use the formula:
     - $\frac{y - y_a}{y_b - y_a} = \frac{x - x_a}{x_b - x_a}$, and you rearrange for y.
   - A line can also have the format $ax + by + c = 0$
   - The product of the gradients of 2 perpendicular lines is -1, such that the gradients are negative reciprocals of each other. If the lines are parallel, then the gradients are the same.

2. Equation of a circle
   - Circles: the equation of a circle is $(x - a)^2 + (y - b)^2 = r^2$, where r is the radius and (a, b) is the centre. You can complete the square to find the equation of the circle, the centre and the radius.
   - If you fully expand the equation of a circle from $(x - a)^2 + (y - b)^2 = r^2$, then you can get an alternative equation in the form $x^2 + y^2 + cx + dy + e = 0$
   - If you have a circle and a line, to find the meeting points, input equation of the line into the equation of the circle and simplify. Use the discriminant, if $b^2 - 4ac > 0$ they meet at 2 points. If $b^2 - 4ac < 0$ they do not meet. If $b^2 - 4ac = 0$ line is a tangent to the circle.

3. Properties of a circle
   - A chord is the line segment that joins 2 points on the circumference of a circle. The perpendicular bisector of a chord will go through the centre of the circle (the perpendicular from the centre to a chord bisects the chord). To find the centre of a circle, find the perpendicular bisectors of 2 chords and the coordinates of their intersection is the centre.
   - The tangent is perpendicular to the radius at the point of intersection.
   - The angle subtended by the arc at the centre of the circle is double the size of the angle subtended by the arc on the circumference
   - The angle in a semicircle is always a right angle
   - Angles in the same segment are equal
   - Opposite angles in a cyclic quadrilateral add to 180 degrees
   - When a tangent meets a chord the alternate segment theorem applies, where the angle between the tangent and chord at the point of contact is equal to the angle in the alternate segment

AM4 Trigonometry

1. The sine (also the ambiguous case), cosine and area of a triangle rules
   - Cosine Rule:
     - $a^2 = b^2 + c^2 - 2bc \cos A,$ or to find the angle: $\cos A = \frac{a^2-b^2-c^2}{-2bc} = \frac{b^2+c^2-a^2}{2bc}$.
     - In a triangle, the smallest angle is opposite the smallest side, and the largest angle is always opposite the largest side.
   - Sine Rule:
     - $\frac{a}{\sin A} = \frac{b}{\sin B} = \frac{c}{\sin C}$ or $\frac{\sin A}{a} = \frac{\sin B}{b} = \frac{\sin C}{c}$
     - The ambiguous case of the sine rule is when you use the sine rule to find missing measures of a triangle, given two sides and an angle opposite one of those sides (SSA). Given the ambiguous case, you can either have no solution for a triangle, one possible triangle or two distinct possible triangles.
   - $\sin(-x) = -\sin(x)$ and $\cos(x) = \cos(-x)$
   - Area of a triangle: $\frac{1}{2} ab \sin C$

2. Radians
   - 1 radian is the angle subtended at the centre of a circle by an arc whose length is equal to the radius of the circle. The circumference of a circle is $2\pi r$ and hence the angle is 2π radians at the centre of the circle.
     - Therefore, $\alpha° = \frac{\pi \theta}{180}$ radians $= \theta$
   - Arc length of circle sector with radius r and angle θ radians is $l = r\theta$.
   - Area of circle sector with radius r and angle θ radians is $\frac{1}{2} r^2 \theta$.
   - Minor arc AB is a shorter arc between points A & B and major arc is a longer arc between points A and B.

3. Key trigonometric values
   - Refer to M5.18

4. Trigonometric graphs
   - Refer to M4.12

5. Trigonometric identities
   - $\tan(x) = \frac{\sin(x)}{\cos(x)}$
   - $\sin(x)^2 + \cos(x)^2 = 1$

6. Solving trigonometric equations
   - Rearrange the equation to have a trigonometric function on one side and a number on the other side. Then solve for the angle, ensuring the solution for your angle is in the given range. You may need to solve quadratics first before you can find the angles.

AM5 Exponentials and logarithms

1. Graph of $y = a^x$
   - Functions in the form $y = a^x$, where a is a constant are exponential functions. They will always pass through the point (0,1).
     - When $a > 1$, it is an increasing function and as a increases a^x grows exponentially. It tends towards 0 as x decreases.
     - When $0 < a < 1$, it is a decreasing function and as a increases a^x tends towards 0. It grows without limit as x decreases.
     - When $x > 0$, $3^x > 2^x$ and when $x < 0$, $3^x < 2^x$

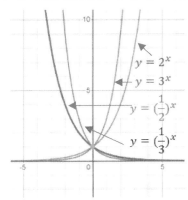

$y = 2^x$
$y = 3^x$
$y = \left(\frac{1}{2}\right)^x$
$y = \left(\frac{1}{3}\right)^x$

   - Note that: $y = \left(\frac{1}{2}\right)^x = (2^{-1})^x = 2^{-x}$

2. Laws of logarithms
   - For any logarithm, if the number that is inside the logarithmic bracket is less than the base, then it will be a fractional answer. You can never take the "log" of a negative number.
   - Log rules:
     - $\log_a n = x$ is equal to $a^x = n$. a is called the base of the log and it cannot be 1
     - $\log_a x + \log_a y = \log_a xy$
     - $\log_a x - \log_a y = \log_a \frac{x}{y}$
     - $\log_a(x^k) = k\log_a x$
     - $\log_a \frac{1}{x} = \log_a x^{-1} = -\log_a x$
     - $\log_a a = 1$
     - $\log_a 1 = 0$
     - $\log_a b = \frac{1}{\log_b a}$
     - $1 + \log_a b = \log_a a + \log_a b = \log_a ab$
     - $\log_a 4 = \log_a 2^2 = 2\log_a 2$
     - $a^b = c \leftrightarrow b = \log_a c$
     - For a number to the power of log of the same number they cancel out: $2^{\log_2 x} = x$

3. Solving equations in the form $a^x = b$
   - To solve equations in the form of $a^x = b$, you take the logarithm of both sides, and sometimes you need to use algebraic manipulation to reach this stage (for example, you may need to solve a quadratic to get two exponential expressions to solve).
   - The graphs of $y = ab^x$ and $y = ax^b$ are both straight lines when you take the logarithm of both sides. But for the first graph $y = ab^x$, it is a straight line when you plot $\log y$ against x and for the second graph $y = ax^b$, it is when you plot $\log y$ against $\log x$.

AM6 Differentiation

1. The derivative of a function
   - The first derivative shows the slope of the function and the rate of change. The first derivative gives the gradient of the tangent to the graph $y = f(x)$ at a point.
   - Second-order derivatives are when you differentiate the expression for the first-order derivative
   - $\frac{dy}{dx} = f'(x) =$ the first derivative
   - $\frac{d^2y}{dx^2} = f''(x) =$ the second derivative

2. Differentiating x^n
   - If you differentiate x^n, you get nx^{n-1}
   - There are some aspects to differentiation, which are not in the specification, but they are still useful to learn:

$f(x)$	$f'(x)$
x^n	nx^{n-1}
e^{kx}	ke^x
$\sin x$	$\cos x$
$\cos x$	$-\sin x$
$\ln x$	$\frac{1}{x}$
$e^{f(x)}$	$f'(x)e^{f(x)}$
$\ln[f(x)]$	$\frac{f'(x)}{f(x)}$

3. Applying differentiation
   - The first derivative tells us whether a function is increasing or decreasing, and by how much it is increasing or decreasing. A positive slope tells us that as x increases, $f(x)$ also increases. A negative slope tells us that as x increases, $f(x)$ decreases.
   - If $\frac{dy}{dx} > 0$ then it is an increasing function and the gradient is greater than 0
   - If $\frac{dy}{dx} < 0$ then it is a decreasing function and the gradient is less than 0
   - If $\frac{dy}{dx} = 0$, then there is a stationary point and it is either a minimum, maximum or a point of inflection.
   - If it is a local maximum then $\frac{d^2y}{dx^2} < 0$, when you substitute in the x value of the point.
   - If it is a local minimum then $\frac{d^2y}{dx^2} > 0$, when you substitute in the x value of the point.
   - A point of inflection is when $\frac{d^2y}{dx^2} = 0$ and $\frac{d^3y}{dx^3} \neq 0$, when you substitute in the x value of the point. It represents a change in the curvature or concavity.
   - If the second derivative is positive, then the first derivative is increasing, so that the slope of the tangent line to the function is increasing as x increases (the curve gets steeper and steeper). The curve is convex.
   - If the second derivative is negative, then the first derivative is decreasing, so that the slope of the tangent line to the function is decreasing as x increases (the slope is getting less and less steep). The curve is concave.
   - If $f''(x) > 0$ for all x then $f(x)$ is a convex function

- If $f''(x) < 0$ for all x then $f(x)$ is a concave function

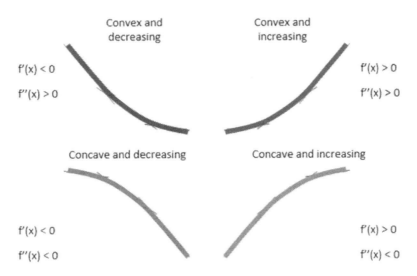

- The gradient of the normal is the negative reciprocal of the gradient of the tangent

AM7 Integration

1. Defining integration
    - Integration represents the area between a curve and the axis

2. Definite and indefinite integrals of x^n
    - To integrate you add one to the power and divide by the new power:
        - $\frac{dy}{dx} = kx^n$ Then $y = \frac{k}{n+1}x^{n+1}$

3. The Fundamental Theorem of Calculus
    - $\int_a^b f(x)dx = F(b) - F(a)$, where $F'(x) = f(x)$
    - $\frac{d}{dx} = \int_a^x f(t)dt = f(x)$

4. Combining integrals with equal or continuous ranges
    - You can combine integrals with either equal or continuous ranges, for example,

$$\int_4^6 f(x) + \int_4^6 g(x) = \int_4^6 (f(x) + g(x))dx$$

$$\int_a^b f(x)dx = -\int_b^a f(x)dx$$

$$\int_3^5 f(x)dx + \int_5^4 f(x)dx = \int_3^5 f(x)dx - \int_4^5 f(x)dx = \int_3^4 f(x)dx$$

5. Trapezium rule
    - $\int_a^b ydx = \frac{1}{2}h(y_0 + 2(y_1 + y_2 + y_3 \dots y_{n-1}) + y_n)$ where $h = \frac{b-a}{n}$ and $y_1 = f(a + ih)$
    - You split the trapezium into equal n strips with width b and find the sum of these areas. Intervals are areas under the curves and ordinates are the lines splitting the curve up. The first ordinate is the y axis and therefore there is always one more ordinate than the number of intervals.

- It is an overestimate if the area of the trapezium is greater than the exact area under the curve, which can be seen if the trapezium lines go "over" the curve line.
- It is an underestimate if the area of the trapezium is lower than the exact area under the curve, which can be seen if the trapezium lines go "under" the curve line.

6. Differential equations
   - Differential equations: such as $\frac{dy}{dx} = \frac{x+1}{y}$. You rearrange to get all the x terms on one side and all the y terms on the other side. Then you can integrate both sides.
   - $\frac{dy}{dx} = \frac{x+1}{y}$ can be rearranged to give $ydy = x + 1\, dx$. Then you integrate both sides to get $\int y\, dy = \int (x+1)dx$ which becomes $\frac{1}{2}y^2 = \frac{1}{2}x^2 + x + c$
   - Rearrange to make y the subject of the formula

AM8 Graphs of functions

1. Sketch common functions
   - Graphs have an alternating pattern, the quadratics and quartic have a curved-like shape like a bowl. cubics and quintics have a similar wave-like shape.
   - Curve sketching step by step method:
     - Find the roots and intercepts at both the axis. Substitute in $x = 0$ & $y = 0$.
     - Is it an even or odd function? An even function is where it is symmetrical in the y axis (reciprocal graphs), and an odd function is where it is not (cubic graphs). Even function: $f(x) = f(-x)$ and an odd function $-f(x) = f(-x)$
     - Is it a periodic function such as the sin graph?
     - Are there any asymptotes (horizontal or vertical)? What happens as the graph approaches the vertical asymptotes?
     - What happens as $x \to \pm\infty$?
     - Differentiate the function and find any turning points and find the second derivative to determine whether they are maximum or minimum points.
     - Sketching lines uses the format $y = mx + c$, where m is the gradient and c is the y intercept. The method for sketching quadratics and trigonometric functions has been explained previously.

2. Graph transformations
   - If a is a positive integer, then:

$y = f(x)$	No transformation
$y = f(x) + a$	Shift the graph up a units. Vector $\begin{pmatrix} 0 \\ a \end{pmatrix}$
$y = f(x) - a$	Shift the graph down a units. Vector $\begin{pmatrix} 0 \\ -a \end{pmatrix}$
$y = f(x + a)$	Shift the graph left a units. Vector $\begin{pmatrix} -a \\ 0 \end{pmatrix}$
$y = f(x - a)$	Shift the graph right a units. Vector $\begin{pmatrix} a \\ 0 \end{pmatrix}$
$y = -f(x)$	Reflect the graph in the x axis.
$y = f(-x)$	Reflect in the y axis.
$y = af(x)$	Stretch the graph in the y−axis (vertically) by a scale factor of a
$y = f(ax)$	Stretch the graph in the x−axis (horizontally) by a scale factor of $\frac{1}{a}$

- Key graph transformation notes: If you have different transformations affecting the same coordinate then the order you do it in matters. $y = Af(Bx + C) + D$ perform operations in order: $CBAD$.
  - Start inside the brackets where you look for a horizontal shift (if there is no horizontal shift then a vertical shift inside the brackets).
  - Deal with multiplication (stretch or compression) outside the brackets
  - Deal with reflections
  - Deal with addition/subtraction (vertical shift outside the brackets)

3. Changing m and c in $y = mx + c$
   - For $y = mx + c$, increasing m will make the gradient steeper and increasing c will shift the curve upwards

4. Changing a, b and c in $y = a(x + b)^2 + c$
   - In the curve $y = a(x + b)^2$: a is the stretch vertically. b is the horizontal shifts and c is a vertical shift

5. Using differentiation to graph a function
   - A stationary point is where the first derivative is equal to 0, a graph is increasing when the first derivative is greater than 0 and a graph is decreasing when the first derivative is less than 0.

6. Finding where a graph intersects the coordinates axis and finding real roots
   - A function intersects the y axis when $x = 0$ and it intersects the $x -$ axis when y is equal to 0.
     - Quadratic Graphs: to sketch graphs that are in the form $f(x) = ax^2 + bx + c$
     - Find $y -$ intercept when $x = 0$
     - Find the maximum or minimum point by completing the square: $f(x) = a(x + p)^2 + q$, where the turning point is $(-p, q)$
     - Find the two roots when $y = 0$
     - If the x^2 coefficient is positive, then it forms a U-shaped parabola. If the x^2 coefficient is negative, then it forms a ∩-shaped parabola
       - e.g. $y = 4 - 7x - 2x^2$, Firstly, you complete the square: $y = -2(x + \frac{7}{4})^2 + \frac{81}{8}$. Overall, the roots of the equation are $x = \frac{1}{2}$ and -4, the y-intercept is 4 and the maximum point is $\left(-\frac{7}{4}, \frac{81}{8}\right)$.
   - To find the number of roots:
     - Method 1: differentiate the equation and then factorise it. This gives the number of turning points and then find the exact coordinates of the turning points. Find the second derivative to see if it is a maximum or a minimum. Then plot this graph and it will show the number of real roots.
     - Method 2: if you cannot immediately spot how to factorise, you can input the numbers into the function starting from -2 and working up to 2 and see if any of these equate the expression to 0. They are commonly used factors. If you find one, then this becomes a root and you then use polynomial long division to simplify the expression.

7. The interpretations of intersecting graphs, their simultaneous equations and the solutions
   - To find how many times two curves intersect, you equate them to each other and then if there is one solution, they meet once, if there are two, they meet twice. If the discriminant is negative, they don't meet. If the discriminant is equal to 1 then there is one solution. If the discriminant is positive, then the curves meet more than once.

Other Useful Points

1. To find the horizontal asymptotes of a function, which is useful to sketch graphs:
   - If the numerator's highest degree polynomial is the same as the denominator's highest degree polynomial, then divide the coefficients of each $\frac{\text{numerator highest degree}}{\text{denominator highest degree}}$. This gives the horizontal $y = z$ asymptote. For example, $y = \frac{5x}{x-6}$, as the degrees are the same, divide the leading coefficients of the numerator and the denominator, $\frac{5}{1} = 5$. Therefore, horizontal asymptote at $y = 5$.
   - If the highest degree polynomial in the numerator is a lower degree than that in the denominator then there is a horizontal asymptote at $y = 0$. For example, $y = \frac{6}{(x-3)(6-x)}$, as the degree is the numerator is lower, there is a horizontal asymptote at $y = 0$.
   - If the highest degree polynomial in the numerator is a higher degree than that in the denominator, then there is no horizontal asymptote. For example, $y = \frac{7x^2}{x+11}$, as the degree in the numerator is greater than in the denominator, there is no horizontal asymptote

2. Certain prefixes for quantities are essential to know:

Prefix	Scale
Giga	10^9
Mega	10^6
Kilo	10^3
Deci	10^{-1}
Centi	10^{-2}
Milli	10^{-3}
Micro	10^{-6}
Nano	10^{-9}

300 Mathematics Questions

This next section of the book contains 300 Mathematics questions, which were carefully crafted based on the ECAA specification.

We have purposefully included certain questions that are easier than that which you will find in the ECAA, to test the foundation of your knowledge. Additionally, there are numerous questions which may be harder than that which you will find in the ECAA, which were included to push the boundaries of your mathematical ability and maximise your preparation.

We suggest that you complete these questions in small blocks, perhaps 20 questions every other day. There is no need to answer the questions under strict time conditions, however, it may be beneficial to work through each question as fast as possible, whilst maintaining accuracy. You could use a stopwatch out and try and minimise the time required to answer every question.

To build up your mental maths, we have tried to include numerous questions which require complex and long calculations with challenging numbers and the questions do not always provide simple round answers.

Do not use a calculator. You do not have a calculator in the ECAA exam; therefore, all your practise should be completed without the use of a calculator. There may be a temptation to use a calculator to perform the complex calculations that you "know how to do" but do not want to spend time doing, however, do not succumb to this. By doing these complex calculations yourself, it will speed up your mental maths and increase your accuracy. This is essential in the ECAA, to prevent silly mistakes and to finish the paper on time.

There is no order to the difficulty of the questions in this book (i.e. question 1 is not necessarily the easiest question and question 300 is not necessarily the hardest). However, for questions 1-100, we ensured to only offer 4 multiple-choice options, but as the questions progress to 101-300, there are commonly more than 4 options to choose from. This reflects the progression in your ability and skill as you practise more questions and increases the challenge in answering the questions.

Suggested use:

1. Work at a clear desk with no clutter: you will only need a pen and this ECAA book. There is space underneath each question to write your answer.
2. Always set a target number of questions you want to complete in one sitting, for example, 20. Begin answering the questions, and start a stopwatch at the same time.
3. Work through the questions rapidly but accurately and move on if you get stuck. Work with your full concentration, without background noise (e.g. the TV) and work on your own, with no help from friends.
4. While completing the section, resist the urge to check the answers or peek at the worked solutions, and if you cannot do a question, then leave it and move on.
5. After completing the set of questions, stop the timer and record the time it took. Then, return to any questions that you could not answer and without any time pressure attempt to answer them again.
6. After you have revisited questions, use the answer list (not the worked answers) to mark the questions and record your score. For any questions which you got incorrect, without looking at the worked answers, go back and try the question again to try and derive the correct answer. If you still cannot solve it, then go to the worked answers.
7. Read through all the worked answers for the question set you completed, even if you got the answer correct, look to see if the worked solution performed the calculation with a shorter method. Try and learn from the worked answers to improve your efficiency.

Tracking your work

We recommend making a table on Excel to track your progress through the book. Our suggested table will have the question numbers from 1 to 300 as the first column. Then you put a 1 (correct) or 0 (incorrect) in the second column, and as you progress through the book you can track the number of questions you answered correctly and the number of questions you got wrong. The third column is for notes, namely, you can put a "*" next to any question (whether you got it correct or not) which you found extremely challenging and which you would like to revisit later.

Naturally, you can produce any version of this table that suits you, perhaps adding a key to include aspects such as careless mistakes, not reading the questions carefully, timing issues or content weakness comments etc.

The Excel table headers have a small arrow next to them, which will allow you to filter the questions. For example, you can filter to find all the questions which have "*" in the third column. This will give you all the challenging question numbers.

An example table is shown below:

Q	Result	Notes		Key	
1	1	*		1	Correct
2	1			0	Incorrect
3	0	CM		Q	Mis-understanding/ not reading the question
4	1			T	Timing issues
...	...			CW	Content weakness
298	0	T		*	Challenging question - revisit
299	1			CM	Careless mistake
300	0	Q			

Total correct	250

The book does not have to be a one-time use! Start revising early, such as Year 12 summer, and spend a few weeks completing the book. Then, revise for the ECAA from other sources such as the past papers on the website, or the links provided above, and then after a few weeks return to this book. You can reattempt all the questions, and you will likely have forgotten the majority of specific answers by then, or you can pick and choose the hardest questions to reattempt.

If you do reattempt all the questions, create a new column on the Excel Sheet, and then you can compare your score and accuracy from both attempts.

Good luck!

300 Maths Questions

1. A circle has equation $x^2 + y^2 + 8x + 4y - 29 = 0$. What is the radius of this circle?

A $\sqrt{29}$ C $\sqrt{109}$

B   7   D   10

2. A curve has an equation $y = 5x^3 - 12x^2 + 6x^{\frac{1}{2}}$. What is the gradient of the normal when $x = 2$?

A $\dfrac{-8+\sqrt{2}}{93}$ C $\dfrac{(24+3\sqrt{2})}{2}$

B $-7 + 6\sqrt{2}$ D   15

3. A function f is given by $f(x) = 2x^2 - 2x - 9$. Which of the following describes the nature of the roots of $f(x) = 0$?

A   No real roots   C   Real distinct roots

B   Equal roots   D   Rational distinct roots

4. What is the coefficient of the x^4 term in the following expansion: $(1 + x + x^2)^3$?

A   3

B $\frac{1}{2}$

C   1

D   6

5. When $x^2 + 14x + \frac{11}{2}$ is written in the form of $(x + p)^2 + q$, what are the values of p and q?

A $p = 7$ and $q = -\frac{87}{2}$

B $p = 14$ and $q = -\frac{11}{2}$

C $p = -14$ and $q = \frac{11}{2}$

D $p = -7$ and $q = \frac{87}{2}$

6. What is the value of the expression below?

$$\frac{1}{\sqrt{1} + \sqrt{2}} + \frac{1}{\sqrt{2} + \sqrt{3}} + \frac{1}{\sqrt{3} + \sqrt{4}} + \frac{1}{\sqrt{4} + \sqrt{5}} \cdots + \frac{1}{\sqrt{35} + \sqrt{36}}$$

A   6

B   5

C $\sqrt{35} - \sqrt{2}$

D $360 + \frac{5\sqrt{3}}{\sqrt{125\sqrt{2}}}$

7. What is the solution of $2x^2 - 6x < 36$, where x is a real number?

A $-3 < x < 6$ C $x > 3$ and $x < -6$

B $3 < x < 6$ D $x = -3$ and $x = 6$

8. What is the product of the gradient of the line parallel to $3y + 2x = 6$ and the gradient of the line perpendicular to $5y + 3x = 11$?

A $\dfrac{2}{5}$ C $-\dfrac{10}{9}$

B $\dfrac{5}{2}$ D $-\dfrac{2}{3}$

9. A function $f(x)$ is defined as $f(x) = x^3 - 5x^2 + 4x + 3$. What is the remainder when $f(x)$ is divided by $(x - 2)$?

A $\dfrac{1}{2}$ C   1

B -1 D   6

10. There are 10 marbles in a bag, 6 are pink and 4 are orange. You take two out of the bag at random without replacement. Given that at least one of them was orange, what is the probability the next one is orange?

A $\dfrac{7}{20}$ C $\dfrac{1}{2}$

B $\dfrac{7}{30}$ D $\dfrac{1}{3}$

11. If $3x - y = 15$, what is the value of $\dfrac{8^x}{2^y}$?

A 4^2 C 2^{15}

B $\dfrac{8^{15}}{2^3}$ D   Insufficient information

12. Given that $\left(\sqrt{3}\right)^m = \dfrac{3^{2x}}{81^y}$, express m in terms of x and y.

A $m = 4x - 8y$ C $m = 3x - 9y$

B $m = 2x - 4y$ D $m = x + y$

43

13. Given that $a^{5x}b^{2x}c^x d^{-3x} = 4$, where a, b, c and d are all positive real numbers, then $x =$

A $\quad \dfrac{4}{\log\left(\frac{a^5 b^2 c}{d^3}\right)}$

C $\quad \dfrac{4d^3}{a^5 b^2 c}$

B $\quad \dfrac{\log(4)}{\log\left(\frac{a^5 b^2 c}{d^3}\right)}$

D $\quad 4 - \dfrac{a^5 b^2 c}{d^3}$

14. If $3^{x+2} \times 9^{\frac{3}{2}x} = 27^{27}$, what is the value of x?

A $\quad 3$

C $\quad \dfrac{52}{3}$

B $\quad \dfrac{27}{2}$

D $\quad \dfrac{79}{4}$

15. Solve the inequality: $\dfrac{x}{x-10} > \dfrac{1}{2}$

A $\quad x < -10$ or $x > 10$

C $\quad -5 < x < 5$

B $\quad -10 < x < 10$

D $\quad x < 10$ or $x > 20$

16. The roots to the equation $3x^2 - 10x - k = 0$, differ by $\frac{14}{3}$. What is the value of k?

A -8

B 4

C $\frac{11}{3}$

D 8

17. What is the sum of the solutions of the equation $(3^x)^2 - 13(3^x) = -40$?

A $\frac{13}{\log 3}$

B 13

C $\frac{\log_{10} 40}{\log_{10} 3}$

D $\log_{10} \frac{40}{3}$

18. If $f(x) = 2x^2 - 4x + 8$, what is the coordinates of the minimum of $y = f(x - 2)$

A $(-3, -6)$

B $(3,6)$

C $(1,6)$

D $(4, -3)$

45

19. If $f(x) = -3x^2 + 5x + 8$, what are the coordinates of the minimum of $y = -4f(x+1)$

A $(-\frac{1}{6}, -\frac{121}{3})$

B $(\frac{5}{6}, \frac{121}{12})$

C $(11, -4)$

D $(-\frac{1}{6}, -\frac{121}{12})$

20. A sequence has the property that $a_{n+1} = \frac{a_n}{a_{n-1}}$. Given that $a_1 = 3$ and $a_2 = 5$, what is a_{2020}

A $\frac{1}{5}$

B   3

C $\frac{5}{3}$

D $\frac{1}{3}$

21. Which of the following statements is true for the equation $2x^3 - x^2 - 13x - 6$?

A   It has no real roots

B   It has three real roots

C   It has two real roots and one imaginary root

D   Insufficient information to find the number of roots

22. What is the greatest value of the function $f(x) = (4\cos^2(11x - 4) + 2)^3$?

A   8

B   216

C   1

D   0

23. How many stationary points does the function $y = -3x^3 - 7x^2 + x - 11$ have?

A   0

B   2

C   1

D   3

24. The equation $4^x - 2^{x+3} = m$ has one or more solutions when

A $m \leq 16$

B $m \geq 4$

C $m \geq -16$

D $m \geq 16$

25. The 4th, 5th and 6th terms in a geometric sequence are: $x + 6, 2x$ and $3x - 4$ respectively. What is the sum of the two possible values for x?

A $2\ and\ 12$ C $6\ and\ 14$

B 20 D 14

26. $f(x) = x^5 + ax^4 + bx^3 + 3x^2$. When $f(x)$ is divided by $(x - 1)$, the remainder is 12 and when $f(x)$ is divided by $(x + 2)$, the remainder is also 12. What is the product of a and b?

A   16   C   4

B   5   D   28

27. In an arithmetic progression, the sum of the first 20 terms is 350 and the sum of the next 15 terms is 3,150. Find the common difference.

A   11   C   6

B   −87   D   13

28. A rectangle has an area of $\sqrt{150}$ and it has a side length of $3 + 2\sqrt{3}$. What is the perimeter of the rectangle?

A $\quad 6 + 4\sqrt{3} - 10\sqrt{6} + 20\sqrt{2}$

B $\quad -5\sqrt{6} + 10\sqrt{2}$

C $\quad 2(\sqrt{150} - (3 + 2\sqrt{3}))$

D $\quad 12 + 8\sqrt{3}$

29. Rationalise the following expression: $5 + \dfrac{6\sqrt{2} - 5\sqrt{3}}{\sqrt{3} - \sqrt{2}}$

A $\quad 12 + 3\sqrt{6}$

B $\quad \sqrt{3} + \sqrt{6}$

C $\quad 2 + \sqrt{6}$

D $\quad 2 + 4\sqrt{6}$

30. If $f(x) = 4x^2 + 6x + 9$, what is the coordinates of the minimum of $y = 11f(2x + 3)$

A $\quad \left(\dfrac{-6}{8}, \dfrac{27}{16}\right)$

B $\quad \left(\dfrac{-15}{8}, \dfrac{297}{4}\right)$

C $\quad \left(-\dfrac{15}{8}, \dfrac{207}{8}\right)$

D $\quad \left(-\dfrac{27}{8}, \dfrac{207}{15}\right)$

31. For this question we assume that for any pizza restaurant, **every** time a guest eats, they leave a part of their pizza behind as unwanted leftovers for the restaurant to clear away (no take away). A very unhygienic restaurant, uses the leftovers of 9 pizzas to make it into a new pizza to serve. How many overall **full** pizzas does 681 new pizzas provide (the overall number should include the initial 681)?

A   764

C   765

B   756

D   766.25

32. What is the sum of values of a and b in the solution to the equation below, when a is the largest value it can take?

$$\frac{1}{a} + \frac{1}{b} = \frac{1}{6}$$

A   6

C   5

B   49

D   20

33. What is the distance between the points (3,1,5) and (6,3,6)?

A $\sqrt{13}$

C   8

B   5

D $\sqrt{14}$

50

34. If three fair coins are tossed, what is the probability of getting at most two tails?

A $\dfrac{7}{8}$ C $\dfrac{7}{18}$

B $\dfrac{3}{4}$ D $\dfrac{5}{7}$

35. If a coin is tossed 20 times, which is the following is the correct expression for the probability of getting 5 heads?

A $20C5 \times 0.5^5$ C $20C5 \times 0.5^5 \times 0.5^{20}$

B $20C15 \times 15^{\frac{1}{2}} \times 5^{\frac{1}{2}}$ D $20C15 \times 0.5^5 \times 0.5^{15}$

36. There is a 5-sided spinner, which is painted with 5 colours of equal area: red, blue, green, yellow and pink. What is the probability of getting 11 reds when it is spun 30 times?

A $30C11 \times \left(\dfrac{1}{5}\right)^{19} \times \left(\dfrac{4}{5}\right)^{11}$ C $\left(\dfrac{1}{5}\right)^{11} \times \left(\dfrac{4}{5}\right)^{19}$

B $30C5 \times 11^{\frac{1}{5}} \times 19^{\frac{4}{5}}$ D $30C19 \times \left(\dfrac{1}{5}\right)^{11} \times \left(\dfrac{4}{5}\right)^{19}$

37. If $f(x) = x^4 - 2x^3 + px^2 + qx + r$, and when $f(x)$ is divided by $(x - 2)$, the remainder is -24 and when it is divided by $(x + 4)$, the remainder is 240. If $x = -1$ is a solution to the polynomial, then find the product of p, q and r.

A   36

B -144

C   42

D -256

38. How many permutations are there to write the word "$onomatopoeia$"?

A $\frac{12!}{4! \times 2!}$

B $12!$

C $\frac{12!}{6! \times 4!}$

D   1

39. How many ways can the results of 5 cricket matches be forecast, such that each match can either be a home win, a draw or an away win?

A   243

B   125

C   15

D   25

40. If an infinite geometric series with a first term 4, converges to the sum of 6, find the 4th term in the sequence.

A $\dfrac{4}{9}$

B $\dfrac{4}{81}$

C $\dfrac{1}{3}$

D $\dfrac{4}{27}$

41. Does the line $y = x$ meet with the circle $x^2 - 4x + 4 + y^2 - 20y - 100 = 18$?

A   Yes, at one point

B   No

C   Insufficient information

D   Yes, at two points

42. The probability that I fall over when cycling is 0.7 if it is a rainy day, and 0.2 on a clear day. Suppose the probability that it rains on any day is 0.6, find the probability that it was a rainy day given that I did not fall over. *For the purpose of the question assume that every day can be categorised into raining or not raining.*

A $\dfrac{3}{10}$

B $\dfrac{21}{50}$

C $\dfrac{9}{25}$

D $\dfrac{9}{50}$

43. The graph $y = \log_{10}\left(\frac{1}{3x^2+17x-56}\right)$, has asymptotes at $x = a$ and $x = b$, as well as roots at $x = c$ and $x = d$. Find $abcd$.

A 0

C $4 + \sqrt{6}$

B $\frac{1064}{3}$

D $\frac{1164}{3}$

44. Let $f(x)$ be any quadratic polynomial in the form $ax^2 + bx + c$. The remainder is 3, when it is divided by the linear function $(x - 1)$, it has a remainder of 12, when it is divided by $(x - 2)$, and finally the remainder is 0, when it is divided by $(x + 2)$. What is the value of $a - b + c$?

A $a = 2, b = 3 \text{ and } c = -2$

C 3

B -3

D $a = 3, b = 4 \text{ and } c = 4$

45. If House A costs £3.86×10^6 and House B costs £4.55×10^7, what is the difference between their prices in standard form?

A 0.69×10^1

C 4.164×10^7

B 6.9×10^{13}

D $41,640,000$

54

46. If $f(x)$ is a quadratic function in x and the graph $y = f(x)$ passes through a point $(3,3)$ and has a minimum point at $(1.5, -1.5)$. Which of the following is the correct equation?

A $y = x^2 - 3x + 3$

B $y = (x - 1.5)^2 + 3.75$

C $y = 2x^2 + 6x + 3$

D $y = 2x^2 - 6x + 3$

47. Find the coefficient of the x^3 term in the expansion of $(1 + x)(2x + 5)^4$

A   760

B   600

C   160

D   176

48. Find the coefficient of the x^3 term in the expansion of $(3 + 2x)^2 \left(2x + \frac{1}{x}\right)^6$

A   2880

B   2800

C   160

D   2688

49. For an arithmetic sequence, with first term a and common difference d, if the sum of the first 4 terms is equal to the sum of the first 12 terms. What is the relationship between a and d?

A $\quad a = -\dfrac{30}{8}d$

B $\quad 4a = 30d$

C $\quad a = d$

D $\quad 4a = -30d$

50. Which of the following numbers is smallest?

A $\quad \log_2 7$

B $\quad \log_{11} 7$

C $\quad (3^{-3} + 3^{-2})^{-1}$

D $\quad \dfrac{5}{10(\sqrt{2}-1)^2}$

51. The first three terms of a geometric sequence are $p - 3$, $2p - 4$ and $4p - 3$ respectively. What is the sum of the first 3 terms in the sequence?

A $\quad -\dfrac{8}{3}$

B $\quad 39$

C $\quad 25$

D $\quad 7$

52. What is the coefficient of the x^2 term in the following expansion: $(1 + 4x + x^2)^4$?

A   304   C   16

B   4   D   100

53. Solve the equation:

$$5(2^{3x}) + 14(2^{2x}) + 7(2^x) - 2 = 0$$

A $x = -\dfrac{\log 5}{\log 2}$ C $x = -\log 3$

B $x = \dfrac{1}{5}, x = -1, x = -2$ D $x = \dfrac{1}{5}$

54. Rearrange the following equation to make a, the subject of the formula:

$$\frac{1}{a} + \frac{1}{b} = \frac{1}{c}$$

A $\dfrac{cb}{b-c}$ C $\dfrac{b-c}{cb}$

B $b - c$ D $\dfrac{1}{c} - \dfrac{1}{b} - 1$

55. Simplify $17\left(1 - \frac{1}{17^2}\right)^{\frac{1}{2}}$, into surd in the form of $a\sqrt{2}$.

A $24\sqrt{2}$ C $12\sqrt{2}$

B $17\sqrt{2}$ D $10\sqrt{2}$

56. A perfectly round drop of paint with diameter 5mm, falls onto the acrylic surface from the tip of a brush, and creates a circular film of paint with radius 15cm. What is the thickness of the film?

A $\frac{1}{250}\pi\ cm$ C $\frac{1}{2560}\pi\ mm$

B $\frac{1}{1080}\ mm$ D $\frac{1}{135}\ mm$

57. For the geometric progression $q + q^2 + q^3 + q^4 \ldots$ where $q \neq 0$, if the sum to infinity is $4q$, then the common ratio is:

A $\frac{3}{4}\ or\ 0$ C $\frac{5}{6}\ or\ 0$

B $\frac{5}{6}$ D $\frac{3}{4}$

58. By considering the infinite expansion of a geometric series, or otherwise, find the fraction equal to the recurring decimal $0.\dot{5}\dot{4}$

A $\dfrac{2727}{5000}$ C $\dfrac{7}{12}$

B $\dfrac{2700}{4949}$ D $\dfrac{6}{11}$

59. By considering the infinite expansion of a geometric series, or otherwise, find the fraction equal to the recurring decimal $0.6\dot{3}\dot{6}$

A $\dfrac{159}{250}$ C $\dfrac{7}{12}$

B $\dfrac{6363}{1000}$ D $\dfrac{7}{11}$

60. A triangular prism is made from an equilateral triangle of side $x\,cm$ and length $l\,cm$, as shown below. Given that it has a volume $250cm^3$, what is the maximum surface area of the prism?

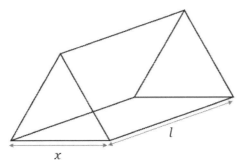

A $150\sqrt{3}\,cm^2$ C $250^{\frac{2}{3}}cm^2$

B $10cm^2$ D   Insufficient information

61. Solve the inequality $x^3 - 5x > 2x^2 - 6$

A $-2 < x < 1, x > 3$

B $1 < x < 3, x < -2$

C $-2 < x < 4$

D $x < -4, x > 5$

62. Solve the inequality $x^3 - 4x^2 > 7x - 10$

A $x \in R$

B $1 < x < 5, x < -2$

C $x < 5, x < -2$

D $-2 < x < 1, x > 5$

63. Solve the inequality $\frac{x(x-2)}{x-3} > \frac{1}{2}$

A $1 < x < \frac{3}{2}, x > 3$

B $1 < x < 3$

C $x < 1, x > \frac{3}{2}$

D $-2 < x < \frac{1}{2}$

64. If the points $(p, q), (2,4)$ *and* $(4,7)$ are collinear, then what is the relationship between p and q?

A $3p - 2q = -2$ C $p = \frac{q}{2}$

B $-3p + 2q = -2$ D $2p + 5q + 6 = 0$

65. What is the locus of the points that are equidistant from the centres of the two circles:

$x^2 - 4x + y^2 - 6y - 15 = 0$ and $(x - 5)^2 + (y + 3)^2 = 25$

A $y = -\frac{1}{2}x + \frac{7}{4}$ C $4y - 2x = -7$

B $y = 2x + 7$ D $y = \frac{1}{2}x - \frac{11}{2}$

66. If the curve $y = x^3$ undergoes the following transformation, in the order given, then what is the equation of the final curve?

A translation of magnitude 4 parallel to the y axis, then a scaling of factor 3 parallel to the x axis, followed by a scaling of factor 5 parallel to the y axis and a reflection in the x axis. Finally, a translation of factor -6 parallel to the y axis.

A $y = -\frac{5x^3}{27} - 2$ C $y = -135x^3 - 26$

B $27y = -5x^3 + 378$ D $27y = -5x^3 - 702$

67. If the curve $y = f(x)$ is transformed using the transformation A, B, C, D such that

$y = Af(Bx + C) + D$, then what is the correct order to perform the transformation?

A $ADBC$ C $BCAD$

B $BCDA$ D $CBAD$

68. What is the equation of a circle with the diameter being the line joining the points $(3,5)$ and $(7,7)$?

A $(x + 5)^2 + (y + 6)^2 = 5$ C $x^2 - 10x + y^2 - 12y + 54 = \sqrt{5}$

B $(x - 5)^2 + (y - 6)^2 = 10$ D $x^2 - 10x + y^2 - 12y + 61 = 5$

69. Which of the following is true for the functions defined by:

$p(x) = 5x - \dfrac{1}{x}$, where $x > 1$ and $q(x) = x^5 + 6x^3$

A p is increasing, q is decreasing   C p is increasing, q is increasing

B p is decreasing, q is increasing   D p is decreasing, q is decreasing

70. Solve the simultaneous equations below:

$$3x^2 + y^2 = 36 + xy$$

$$x = y - 3$$

A $y = \frac{5+\sqrt{37}}{2}$ and $x = \frac{-1+\sqrt{37}}{2}$ or $y = \frac{5-\sqrt{37}}{2}$ and $x = -\frac{1+\sqrt{37}}{2}$

B $y = \frac{5+\sqrt{37}}{4}$ and $x = \frac{-1+\sqrt{37}}{4}$ or $y = \frac{5-\sqrt{37}}{4}$ and $x = -\frac{1+\sqrt{37}}{4}$

C $y = 3$ and $x = 0$ or $y = 6$ and $x = 3$

D $y = 2.5$ and $x = -0.5$ or $y = 1.25$ and $x = -1.75$

71. How many real solutions does the following equation have: $27^x - 9^x = -9 + 3^{x+2}$?

A   0   C   1

B   2   D   3

72. If p and q are both positive numbers, then by considering the equation below, find the product pq, when p is the largest possible value it can be.

$$9(\log_8 p)^2 = 1 - (\log_8 q)^2$$

A   4   C   12

B   2   D   0

73. If the equation: $4x^4 = (2x - p)^2$, has 4 real solutions, then p satisfies the inequality:

A $p < \frac{1}{2}$

C $-\frac{1}{2} < p < \frac{1}{2}$

B $p > -\frac{1}{2}$

D $p > 2$ and $p < -2$

74. Solve the cubic equation: $6x^3 - 5x^2 - 17x + 6 = 0$

A $x = -\frac{3}{2}, x = 2, x = \frac{1}{3}$

C $x = -\frac{5}{2}, x = 2, x = \frac{1}{3}$

B $x = -\frac{3}{2}, x = 2, x = -\frac{1}{3}$

D $x = -\frac{5}{2}, x = 3, x = \frac{1}{4}$

75. For what values of q does the equation $\frac{6}{4}x^4 - 8x^3 + 9x^2 + q = 0$, have 4 real solutions?

A $-\frac{5}{2} < q < \frac{27}{2}$

C $-\frac{5}{2} < q < 0$

B $q \in R$

D $q < 0$

76. Which of the following list of transformations is correct for the expression: $y = \frac{1}{4}(3x^3 + 9) - 5$, from the curve x^3?

A   Stretch by factor $\frac{1}{3}$ in the horizontal direction, then a shift 9 units left horizontally, followed by a stretch vertically by factor $\frac{1}{4}$ and a shift 5 units downward vertically

B   Stretch by factor 3 in the vertical direction, shift upwards $\frac{9}{4}$ units, stretch by factor $\frac{1}{4}$ in the vertical direction and finally a shift by -5 vertically

C   Vertical shift upwards by 3, stretch by factor of 0.75 in the y axis, vertical shift by -5

D   Vertical stretch by factor $\frac{3}{4}$ in the x axis, followed by a shift by $-\frac{11}{4}$ vertically

77. Simplify the following: $x^4 + 12x^3y + 54x^2y^2 + 108xy^3 + 81y^4$

A $(x + 2y)^4$ C $(xy + 3x + 3y)^2$

B $(3x + y)^4$ D $(x + 3y)^4$

78. How many solutions does the following equation have?

$$\log_{4x-4}(x^4 + 2x^3 - 3x^2) = 1$$

A   4   C   0

B   2   D   Infinite solutions

65

79. If a bank account starts with £100 and there is an interest of 5% gained at the end of each year, what is the total in the bank after 4 years?

A   £121.55

C   £428.71

B   £120

D   £120.54

80. If A is directly proportional to $\frac{1}{B^4}$ and if B is increased by 50%, then to the nearest percentage, what is the change in A in percentage terms.

A   20% decrease

C   80% increase

B   20% increase

D   80% decrease

81. How many times are the hands of a clock (hour and minute hand) at right angles in 24 hours?

A   48

C   22

B   6

D   44

82. You have to choose a team of 11 football players out of a group of 7 Brazilian players, 4 English players and 4 Spanish. If you want 5 players from Brazil, 3 from England and 3 from Spain, what is the probability of picking this team?

A $\frac{11}{15}$

C $\frac{32}{65}$

B $\frac{16}{65}$

D Insufficient information

83. You have to make a ring which can have any number of beads. If you have 1 ruby bead, 1 sapphire bead, 1 amethyst bead and 1 emerald bead available, how many different ways are there to make this ring?

A 15

C 64

B 6

D 72

84. You are a waiter at a restaurant, and a family walks in (2 parents and 3 children). How many arrangements can the family be seated in around a rectangular table, if the two parents do not want to sit next to each other? *Note, everyone sits along the same row:*

| Person 1 | Person 2 | Person 3 | Person 4 | Person 5 |

A 120

C 72

B 48

D 119

85. At a funfair, there is a "Make your own burrito" stall. In addition to the bean filling which every burrito has, they offer 8 different topping options (sour cream, tomato, lettuce, cheese, onions, salsa, chilli sauce and rice). There are also 5 different types of tortilla wrap to choose from. How many possible burrito options are there?

A   1360

B   45

C   40

D   1280

86. For the variables x and y, if a graph is drawn that plots x to log (y), then which of the following relationships will produce a linear graph?

A $y = ax^b$

B $y = ab^x$

C $y = mx + c$

D $x^{\log(y)} = y^x$

87. If there are two boxes, box A with x white balls and y black balls, and box B with y white balls and x black balls. One ball is taken out at random from box A and put in box B. Then, if one ball is taken out of box B, what is the probability that it is black?

A $\dfrac{x^2+y(x+1)}{(x+y)(1+x+y)}$

B $\dfrac{x^2+y(x+1)}{(x+y)^2}$

C $\dfrac{x^2+y(x+1)}{2(x+y)(1+x+y)}$

D $\dfrac{x^2+xy}{(x+y)^2}$

88. Solve the following equation for $\frac{x}{y}$

$$2\log(x - 2y) - \log(x) = \log(y)$$

A $1\ or\ 4$

C $2\ or\ 6$

B $1\ or\ \frac{1}{4}$

D $\frac{1}{2}\ or\ \frac{1}{6}$

89. The nth term of an arithmetic sequence is $u_n = 2\ln(p) + (n - 1)\ln(q)$. If $u_5 = \ln(1296)$ and $u_7 = \ln(11664)$. What are the values of p and q, assuming they are both positive integers?

A $p = 5, q = 7$

C $p = 3, q = 4$

B $p = 7, q = 5$

D $p = 4, q = 3$

90. The sum to infinity of a convergent geometric series is 6. If a second convergent geometric series is formed by squaring every term in the first geometric series and has a sum of 30, what is the common ratio of the original series?

A $1\ or\ \frac{1}{11}$

C $\frac{1}{11}$

B $\frac{1}{6}$

D $\frac{1}{6}\ or\ 1$

69

91. In the binomial expansion $(p + 3x^2)^5$, where the coefficient of x^6 is 1215 and $p < 0$, what is the value of p?

A $\quad -\dfrac{3\sqrt{2}}{2}$

B $\quad -\dfrac{5\sqrt{2}}{2}$

C $\quad 3\sqrt{5}$

D $\quad -3\sqrt{5}$

92. Solve the simultaneous equations below:

$$\log_2 x + 3\log_2 y = 2$$

$$\log_3 \frac{1}{x} - 4\log_3 y = -2$$

A $\quad y = -\dfrac{1}{36}$ and $x = -186624$

B $\quad x = \dfrac{256}{729}$ and $y = \dfrac{9}{4}$

C $\quad x = \dfrac{1}{9}$ and $y = 3$

D $\quad x = \dfrac{1}{2}$ and $y = 2$

93. Solve the set of inequalities below:

$$-2x^2 + 5x + 7 \le 0$$

$$x^2 - 9x + 18 \ge 0$$

A $\quad x \le -1$ or $x \ge \dfrac{7}{2}$

B $\quad x \le 3$ or $x \ge 6$

C $\quad x \le -1$ or $x \ge 6$

D $\quad x \le 3$ or $x \ge \dfrac{7}{2}$

94. In a school of 100 pupils, there are three sports played by students: Rugby, Cricket or Football.

5 students play football only, 20 play cricket only and 13 play rugby only. 27 play football and rugby, 15 play cricket and football and 12 play rugby and cricket. 12 students do not play any sport. If one student is chosen at random from the 100 students, and then a second student is chosen from the remaining students, what is the probability that the first student plays football and the second student plays rugby but not cricket.

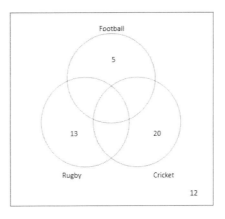

A $\dfrac{19}{110}$ C $\dfrac{25}{132}$

B $\dfrac{171}{1000}$ D $\dfrac{337}{1980}$

95. $\int_1^2 x^2(\sqrt{x} + x^3 - 4x + 1)\, dx$

A $-\dfrac{103}{42} + \dfrac{16\sqrt{2}}{7}$ C $-\dfrac{23}{12} + \dfrac{4\sqrt{2}}{3}$

B $5 + 4\sqrt{2}$ D $-\dfrac{23}{12} + \dfrac{4\sqrt{2}}{3} + c$

96. If a shape, with perimeter 60cm, consists of a rectangular base with a semi-circular top, find the maximum value of the area in terms of π.

Perimeter 60cm

A $\dfrac{1800}{4+\pi}cm^2$

B $24\pi cm^2$

C $\dfrac{60}{4+\pi}cm^2$

D $0cm^2$

97. Solve the following equation for x:

$$\log_2(19x + 30) = 3\log_2(x)$$

A $x = -3, x = -2, x = 5$

B $x = -2, x = 3, x = 5$

C $x = 5$

D $x = 2^{\frac{\log_2 570}{2}}$

98. The mean of a set of 15 numbers if 66 and when a number y is removed from the set, the mean reduces to reach 60. The mean weight of a group of 20 teenagers was $62kg$ and when two teenagers left the group, whose weights were $65kg\ and\ 59kg$, the mean fell to xkg. What is the product of xy.

A   5580

B   9300

C   8370

D   5022

72

99. In the archery target shown below, which is divided into three concentric circle, with radii in the ratio of $1:2:4$. What is the ratio of the area $outer:middle:inner$?

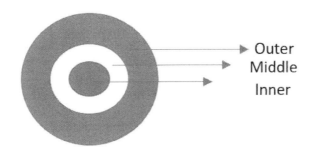

A $1:4:16$

B $1:3:12$

C $1:3:16$

D   Insufficient information

100. If you have 65 coins in a bag, where 1 coin is double headed and the remaining 64 are standard coins. You pick a coin from the bag at random and toss it 6 times and get 6 heads. What is the probability that the next time you flip it you get tails?

A $\frac{1}{2}$

B $\frac{64}{65}$

C 0

D $\frac{1}{4}$

101. What is the area of an equilateral triangle with side length $\frac{3}{2}x$?

A $\dfrac{9x^2 3^{0.5}}{16}$

B $\dfrac{9x 3^{0.5}}{16}$

C $\dfrac{x^2}{2}$

D $\dfrac{9x^2}{8}$

E $\dfrac{x^2 \sqrt{3}}{4}$

F $\dfrac{9x^2}{4}$

102. The ratio of length to width for my lawn is 12:5 and the diagonal is 39 metres. There is a 2m path around the outside. What is the combined area of my lawn and the path?

A   722 metres²

B   760 metres²

C   540 metres²

D   646 metres²

E   More information needed.

103. A square-based pyramid has sides of unit length. What is the height of the line perpendicular to the base connecting to the top vertex?

A $\dfrac{\sqrt{2}}{2}$

B $\sqrt{3}$

C $\sqrt{2}$

D $\dfrac{\sqrt{3}}{2}$

E   1

F   More information needed

104. How many times do $y = 3\tan 2x$ and $y = x$ intersect in the interval $0 \le x \le 2\pi$?

A   0   E   4

B   1   F   5

C   2   G   6

D   3

105. Solve for x, $\log_3(2 - 3x) = \log_9(6x^2 - 19x + 2)$

A $x = -\frac{3}{2}$ or $x = \frac{2}{3}$ D $x = \frac{3}{2}$

B $x = \frac{2}{3}$ or $x = 3$ E   None of the above

C $x = -2$ or $x = -\frac{1}{3}$ F   Need more information to solve

106. Solve $27^x - 3^{x+2} = 0$ for x

A $x = -1$ D $x = 2$

B $x = 0$ E $x = 3$

C $x = 1$

107. Solve for x, $\cos x + \sin x \tan x = \sqrt{2}$, in the range $0 \leq x \leq \frac{\pi}{2}$

A 0 D $\frac{\pi}{3}$

B $\frac{\pi}{6}$ E $\frac{\pi}{2}$

C $\frac{\pi}{4}$

108. How many times do $y = 3x$ and $y = 2^x$ intersect?

A   0   D   3

B   1   E   4

C   2   F   More information needed

109. Given that $f(x) = \frac{x^3+2}{2x}$, calculate $f''(x)$

A $\frac{x^3}{6} + \ln x$ C $x(1 - \frac{1}{x^3})$

B $1 + \frac{2}{x^3}$ D 1

                                E $-x$

110. The volume of grain in a silo is modelled by the following equation:

$V = 2t + 2t^2 - \frac{t^3}{3}$ find the value of t at which the silo fills the fastest.

A   6

B   2

C $2 + \sqrt{6}$

D $3 + \frac{3\sqrt{\frac{20}{3}}}{2}$

E   More information needed

111. Solve for x, $2\log_2(x + 15) - \log_2 x = 6$

A $x = 9 \ or \ x = 25$

B $x = 9$

C $x = -15$

D $x = 15$

E   No real values of x

112. For the domain $0 < x < 1$, which of the following expressions has the largest value?

A $\cos x$

B $\sin x$

C e^x

D $\ln x$

E $\log x$

113. Simplify $\sin^4(x) - \cos^4(x)$

A $\sin^2 x - \cos^2 x$

B $2 \sin x \cos x$

C $2 \sin^2 x - 1$

D $2 \sin x$

114. Solve for x, $\log(3x - 2) + \log(x + 2) = \log(15x + 16)$

A $\frac{1}{3}$

B $-\frac{4}{3}$

C $\frac{20}{3}$

D   1

E   5

F   No solutions

115. Two perpendicular lines have the following equations, what is the value of α?

$y_1 = (\alpha + 2)x + 7$ & $y_2 = (\alpha)x - 3$

A -2

B -1

C   0

D   1

E   2

F   More information is needed

116. Given that $f(x) = \frac{(x+1)(2x-4)}{2x}$, calculate $f'(x)$ and evaluate at $x = 2$

A $\frac{3}{2}$

B   3

C $-\frac{1}{27}$

D   1

E   Not possible to calculate $f'(x)$

117. Let $f(x) = 3x(3 - 2x)$ and $a = 4$. Find the area of the finite region bounded by the origin, the integer root of the curve with equation $y = -\frac{a}{12}f(x + a)$ and the curve $-\frac{a}{4}f(x + a)$.

A -112

B $-\frac{112}{3}$

C $-\frac{56}{3}$

D   56

E   No solution

118. 11 football players from 3 teams line up in a straight line: 3 are wearing a red top, 4 are wearing a blue top and the rest are wearing a green top. How many different arrangements of tops exist?

A   11!

B $\frac{11!}{3!4!4!}$

C   48

D $\frac{11!}{3!+4!+4!}$

E   3! 4! 4!

119. Which of the following sets of equations graph the same graph?

A $\quad 2 - \sin(\pi + x) \ and \ 2 - \cos(x)$

B $\quad 1 - \sin\left(\frac{\pi}{2} - x\right) and \ 1 + \cos(\frac{\pi}{2})$

C $\quad 2 + \sin\left(\frac{3\pi}{2} - 2x\right) and \ 2 + \cos(2x - \pi)$

D $\quad 1 - \sin\left(x - \frac{\pi}{2}\right) and \ 1 - \sin(x)$

E $\quad$ None

120. Given that $\dfrac{1}{24}x = \dfrac{y^{\frac{1}{3}}}{12} - \dfrac{1}{6}$, what is the value of $\dfrac{d^3y}{dx^3}$?

A $\quad \dfrac{5}{12}$

B $\quad \dfrac{5}{6}$

C $\quad \dfrac{3}{4}$

D $\quad 5$

E $\quad 1$

121. If $a.b = \dfrac{a^2b}{2(a-b)}$, what is $3.(3.2)$?

A $\quad$ -18

B $\quad -\dfrac{27}{4}$

C $\quad \dfrac{13}{4}$

D $\quad \dfrac{13}{8}$

E $\quad \dfrac{81}{4}$

122. For what value of n are the areas of the two shapes equal? Assume n is an even integer.

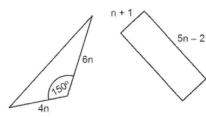

A $n = -4$

B $n = -2$

C $n = 0$

D $n = 2$

E $n = 4$

123. Given that the volume, V m^3, of an unknown 3D shape is related to its length, l m, by the formula $V = \frac{11}{9}\gamma l^4$, where γ is a constant of measure defined as $\frac{9}{2}$. Find the rate of change of volume with respect to length when the length is 2 cm.

A $\frac{44}{9}$

B 44

C $\frac{176}{9}$

D 176

E   None of the above

124. Calculate x

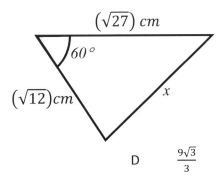

A $\frac{9\sqrt{3}}{2}$

B $\sqrt{21}$

C $\sqrt{39 - 18\sqrt{3}}$

D $\frac{9\sqrt{3}}{3}$

E   No solution

81

125. Let a and b be numbers such that $10 < a < 40$ and $30 < b < 60$. Which of the following represents all possible values of $a - b$?

A $-50 < a - b < -30$

B $-50 < a - b < 10$

C $-30 < a - b < -30$

D $-20 < a - b < 10$

E $-20 < a - b < 20$

126. Given $x = \dfrac{3}{2}y - 1$, evaluate $\dfrac{3^{2x}}{27^y}$

A $\dfrac{1}{3}$

B 0

C 3

D 9

E 27

F 81

G   More information needed

127. $f(x) = (x^2 + 4x - 6)^2$, calculate $f'(-1)$

A -36

B -12

C 1

D 48

E 81

128. Solve for x, $\log_{\frac{1}{2}}\left[\log_8\left(\frac{x^2-2x}{x-3}\right)\right] = 0$

A -3

B 3

C -2

D 12

E No integer solutions

129. How many times does $13\tan(9x)$ intercept the $x-axis$ in the domain $0 \le x \le \frac{\pi}{2}$?

A 1

B 2

C 3

D 4

E 5

F 6

130. Find the gradient of the line perpendicular to $f(x) = x^3 + 2x$ at $x = 1$.

A $-\frac{1}{6}$

B $-\frac{1}{5}$

C 5

D 6

E The graph is assymptotic at $x = 1$

131. Solve for x, $\log(3x - 1) = \log 16 - \log(3x + 1)$

A $\quad -\dfrac{17}{45}$

B $\quad 1$

C $\quad \dfrac{1}{17}$

D $\quad \dfrac{\sqrt{17}}{3}$

E $\quad$ No solutions

132. Solve for x in the domain $-\dfrac{\pi}{2} \leq x \leq \dfrac{\pi}{2}$, $\sqrt{\dfrac{1}{1+\tan^2 x}} = 1$

A $\quad -\dfrac{\pi}{2}$

B $\quad -\dfrac{\pi}{3}$

C $\quad -\dfrac{\pi}{4}$

D $\quad 0$

E $\quad \dfrac{\pi}{4}$

F $\quad \dfrac{\pi}{3}$

G $\quad \dfrac{\pi}{2}$

133. Evaluate $\lim\limits_{x \to 0} \left(\dfrac{x^2 - 1}{x - 1} + 2 \right)$

A $\quad -1$

B $\quad 0$

C $\quad 1$

D $\quad 2$

E $\quad 3$

134. A function, $g(x)$, is defined as $Ae^{Bx} + C$, and it passes through $(0, -6)$ and $(3, -4)$. Given that the line $y = -9$ is an asymptote to the graph, what is the exact value of B?

A -9

B 3

C $\frac{1}{6}\ln\left(\frac{8}{3}\right)$

D $\frac{1}{3}\ln\left(\frac{5}{3}\right)$

E $\ln\left(\frac{8}{3}\right) - 9$

F   None of the above

135. Work out the area of triangle ACD, given that $AB = 6, BC = 2 \ \& \ CD = 3$

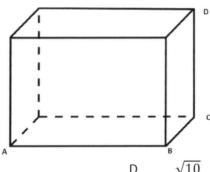

A   3

B   6

C   9

D $\sqrt{10}$

E $2\sqrt{10}$

F $3\sqrt{10}$

136. If $\sin x = 0.8$, what is $\cos(90° - x)$?

A $\frac{4}{5}$

B $\frac{3}{5}$

C $\frac{5}{12}$

D $\frac{5}{13}$

E $\frac{12}{13}$

F $\frac{3}{4}$

85

137. A bag contains counters which are either yellow or green. The ratio of yellow to green is $4:3$. When five yellow and five green counters are removed the ratio becomes $3:2$. How many green counters were there originally?

A   12

B   15

C   18

D   24

E   30

138. If p is prime, how many factors does p^3 have?

A   1

B   2

C   3

D   4

E   5

139. A scientist has three containers of hydrofluoric acid, two circular cones and one circular cylinder and each is 80% full. The diameter and height of both types of containers are $10cm$ and $20cm$ respectively. What is the total volume of the hydrofluoric acid the scientist has in cm^3? (Take $\pi \approx 3$)

A   4000

B $\dfrac{400}{3}$

C $\dfrac{4000}{3}$

D   5000

E $\dfrac{500}{3}$

F $\dfrac{5000}{3}$

140. A large pool in the shape of a cuboid is to be manufactured using 54 m² of sheet metal. The tank has a horizontal base and no top, the height is x metres. The two opposite vertical faces are squares. Given that x can vary, use differentiation to find the maximum value of V.

A   3

B   12

C   36

D   54

E   No cuboid is possible

141. How many integers between 4 and 501 begin and end in the digit 3?

A   9

B   10

C   11

D   48

E   49

F   50

142. Find the exact value of x

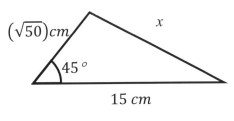

$(\sqrt{50})cm$ x $45\,^{\circ}$ $15\ cm$

A   15

B $5\sqrt{5}$

C $5\sqrt{6}$

D $5\sqrt{7}$

E $5\sqrt{11}$

143. The arithmetic mean of a set of six numbers is 8. When one of the numbers is replaced by the number 6, the average of the set increases to 11. What is the number that was replaced?

A -24

D 0

B -12

E 24

C -11

144. Given $\frac{dy}{dx}$ of $x^3 + y^3 = 0$, for what values of x does $\frac{dy}{dx} = -1$

A -1

D 2

B 0

E All values of x

C 1

145. Six individual gloves are in your drawer. There are two green, two blue and two black gloves. What is the probability you randomly pick two gloves of the same colour?

A 0.1

D $\frac{3}{10}$

B 0.2

E $\frac{1}{3}$

C $\frac{1}{6}$

F $\frac{1}{9}$

146. If $f(x) = x^\pi$, then evaluate $f'(1)$

A π

B $\dfrac{1}{\pi}$

C $\pi x^{\pi-1}$

D $\pi^{-1}x^{\pi-1}$

E 1

147. Given that $f(x) = 5x - 7 + \dfrac{2\sqrt{x}+3}{x}$, calculate $f'(4)$

A 5

B $\dfrac{\sqrt{2}}{2}$

C $\dfrac{57}{4}$

D $\dfrac{75}{16}$

E   None of the above

148. What is the equation of the normal of $y = e^{-x}$ at the point $(-1, e)$?

A $y = \dfrac{x}{e} + 1$

B $y = \dfrac{x}{e} + \dfrac{1}{e} + e$

C $y = 1 - e^{-x}$

D $y = \dfrac{1}{e}x + \dfrac{2}{e}$

E $y = -ex$

149. For what value of x does $f(x) = \frac{1}{2}e^{0.01x}\ln(x)$ cross the $x - axis$?

A   0   D   1

B   0.01   E   Never

C   0.5

150. Given $y = 2x^2 + 3\left(\frac{x}{2} - 3\right)^2$, calculate the value of $\frac{dx}{dy}$ when $x = -1$

A $\frac{2}{7}$ E $-\frac{4}{155}$

B $\frac{7}{2}$ F $\frac{155}{4}$

C $-\frac{2}{29}$ G $x = -1$ not in domain of function

D $-\frac{29}{2}$

151. What is the positive $x - intercept$ of $f'(x)$, if $f(x)$ is $5x^3 + \frac{7}{2}x^2 - 2x + 6$?

A $\frac{1}{5}$ C $\frac{3}{2}$

B $\frac{2}{3}$ D   6

                                          E   No positive $x - intercept$

152. What is the x coordinate of the positive stationary point of $f(x) = x^3 - 61x + \frac{32}{3} - (14x + 1)(x - 3)$?

A $\frac{2}{3}$

B   3

C   10

D   12

E $\frac{41}{3}$

153. If $(x + 1)^2 = 4$ and $(x - 1)^2 = 16$, what is the value of x?

A -3

B -1

C   1

D   3

E   5

154. What is the area bounded between the functions $f(x)$ and $g(x)$? $f(x) = \frac{1}{2}x^2 - \frac{9}{2}x + 11$ and $g(x) = x^2 - 9x + 11$?

A $\frac{729}{6}$

B $-\frac{243}{12}$

C   9

D $\frac{243}{4}$

E $\frac{729}{4}$

155. If each digit in an integer is greater than the digit to the left, the integer is said to be 'monotonic'. For example, 12 is a monotonic integer since 2 > 1. How many positive two-digit monotonic integers are there?

A   28

B   32

C   36

D   40

E   44

156. If the expression, $\frac{3-i}{2+4i}$, is written in the form $a + bi$, where a & b are real numbers, what is the value of a? (*Note: $i = \sqrt{-1}$*)

A $-\frac{3}{2}$

B $-\frac{7}{10}$

C $\frac{1}{10}$

D $\frac{4}{13}$

E $\frac{3}{2}$

F   4

157. What is x, given x is an integer? $\log[\log(x)] + \log[\log(x^3 - 2)] = 0$

A   0

B   1

C   2

D $\sqrt[3]{3}$

E   No solutions

158. In the figure below, a square is inscribed in a circle. If the area of the square is 36, what is the perimeter of the shaded region?

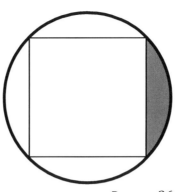

A $6 + \frac{3\sqrt{2}}{2}\pi$

B $6 + 3\pi$

C $6 + 3\sqrt{2}\pi$

D $36 + 6\sqrt{2}\pi$

E $\frac{9}{2}\pi - 9$

159. Given $y = \begin{cases} -\frac{x}{2} + 9, & x \le -3 \\ 2x^2 - 2, & x > -3 \end{cases}$, what is the product of the values of x which satisfy $y = 16$?

A -3

B 3

C -42

D 42

E -112

F 112

G -126

H 126

I   None of the above

160. What is the gradient function of $2x^4 + 2x - 1$?

A $\frac{2x^5}{5} + x^2 - x$

B $6x^2 + 1$

C $8x^3 + 2$

D $2x^2 + 2$

E   All of the above

161. Evaluate $\frac{d^2y}{dx^2}$ when $x = 1$, given $y = \frac{1}{4}x^4 + \frac{1}{3}x^3 + \frac{1}{2}x^2$

A   0

B $\frac{13}{12}$

C   3

D   6

E   8

F   None of the above

162. How many times do $\frac{1}{3}\cos x$ and $\frac{1}{2}\sin x$ meet in the interval $10 \le x \le 200°$?

A   0

B   1

C   2

D   3

E   4

F   5

163. Let a and b be numbers such that $a^3 = b^2$. Which of the following is equivalent to $b\sqrt{a}$?

A $b^{\frac{2}{3}}$

B $b^{\frac{4}{3}}$

C b^2

D b^3

E b^4

94

164. How many times do $3 \sin x$ and $\dfrac{3}{\cos\left(x-\frac{\pi}{2}\right)}$ intersect in the interval $0 \le x \le 2\pi$?

A   0

B   1

C   2

D   3

E   4

F   None of the above

165. The regional manager for McRonald's opens a new outlet. For the new outlet, the manager estimates that, during opening hours, an average of 90 customers per hour enter the outlet and each of them stays an average of $\frac{1}{5}$ hours. What is the average number of customers in the store?

A   10

B   12

C   15

D   18

E   21

F   45

166. What is the value of x?

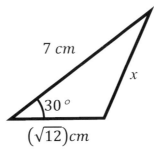

A $2\sqrt{3}$

B $7\sqrt{2}$

C 7

D $3\sqrt{3}$

E $\sqrt{19}$

167. An integer is subtracted from its square. Which of the following could be the result?

A   A negative integer

B   An odd integer

C   The product of two consecutive even integers

D   The product of two consecutive odd integers

E   The product of two consecutive integers

168. Three students (α, β and γ) are competing for the role of school captain. α has a 0.4 chance of being selected and a 0.6 chance of abolishing mandatory uniform rules. β has a 0.25 chance of being selected and a 0.5 chance of abolishing mandatory uniform rules. γ has a 0.1 chance of abolishing mandatory uniform rules, one of the three students must be chosen for the role. What is the probability that school uniforms will be abolished?

A   0.24   D   0.4

B   0.25   E   0.5

C   0.3   F   0.6

169. If x is the mean of m and 9, y is the average of $2m$ and 15, and z is the average of $3m$ and 18. What is the average of x, y, and z in terms of m?

A $m + 6$ D $3m + 21$

B $m + 7$ E   None of the above

C $2m + 14$

170. $h(x) = \dfrac{e^3}{(x^2+1)^{-1}}$, calculate $h'(2)$

A $4e$ D $4e^3 + e^3$

B $4e^3$ E e^3

C $5e^3 + 4$ F $5e^3$

171. What solution of x is obtained from this pair of simultaneous equations? $\begin{cases} \log_{7\sqrt7}(x-4) = \frac{2}{3} - \log_{7\sqrt7}(x-10) \\ (2^x)^x = 4^{6-\frac{x}{2}} \end{cases}$

A -4 D 11

B 3 E 14

C 4 F   No solutions

172. Given $\tan\theta = \cos\theta + 3\tan\theta - \dfrac{2}{\cos\theta}$. Solve for θ, where θ is the first positive integer value to satisfy the equation.

A $0°$ F $120°$

B $30°$ G $135°$

C $45°$ H $150°$

D $60°$ I   No such values exist

E $90°$

173. If $x > 3$, which of the following is equivalent to $\dfrac{1}{\frac{1}{x+2}+\frac{1}{x+3}}$?

A $\dfrac{2x+5}{x^2+5x+6}$

B $\dfrac{x^2+5x+6}{2x+5}$

C $2x+5$

D $x^2 + 5x + 6$

174. On Day 1 a golden pineapple is sold at £x, on Day 2 it is discounted by 20%, then on Day 3 there is a special one-day further 30% off on all items. What is the overall price reduction of the shirt as a percentage of x?

A   6%

B   44%

C   50%

D   56%

E   94%

175. There exists a right-angle triangle with side lengths a, b and $\sqrt{a^2 + b^2}$, with the latter being the hypotenuse. One of the angles measures $\tan^{-1}\left(\frac{a}{b}\right)$. What is the value of $\cos\left[\tan^{-1}\left(\frac{a}{b}\right)\right]$?

A $\dfrac{a}{b}$

B $\dfrac{b}{a}$

C $\dfrac{a}{\sqrt{a^2+b^2}}$

D $\dfrac{b}{\sqrt{a^2+b^2}}$

E $\dfrac{\sqrt{a^2+b^2}}{a}$

176. Solve for x, $(10)^{\log(x-2)} = 100$

A   2

B   10

C   12

D   102

E   1002

F   None of the above

177. Let m be an even positive integer. How many possible values of m satisfy $\sqrt{m+7} < 3$?

A   0

B   1

C   2

D   3

E   4

F   None of the above

178. Simplify $8^{\log_2(\log_8 x)}$

A $(\log_8 x)^3$

B   8

C $\log_8 x$

D   3

E $\log_8 2$

179. $f(x) = \frac{(3x+2)^2}{x^{0.5}}$, calculate $f'(1)$

A $\frac{5}{2}$ D $\frac{35}{2}$

B   5   E   25

C $\frac{25}{2}$ F   35

180. Given that $\int_{11}^{0} f(x)\,dx = 19.2$, what is the value of $\int_{0}^{11}[f(x) + 2]\,dx$?

A -17.2 D   41.2

B   2.8   E   Insufficient information

C   21.2

181. $f(x) = \frac{(3-4\sqrt{x})^2}{\sqrt{x}}$. What is the value of $f'(9)$?

A   1   D   9

B $\frac{5}{2}$ E   27

C   3

182. What is the size of the angle labelled x?

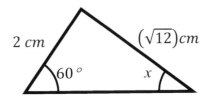

2 cm $(\sqrt{12})cm$

$60°$ x

A $45°$

B $60°$

C $\dfrac{\pi}{3}$

D $\dfrac{\pi}{2}$

E $\dfrac{\pi}{6}$

183. What is a in the following equation? $\lim\limits_{x \to a} e^x = 0$

A $-\infty$

B -1

C 0

D 1

E ∞

184. Find the complete set of values of the real constant α for which the expression, $x^2 + 4x + \alpha x - 2\alpha + 4$ is positive for all real values of x.

A $-16 < \alpha < 0$

B $\alpha < -16$ or $\alpha > 0$

C $-2\sqrt{6} - 5 < \alpha < 2\sqrt{6} - 5$

D $\alpha < -2\sqrt{6} - 5$ or $\alpha > 2\sqrt{6} - 5$

E $-4 < \alpha < \dfrac{1}{4}$

F $\alpha < -4$ or $k > \dfrac{1}{4}$

G $0 < \alpha < 6$

H $\alpha < 0$ or $k > 6$

185. $\log_{\frac{1}{x}}(216) = 3$, what is x?

A $\frac{1}{6}$

B 6

C $\frac{1}{3}$

D 3

E 2

F $\frac{1}{2}$

G None of the above

186. If a and b are numbers such that $(a-4)(b+6) = 0$, then what is the smallest possible value of $a^2 + b^2$?

A 52

B 16

C 36

D 0

E −2

187. What is the value of $\lim\limits_{x \to 3} \frac{x^2-9}{x-3}$?

A 0

B 1

C 3

D 6

E ∞

188. If $\frac{24x^2-12x-47}{ax-3} = -4x+4 - \frac{35}{ax-3}$, what value does a take?

A 3

B −3

C 6

D −6

E 8

F −8

G None of the above

189. Solve for x in the interval $0 \le x \le \frac{\pi}{2}$, $2\sin^2 x + 2 = 7\cos x$

A 0

B $\frac{\pi}{6}$

C $\frac{\pi}{4}$

D $\frac{\pi}{3}$

E $\frac{\pi}{2}$

190. The minimum value of $e^{-x} + 2e^x$ occurs at what value of x?

A 0

B 1

C $2\sqrt{2}$

D $-\frac{1}{2}\log_e 2$

E None of the above

191. $P(B|A) = \frac{2}{3}, P(A|B) = \frac{1}{3}, P(A'|B') = \frac{5}{6}$. Find $P(B)$.

A $\quad \frac{1}{12}$

D $\quad \frac{5}{12}$

B $\quad \frac{1}{3}$

E $\quad \frac{18}{19}$

C $\quad \frac{3}{5}$

F $\quad$ None of the above

192. Given $f(3) = 0$, calculate the other positive root of $f(x) = x^3 - 10x^2 - 23x + 132$

A $\quad$ 2

D $\quad$ 6

B $\quad$ 3

E $\quad$ 11

C $\quad$ 4

F $\quad$ 12

193. Evaluate $\frac{d^2y}{dx^2}$ when $x = 2$, given $xy = 2$

A $\quad -1$

D $\quad \frac{1}{2}$

B $\quad -\frac{1}{2}$

E $\quad$ 1

C $\quad \frac{1}{8}$

194. What is the $y-$ intercept of $y = \cos\left(\frac{\pi}{3} + 32x\right)$?

A $\frac{1}{2}$

B   1

C   16

D   32

E   None of the above

195. What is the horizontal asymptote as $x \to -\infty$ for $f(x) = \left(\frac{x^2+3x+1}{4x^2-9}\right)^3$?

A $-\frac{3}{2}$

B $\frac{1}{64}$

C $\frac{1}{4}$

D $\frac{3}{2}$

E   No horizontal asymptote

196. Amy is two years older than Bill. The square of Amy's age in years is 36 greater than the square of Bill's age in years. What is the sum of Amy's age and Bill's age in 3 years?

A   8

B   10

C   18

D   24

E   None of the above

197. The graph of the polynomial function is sketched, $y = ax^7 + bx^6 + cx^5 + dx^4 + ex^3 + fx^2 + gx + h$, where a, b, c, d, e, f, g and h are real constants, where $a \neq 0$. Which of the following is not possible?

A   The graph has two local minima and two local maxima

B   The graph has one local minimum and two local maximum

C   The graph has one local minimum and one local maximum

D   The graph has no local minima or local maxima

198. $f(x) = (x^3 + 2x)(\sqrt{x})$, what is the gradient of $f''(x)$ at $x = 4$?

A $\dfrac{283}{4}$

B $\dfrac{837}{32}$

C   118

D   144

E   Assymptotic at $x = 4$

199. Find the coefficient of x in the expression:

$$(1 + x)^0 + (1 + x)^2 + (1 + x)^4 + (1 + x)^6 + \cdots + (1 + x)^{78} + (1 + x)^{80}$$

A   40

B   41

C   80

D   164

E   324

F   1640

G   3240

H   3280

200. What is the length of the side labelled x?

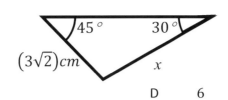

A $3\sqrt{2}$ D   6

B   3   E   None of the above

C $6\sqrt{2}$

201. What value of a satisfies the following statement $\int_1^4 (2x^3 + ax^{-\frac{1}{2}} + 5) \, dx = \frac{301}{2}$?

A   2   D   5

B   3   E   6

C   4   F   7

202. What value of a gives the minimum value to the following integral $\int_{-1}^{1} (x^3 - ax^{-3}) \, dx$?

A   2   D   5

B   3   E   6

C   4   F   Any value of a leads to the minimum value

203. Find the value of b for which $\int_{-2}^{4}(4x - 2b^2)\,dx$ has the maximum possible value.

A -2 D   1

B -1 E   2

C   0   F   3

204. Evaluate $\int_{-2}^{2}(2x - 3)\,dx - \int_{-2}^{2}(x + 1)^2\,dx$

A -12 D $\dfrac{8}{3}$

B $\dfrac{28}{3}$ E $\dfrac{64}{3}$

C $\dfrac{-8}{3}$ F $-\dfrac{64}{3}$

205. Find the area of the shape that is bounded by the x-axis, lines $x = 0$ & $x = 2$ and the polynomial $x^2 + 3x + 4$.

A $\dfrac{100}{3}$ D $\dfrac{3}{2}$

B $\dfrac{50}{3}$ E $-\dfrac{3}{2}$

C   0   F $\dfrac{3}{4}$

206. Find the area enclosed between the lines $y = 4x$ and $y = x^2$

A $\frac{8}{3}$ D   36

B   8   E $\frac{32}{3}$

C $\frac{64}{3}$ F   More information is needed

207. Find the value of a in $\int_1^a \left(\frac{1}{2}x - \frac{1}{2}\right) dx = \frac{49}{4}$

A   9   D   6

B   8   E   5

C   7   F   4

208. Evaluate the following: $\int_1^5 (x^2 + 3x + 10)\, dx - \int_3^5 (x^2 + 3x + 10)\, dx$

A $\frac{352}{3}$ E $\frac{112}{3}$

B $\frac{-352}{3}$ F $\frac{-112}{3}$

C $\frac{230}{3}$ G $\frac{-122}{3}$

D $\frac{-230}{3}$ H $\frac{122}{3}$

209. What is area of the shaded region on the graph?

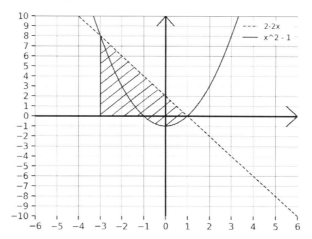

A $15 + \dfrac{7}{3}$

B $15 - \dfrac{7}{3}$

C $\dfrac{4}{3}$

D $\dfrac{-4}{3}$

E 16

F $16 - \dfrac{4}{3}$

G More information is needed

210. What are two possible values for Z in $\int_{1}^{4}(4x - Z)dx = Z^2 - 2Z$

A $Z = 5$ and $Z = -6$

B $Z = -5$ and $Z = 6$

D $Z = 4$ and $Z = 1$

E $Z = -1$ and $Z = 4$

C $Z = 2$ and $Z = -3$

F $Z = -2$ and $Z = 3$

211. What is the value of k in $\int_1^k \frac{1}{\sqrt{x}}\, dx = 4$?

A   3

B   4

C   9

D   16

E   36

F   49

212. The gradient function of a line is $\frac{dy}{dx} = x^2 + 12$, and it passes through the point $(3, 28)$. What is the function of this line?

A $\frac{x^3}{3} + 12x - 17$

B $3x^2 + 28x - 34$

C $x^3 + 6x + 28$

D $x^3 - 12x + 17$

E $x^2 - 6x + 28$

F $\frac{x^3}{3} + 12x^2 + 28x + 3$

213. Find the area between the curves x^2 and $0.5x^2 + 8$.

A   4

B $\frac{14}{3}$

C $\frac{-14}{3}$

D $\frac{128}{3}$

E   8

F $\frac{64}{3}$

214. Evaluate $\int_{-1}^{1}(x)^5\,dx$

A   1

B   2

C   0

D $\frac{1}{32}$

E -1

F -2

G   More information is needed

215. Evaluate $\int_{-2}^{2}(3x^3 + 1 + 3x^{-3})\,dx$

A   2

D   4

B $\frac{5}{3}$

C   6

E $\frac{16}{3}$

F   None of the above

216. Given that $\dfrac{dy}{dx} = \dfrac{6x^2 + 3x^{\frac{1}{2}}}{x^{\frac{1}{2}}}$ and that $y = 88.8$ when $x = 4$, what is equation of the original line?

A $\dfrac{12x^{\frac{5}{2}}}{5} + 3x$

B $\dfrac{12x^{\frac{5}{2}}}{5} + 3x + 28.8$

C $6x^{\frac{3}{2}} + 3 - 88.8$

D $6x^{\frac{3}{2}} - 3x - 88.8$

E $9x^{\frac{1}{2}} + 28.8$

F $9x^{\frac{1}{2}} - 88.8$

217. Evaluate $\int_1^1 \frac{(x+1)^2}{x^{0.5}} dx$

A   Undefined

B $\frac{1}{2}$

C $\frac{1}{3}$

D   0

E $\frac{1}{\sqrt{x}}$

F $x^{\frac{3}{2}}$

218. $f(x) = (1 + x)^4$. Find the area under the curve, between the lines $x = 0$, $x = 2$, and the x-axis.

A $\frac{32}{5}$

B   4

C $\frac{3124}{5}$

D $\frac{64}{3}$

E $\frac{242}{5}$

F   Undefined

219. What is the value of b in $\int_b^5 \left(\frac{2}{\sqrt{x}}\right) dx = 4\sqrt{5} - 4$?

A   1

B   2

C $\frac{1}{5}$

D   3

E   4

F $\frac{1}{\sqrt{5}}$

220. Find the area enclosed by the lines $(x^2 + 4x)$ and $(-x^2 - 4x)$.

A $\dfrac{32}{3}$ D $-\dfrac{16}{3}$

B $\dfrac{64}{3}$ E $-\dfrac{48}{3}$

C $\dfrac{128}{3}$

221. If $\int_1^2 (px^3 + qx^2)dx = \dfrac{29}{2}$ and $\int_{-1}^1 (qx^2 - px)dx = 2$, what are the values of p and q?

A $p = 4$ and $q = -2$ D $p = -2$ and $q = -3$

B $p = 2$ and $q = 5$ E $p = 2$ and $q = 3$

C $p = 7$ and $q = 7$ F   More information needed

222. What are two possible values for B in $\int_1^2 (2x^2 + B)dx = -B^2 + \dfrac{32}{3}$?

A $B = 3$ and $B = -2$ D $B = 2$ and $B = -2$

B $B = 2$ and $B = -3$ E $B = 1$ and $B = 8$

C $B = \dfrac{3}{2}$ and $B = \dfrac{1}{2}$ F $B = -5$ and $B = -6$

114

223. What is the area enclosed between the curve $f(x) = x(x + 2)(2 - x)$ and the x-axis?

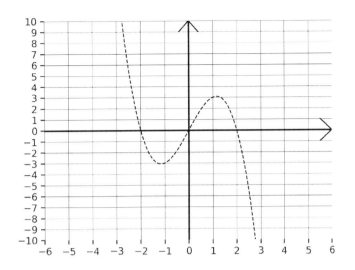

A   4

B   8

C   −8

D   12

E   2

F   5

224. Evaluate $\int_1^2 (x^2 + 5 + x^{-2})\, dx$

A $\dfrac{47}{6}$

B $\dfrac{94}{4}$

C $\dfrac{12}{5}$

D $\dfrac{147}{4}$

E $\dfrac{543}{10}$

F   More information is needed

225. Evaluate the following: $\int_{-5}^{-1}(x+4) + \int_{-1}^{-2}(x+4)$

A   4

B $-\dfrac{5}{2}$

C $\dfrac{4}{5}$

D $\dfrac{1}{2}$

E $\dfrac{3}{2}$

F   6

226. $f(x) = \dfrac{x^3+x^2-10x+8}{x-2}$, what is the minimum point of $f(x+1)$?

A $(-2.5, -6.25)$

B $(-8, 36)$

C $(-3, -4)$

D $(-1, -6)$

E $(6, 50)$

227. What are the asymptotes of $[f(x) + 5]$, where $f(x) = \dfrac{1}{x+5}$?

A $x = 5$ and $y = 5$

B $x = -5$ and $y = 5$

C $x = 5$ and $y = -5$

D $x = -5$ and $y = -5$

E $x = 10$ and $y - 10$

228. $f(x) = x(x-4)(x+2)$. What are the roots of $f\left(\frac{1}{2}x + 2.5\right)$?

A $[(-9,0),(-5,0),(3,0)]$ D $[(8,0),(5,0),(7,0)]$

B $[(-6,0),(-7.5,0),(3.5,0)]$ E $[(10,0),(-5.5,0),(7.5,0)]$

C $[(2.5,0),(-5,0),(7.5,0)]$ F $[(0,0),(2,0),(-1,0)]$

229. What is the asymptote of $[2f(x) + 10]$, where $f(x) = log(x)$?

A $x = -3$ D $x = 2$

B $x = -2$ E $x = 10$

C $x = 0$ F $x = 12$

230. $f(x) = x^4$. What are the transformations applied to $f(x)$ when it is $f(x) = 0.5(0.5x^4 - 3) + 3$?

A   Vertical stretch of 0.5 and shift of $\begin{pmatrix} 0 \\ 4.5 \end{pmatrix}$

B   Vertical stretch of 0.25 and shift of $\begin{pmatrix} 0 \\ 1.5 \end{pmatrix}$

C   Horizontal stretch of 0.5 and shift of $\begin{pmatrix} 0 \\ 2.5 \end{pmatrix}$

D   Horizontal stretch of 0.25 and shift of $\begin{pmatrix} 0 \\ 3 \end{pmatrix}$

E   Horizontal stretch of 0.5, followed by a vertical stretch of 0.25 and shift of $\begin{pmatrix} 0 \\ 1.5 \end{pmatrix}$

231. Which of the following diagrams correctly represents $f(x) = (x+1)^3 - 9(x+1)$

A

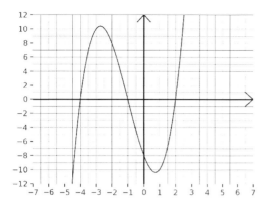

B

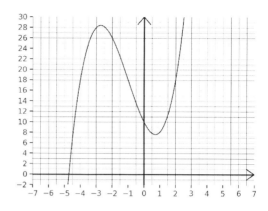

C

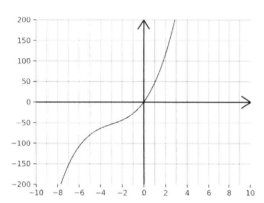

D

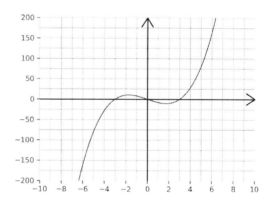

232. $f(x) = x^2(x-8)$, what are the roots of $f\left(\frac{4}{3}x + 5\right)$?

A $\left(\frac{4}{3}, 0\right)$ and $(5, 0)$

B $(-5, 0)$ and $(8, 0)$

C $\left(\frac{-4}{3}, 0\right)$ and $(-5, 0)$

D $(8, 0)$ and $(0, 0)$

E $\left(\frac{-15}{4}, 0\right)$ and $\left(\frac{9}{4}, 0\right)$

F $f\left(\frac{4}{3}x + 5\right)$ has no real roots

233. A plumber charges a flat fee and daily rate for every job that they complete. Job A takes 5 days and charges £1365. Job B takes 8 days and chargers £1374. What is the equation linking the time taken to finish a job ($t, in\ days$) and its cost?

A $\quad C = 3x - 1350$

B $\quad C = 3x + 1350$

C $\quad C = 6x - 1280$

D $\quad C = 6x + 1280$

E $\quad C = 10x - 975$

F $\quad C = 10x + 975$

234. A line passes through points A and B, which have the coordinates $(0, 10)$ and $(k, 7)$ respectively, and its gradient is $\frac{-3}{7}$. What is the value of k?

A $\quad \frac{1}{3}$

B $\quad \frac{1}{27}$

C $\quad 5$

D $\quad 6$

E $\quad 7$

F $\quad 8$

235. $f(x) = x^2 + bx + 4$. What is the value of b, if the minimum point of this quadratic is $(-1, 3)$?

A $\quad 2$

B $\quad -2$

C $\quad 4$

D $\quad -4$

E $\quad \frac{1}{2}$

F $\quad \frac{1}{4}$

236. $f(x) = x^2 + 2x + k$. For what value of k is the minimum point of $f(x) = (-1, 6.25)$?

A   5.25

B   6.25

C   7.25

D   12.50

E   13.50

F   More information is needed

237. $y = \frac{1}{(x+a)^4} - 9$ passes through the origin. Find the two possible values of a.

A $\pm\frac{1}{\sqrt{3}}$

B $\pm\frac{1}{3}$

C ± 3

D $\pm 3\sqrt{3}$

E ± 9

F   More information is needed

238. I want to move the graph of $f(x) = x^2$ by 3 to the right, and then vertically stretch it by a factor of -3. What is the correct transformation?

A $3(\frac{1}{3}x^2 - 9)$

B $\frac{1}{3}(3x^2 + 9)$

C $3(-x^2 + 3)$

D $3(x^2 + 3)$

E $-3(x - 3)^2$

239. $f(x) = ax^2 + bx + c$ passes through the point $(2, 10)$. The gradient of $f(x)$ is 0 at the point $(-3, 15)$. What are the values of $a, b,$ and c?

A $f(x) = x^2 - 4x + 14$

B $f(x) = \frac{-1}{5}x^2 - \frac{6}{5}x + \frac{66}{5}$

C $f(x) = 15x^2 - 6x + 6$

D $f(x) = -x^2 + 6x + \frac{66}{5}$

E $f(x) = \frac{1}{5}x^2 + \frac{6}{5}x - \frac{66}{5}$

F $f(x) = -15x^2 + 6x - 6$

240. $f(x) = \frac{x^3}{3} - \frac{5x^2}{2} + 6x$. For what values of x is $f(x)$ increasing?

A $x < 4$ and $x > 6$

B $x < -4$ and $x > 6$

C $x < -4$ and $x > -6$

D $x < -2$ and $x > -3$

E $x < -2$ and $x > 3$

F $x < 2$ and $x > 3$

241. What are the x-coordinates of the stationary points of $\frac{6}{x} + 2x - 41$?

A $\sqrt{3}$ and $-\sqrt{3}$

B $\frac{1}{\sqrt{3}}$ and $-\frac{1}{\sqrt{3}}$

C -48 and -38

D   1 and -1

E $\frac{6}{x} + 2x - 41$ has no stationary points

121

242. What are the x-coordinates of the stationary points of $f(x) = \frac{x^4}{4} + \frac{2}{3}x^3 - \frac{x^2}{2} - 2x$, if one of the stationary points occurs at $x = -1$?

A $(x = 2), (x = -2)\ and\ (x = -1)$ D $(x = -1), (x = -6)$ and $(x = 6)$

B $(x = 4), (x = -4)$ and $(x = -1)$ E $(x = -1), (x = -2)$ and $(x = 1)$

C $(x = 2), (x = -2)$ and $(x = 0)$ F   More information is needed

243. $f(x) = \frac{x^3}{3} + ax^2 - 6x$. What is the value of a, if $f(x)$ is increasing for $x > 2\ and\ x < -3$?

A   0.5   D $\frac{1}{5}$

B $\frac{1}{3}$ E $\frac{1}{8}$

C $\frac{1}{4}$ F   0.75

244. $f(x) = ax^3 + bx^2 + cx + 5$. The gradient of $f(x)$ is 0 when $x = 3$ & $x = -4$. What are the values of a and b if $c = -12$?

A $a = \frac{1}{5}$ and $b = \frac{1}{4}$ D $a = \frac{1}{3}$ and $b = \frac{1}{2}$

B $a = \frac{1}{4}$ and $b = \frac{1}{3}$ E $a = 1$ and $b = -1$

C $a = \frac{1}{7}$ and $b = \frac{1}{6}$ F $a = \frac{1}{6}$ and $b = \frac{1}{5}$

245. $f(x) = ax^2 + bx + c$ passes through the point $(0, 3)$. The gradient of $f(x)$ is 0 at the point $(-0.5, 2.25)$, what are the values of a, b and c?

A $f(x) = -3x^2 - 3x - 3$

B $f(x) = 3x^2 + 3x + 3$

C $f(x) = 6x^2 + 2x + 12$

D $f(x) = -0.5x^2 + 2.25x - 10$

E $f(x) = 2.25x^2 + 3x - 3$

F $f(x) = 15 - 6x + 12$

246. $f(x) = x^2 + 2x$. Where does the normal to $f(x)$, when $x = 1$, intersect the y-axis?

A $(0, 6.5)$

B $(6.5, 0)$

C $(0, 3.25)$

D $(3.25, 0)$

E $(0, 1)$

F $(1, 0)$

247. $f(x) = x^3 + 3x^2 + 2x - 6$. $(x - 1)$ is a factor of $f(x)$. How many real roots does $f(x)$ have?

A   0

B   1

C   2

D   3

E   More information is needed

248. $f(x) = x^2 + 3x + 5$. Where does the tangent of $f(x)$, when $x = 0$, intersect the x-axis?

A $\left(\frac{-5}{3}, 0\right)$ D $\left(0, -\frac{5}{3}\right)$

B $\left(\frac{-3}{5}, 0\right)$ E $(1, 3)$

C $\left(0, \frac{3}{5}\right)$ F $(3, 1)$

249. $f(x) = e^x$ and $g(x) = 8e^{-x} - 2$. What are the coordinates of the point of intersection of $f(x)$ and $g(x)$?

A $(e^2, 0)$ D $(0, 2)$

B $(\ln(2), 2)$ E $\left(\frac{1}{\ln(4)}, -2\right)$

C $(0, \ln(4))$ F   No such point exists

250. $f(x) = \ln(x + 5) + \ln\left[(x - 2) + \frac{1}{x+5}\right]$. Where does $f(x)$ intersect the x-axis?

A $(\ln(2), 0)$ D $(-5, 0)$

B $(e^2, 0)$ E $(\ln(5), 0)$

C $(2, 0)$ F $(e^5, 0)$

251. Which of the following statements about divisibility are correct?

    i.   "Take the last digit of a number and double it, then subtract the result from the rest of the original number (excluding the last digit). If the result of that subtraction is divisible by 7, so is the original number"

    ii.   "If the sum of the digits for a number is divisible by 3, then the number is divisible by 3"

    iii.   "A number is divisible by 4 if the last two digits are divisible by 4"

A	i		E	i & iii
B	ii		F	ii & iii
C	iii		G	i, ii & iii
D	i & ii			

252. What is the fourth root of 38416?

A	7		D	18
B	14		E	28
C	16		F	36

253. What is the third root of 5832?

A	9		D	16
B	12		E	18
C	14		F	22

254. Plumber A takes 5 days to finish a job. Plumber B takes 3 days to finish a job. Plumber C takes 7 days to finish a job. They work every day of the week, and all start new jobs on day 1. On what day do they all finish a job on the same day, for the second time?

A	Day 21	D	Day 175
B	Day 35	E	Day 210
C	Day 105	F	Day 245

255. John is refurbishing the wiring in his garage. He buys 200m of electrical cable. Each section of wiring needs 10 metres of electrical cable. The length of electrical cable that he purchases is correct to the nearest metre. The length of electrical cable that he needs for each section is correct to the nearest half metre. After he has made 19 runs, what is the maximum length of cable that could remain unused?

A	4.75	C	14.25
B	5.75	D	15.25

256. A soda bottling plant stores unbottled soda in large tanks which have a capacity of 1000 litres, to the nearest 100 litres. This soda is then transferred into smaller tanks, on transportation trucks, which have a capacity of 110 litres, to the nearest 10 litres. What is the minimum number of small tanks each truck needs, to ensure that it can always hold the contents of a large tank?

A	8	C	10
B	9	D	11

257. The length of a field is 40m, to the nearest 10 metres. The width of a field is 50m, to the nearest 10 metres. A farmer wants to distribute seeds across the field evenly, at a cost of £20 per square metre to the nearest ten pounds. What is the difference between the minimum possible and maximum possible cost of distributing seeds onto this field?

A   £6000

B   £19125

C   £13500

D   £20375

E   £45625

F   £38250

258. Person A and Person B share some sweets in the ratio $4:7$. Person A then gives Person B 6 sweets. Person B then gives person A 2 sweets. The ratio of sweets (for Person A: Person B) is now $10:23$. How many sweets did they have initially?

A   Person A $=4$ and Person B $=7$

B   Person A $=7$ and Person B $=16$

C   Person A $=8$ and Person B $=56$

D   Person A $=88$ and Person B $=154$

E   Person A $=24$ and Person B $=42$

F   More information is needed

259. If the ratio of $a:b=3:7$ and $b:c=5:11$, what is the ratio of $c:a$?

A $77:15$

B $15:77$

C $5:11$

D $11:5$

E $3:7$

F $7:3$

260. The ratio of red to blue balls in a bag is $2:5$. 3 blue balls are removed from the bag, and 6 red balls are added to the bag. The ratio of blue to red balls is now $(3x + 1):(4x + 2)$. What is the value of x?

A   10

B   9

C   8

D   5

E   6

F   2

261. If the ratio of $x:y$ is $8:21$, and $y:z$ is $3:2$. What is the simplest form of the ratio of $x:z$?

A $16:63$

B $2:3$

C $4:7$

D $8:21$

E $12:21$

F $21:12$

262. $A = \dfrac{n^3+n^2+a}{n-a}$. What is the rearranged form of this formula with a as the subject?

A $a = \dfrac{n(A-n^2-n)}{A+1}$

B $a = \dfrac{n(A-n^2+n)}{A+1}$

C $a = \dfrac{n(A+n^2-n)}{A-\frac{3}{2}}$

D $a = \dfrac{-n(A-n^2+n)}{A-1}$

E $a = \dfrac{n(A-n^2+n)}{A-2}$

F $a = \dfrac{-n(A-n^2+n)}{A+2}$

263. $y = \sqrt[a]{\dfrac{2x+1}{\sqrt{2w}}}$ What is the rearranged form of the formula with w as the subject?

A $w = \left(\dfrac{2x+1}{y^a}\right)^2$

D $w = \dfrac{\left(\frac{2x+1}{y^a}\right)^2}{2}$

B $w = \left(\dfrac{2x+1}{y^a}\right)$

E $w = \dfrac{(2x+1)^2}{y^a}$

C $w = \dfrac{\left(\frac{2x+1}{y}\right)^2}{2}$

F $w = \dfrac{\left(\frac{2x+1}{y^2}\right)^2}{2}$

264. $C = 4\sqrt{\dfrac{2x}{\sqrt{2\sqrt{y}}}}$ What is the rearranged form of the formula with y as the subject?

A $y = \dfrac{\left(1024x^2\right)^2}{c^8}$

D $y = \dfrac{(512)^2 x^4}{c^8}$

B $y = \dfrac{(512)^2 x^4}{c^8}$

E $y = \left(\dfrac{(512)^2 x^4}{c^8}\right)^2$

C $y = \dfrac{\left(1024x^2\right)^2}{c^4}$

265. Which of the following diagrams correctly show the graph of $f(x) = \tan(2x)$, in the following range: $4410 \leq x \leq 4500$, where x is measured in degrees?

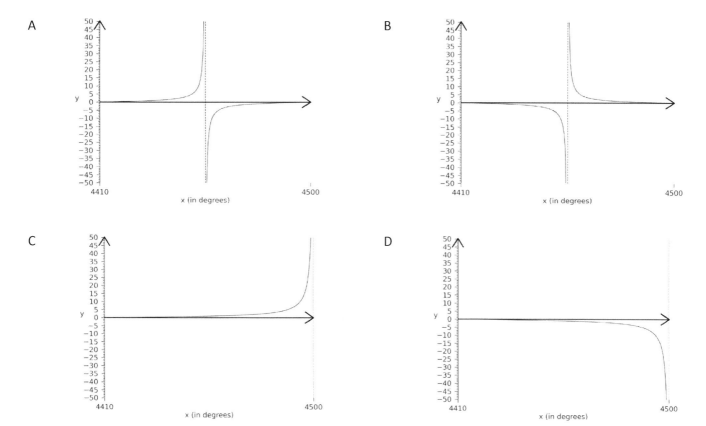

A

B

C

D

266. Which of the following diagrams correctly show the graph of $f(x) = \sin(30t) + 4$, when $0 \leq t \leq 12$, where t is measured in degrees?

A

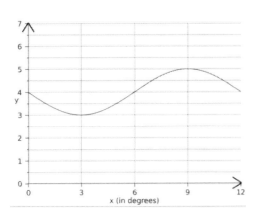

B

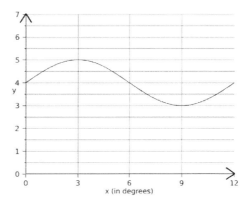

C

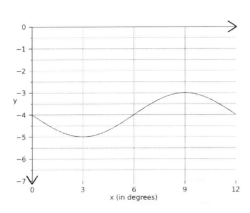

D

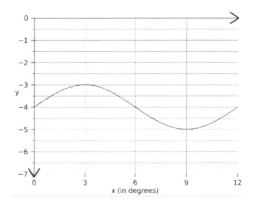

267. How many times do the graphs of $[\sin(15x) + 10]$ & $[\cos(15x) + 10]$ intersect in the range $0 \leq x \leq 24$, where x is measured in degrees?

A   No intersections

B   1

C   2

G   155

D   3

E   4

F   30

268. $\dfrac{\frac{1}{b}}{\frac{1}{b}+1} = b$. What are the possible values of b?

A $1+\sqrt{5}\ \&\ -1-\sqrt{5}$

B $\dfrac{\sqrt{5}}{2}$

C $\dfrac{-1+\sqrt{5}}{2}\ \&\ \dfrac{-1-\sqrt{5}}{2}$

D -1

E   No solutions

269. ABCD is a rhombus. Angle BAD = 50° and Angle ADC = 130°. What are the values of x and y?

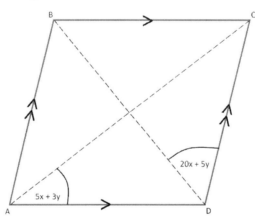

A $x = 5, y = 2$

B $x = 3, y = 4$

C $x = 2, y = 5$

D $x = 4, y = 3$

E $x = 5, y = 5$

F   More information is needed

270. Triangles A and B are similar. The area of triangle $A = 10$. The area of Triangle $B = 22.5$. What is the value of x?

A   2

B   4

C   3

D   6

E   5

F   10

271. $Mass = Volume \times Density$. A large sculpture has a mass of 875 kg. A smaller (but mathematically similar) statue is made that is $\frac{3}{5}$ the height of the original sculpture. The small statue and the large sculpture are both made of the same material. What is the mass of the smaller statue?

A   189kg

B   272kg

C   315kg

D   525kg

E   615kg

F   More information is needed

272. What is the value of a and b in the following diagram?

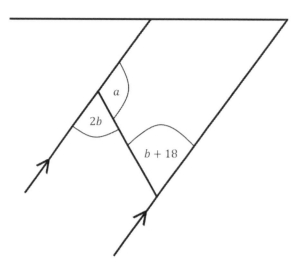

A $b = 72, a = 108$	D $a = 60, b = 120$
B $a = 108, b = 72$	E $a = 144, b = 18$
C $a = 120, b = 60$	F $b = 144, a = 18$

273. One quarter of the exterior angles of a polygon are 24°, one quarter are 32°, one quarter are 12°, and one quarter are 4°. How many sides does this polygon have?

A 10	D 21
B 20	E 19
C 18	F 30

274. In the diagram below, A is the centre of a regular polygon. What is the value of the sum of x and y?

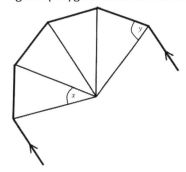

A   108°

B   112°

C   120°

D   128°

E   135°

F   150°

275. BD bisects angle ADC. ACFE is a parallelogram. What is the size of angle CBD?

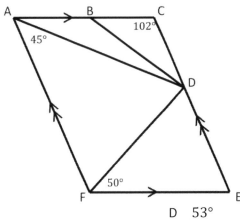

A   45°

B   48.25°

C   51.5°

D   53°

E   55.5°

F   60°

276. ABCG is a parallelogram. DEFG is a parallelogram. What is the value of angle x?

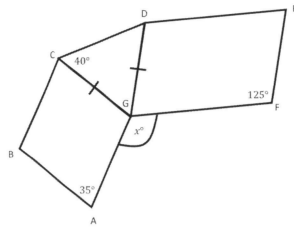

A   35°

B   45°

C   60°

D   70°

E   80°

F   More information is needed

277. A shape has the coordinates $(3, -4)$, $(1, 0)$, $(-2, 0)$, $(-1, -4)$. It is reflected in the line $y = 2$, then translated by the vector $\binom{1}{0}$. What are its new coordinates?

A $[(-1, 2), (2, 2), (0, 6), (4, 6)]$

B $[(-1, 4), (2, 4), (0, 8), (4, 8)]$

C $[(-2, 4), (1, 4), (-1, 8), (3, 8)]$

D $[(-2, 2), (1, 2), (-1, 6), (3, 6)]$

E $[(-2, 3), (1, 3), (-1, 7), (3, 7)]$

F $[(0, 8), (4, 8), (3, 4), (-1, 4)]$

278. A triangle has the points $[(4,4), (8,4), (6,8)]$. It is rotated $180°$ about the point $(6,8)$. It is then reflected in the y-axis. It is then reflected in the x-axis. What are the new coordinates of the triangle?

A $[(4,12), (8,12), (6,8)]$

B $[(-4,12), (-8,4), (-6,8)]$

C $[(-4,4), (-8,4), (-6,8)]$

D $[(4,4), (8,4), (6,8)]$

E $[(-4,-12), (-8,-12), (-6,-8)]$

279. GE is a diameter of the circle. CZ is a tangent to the circle, at point G. O is the centre of the circle. What is the value of a and b? *(Note: diagram not to scale)*

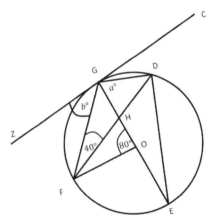

A $b = 50, a = 40$

B $a = 50, b = 40$

C $b = 65, a = 30$

D $a = 65, b = 30$

E $a = 40, b = 20$

F $b = 40, a = 20$

280. A, B, C and D lie on the circumference of the circle. O is the centre of the circle. What is the value of a and b?

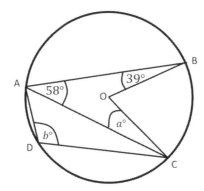

A $\qquad$ $a = 19°, b = 109°$ $\qquad\qquad$ D $\qquad$ $a = 39°, b = 109°$

B $\qquad$ $a = 32°, b = 58°$ $\qquad\qquad$ E $\qquad$ $a = 39°, b = 71°$

C $\qquad$ $a = 32°, b = 135°$ $\qquad\qquad$ F $\qquad$ $a = 19°, b = 71°$

281. A builder specialises in building sheds, all of which are mathematically similar to each other. The manufacturing cost of a shed is made of two parts: the cost of bricks (proportional to volume) and the cost to paint the shed. A small shed costs £1000 to make - £800 in brick costs and £200 to paint. The ratio of respective sides lengths, for a small shed: large shed, is $2: 1$. What is the combined cost to build a small shed and a large shed?

A $\qquad$ £2500 $\qquad\qquad$ D $\qquad$ £8200

B $\qquad$ £7200 $\qquad\qquad$ E $\qquad$ £10000

C $\qquad$ £6400 $\qquad\qquad$ F $\qquad$ More information is needed

282. A parallelogram has the points: $(1,0), (4,0), (6,5), (9,5)$. It is reflected in the line $y = x$. It is then translated by $\binom{-5}{5}$. What are the points of the parallelogram after the transformations?

A $[(-5,6), (-5,9), (0,11), (0,14)]$ D $[(6,2), (6,5), (7,9), (7,12)]$

B $[(1,1), (1,4), (6,6), (6,9)]$ E $[(-1,5), (-4,5), (-6,10), (-9,10)]$

C $[(2,1), (2,4), (5,8), (5,11)]$

283. An irregular polygon has 12 sides. Two of the exterior angles are $12°$, and 4 of the exterior angles are $6°$. The remaining exterior angles are the same size. What is their size?

A $12°$ D $52°$

B $39°$ E $42°$

C $33°$ F $45°$

284. S_1 and S_2 are quadratic sequences. $S_1 = (10, 19, 32, 49, 70, \dots)$ and $S_2 = (6, 7, 10, 15, 22, \dots)$ S_3 is also a sequence, and is made from the product of each corresponding term of S_1 and S_2. For example, the first term of S_3 would be $10 \times 6 = 60$, and the second term of S_3 would be 19×7. What is the formula for the nth term of S_3?

A $3n^4 - 2n^3 - n^2 + n + 3$ D $2n^4 - n^3 + 13n^2 + 11n + 35$

B $x^4 - 13x^2 + 15$ E   More information is needed

C $4n^2 + 15n - 18$

285. What is the nth term of the following sequence: $8, 8, 10, 14, 20$?

A $n^2 + 3n - 10$ D $-2n^2 - 10n + 12$

B $2n^2 + 10n - 12$ E $n^2 + 2n - 6$

C $n^2 - 3n + 10$

286. For quadratic sequence A, the second difference is 2, the 0th term is 10. Which of the following formulas could be the formula for the nth term of sequence A?

         i) $2n^2 + 5n + 10$

         ii) $n^2 - 15.5n + 10$

         iii) $2n^2 - 10$

A   i   E   i & iii

B   ii   F   ii & iii

C   iii   G   i, ii & iii

D   i & ii

287. S_1 is a quadratic sequence with the following terms: $(24, 56, 100, 156, 224, \dots)$ S_2 is a linear sequence with the following terms: $(6, 8, 10, 12, 14)$? S_3 is sequence that is derived by dividing each term of S_1 by its corresponding term in S_2.

For example, the first term of S_3 would be $\frac{24}{6} = 4$, and the second term of S_3 would be $\frac{56}{8} = 7$. What is the formula for the nth term of the S_3?

A $6n^2 + 16n - 4$ D $3n + 1$

B $6n^2 - 16n + 4$ E   More information is needed

C $3n - 1$

288. The formula for the nth term of a quadratic sequence is $3n^2 + 6n + 2$. Two consecutive terms of this quadratic sequence have a difference of 57. What are their term numbers?

A   11 and 12

B   9 and 10

C   6 and 7

D   10 and 11

E   7 and 8

F   8 and 9

289. A fitness company manufactures dumbbells, all of which are mathematically similar to each other. The manufacturing cost of a dumbbell is made of two parts: the cost of raw material (proportional to volume) and the cost to paint the dumbbells. A 5kg dumbbell costs £7 to make - £5 in raw material costs and £2 to paint. The ratio of the lengths of a 10kg dumbbell and 5kg dumbbell is 4: 2. What is the difference in the cost of manufacturing a 10kg dumbbell in comparison to a 5kg dumbbell?

A   £41

B   £21

C   £15

D   £36

E   £40

F   £42

290. The diagram below shows a frustrum. What is the height of the cone that the frustrum is from?

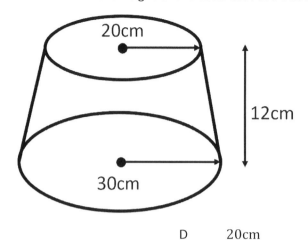

20cm

12cm

30cm

A   36cm

B   28cm

C   24cm

D   20cm

E   More information is needed

291. $\binom{y}{y} - \binom{4x}{2x^2+3x} = \binom{6}{5}$ What is the value of x and y?

A $(x = 4, y = 22)$ and $(x = 2, y = 14)$

B $(x = 1, y = 10)$ and $(x = -0.5, y = 4)$

C $(x = 2, y = 19)$ and $(x = 4, y = 49)$

D $(x = 3, y = 18)$ and $(x = 5, y = 26)$

292. $\begin{pmatrix} 2x \\ x \\ 2x \end{pmatrix} + \begin{pmatrix} 2y \\ -2y \\ 3y \end{pmatrix} + \begin{pmatrix} -2z \\ 3z \\ z \end{pmatrix} = \begin{pmatrix} 8 \\ -6 \\ 7 \end{pmatrix}$ What is the value of x, y, and z?

A $x = 5, y = -5,$ and $z = 0$

B $x = -11, y = -1,$ and $z = 1$

C $x = 1, y = 1,$ and $z = 2$

D $x = 2, y = 6,$ and $z = 12$

E $x = 1, y = 2,$ and $z = -1$

F   More information is needed

293. The table below shows the number of shoes owned by some students in a class. For students that own up to and including 4 shoes, the mean number of shoes is 3. For students who own more than one shoe, the mean number of shoes is 4. What are the total number of students in the class?

Number of shoes	Frequency
1	4
2	x
3	6
4	y
5	10

A $x = 10, y = 2$

B $x = 1, y = 4$

C $x = 2, y = 10$

D $x = 5, y = 2$

E $x = 3, y = 3$

F $x = 1, y = 1$

G   More information is needed

294. The pie chart below describes the favourite colour of 180 children in a school. How many kids have favourite colours of red and yellow?

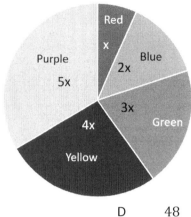

A   0

B   12

C   24

D   48

E   60

F   More information is needed

295. The histogram below represents the heights of students in a large class. If 42 students were recorded in the following class $175 < x \leq 185$, how many students had a height above 195cm?

A   3

B   6

C   9

D   7

E   1

F   More information is needed

296. The heights of plants in a greenhouse are split into categories. The heights range from 10cm to 70cm. There are 160 plants in the $60 < h \leq 70$ category. There are 110 more plants in the $40 < h \leq 50$ than in the $10 < h \leq 20$ category. There are 52 plants in the $30 < h \leq 40$. There are 82 plants in the $10 < h \leq 40$. There are 430 plants in the $40 < h \leq 70$ category. There are 8 plants in the $10 < h \leq 20$ category. There are 512 plants in total. How many categories have between 30 and 155 plants?

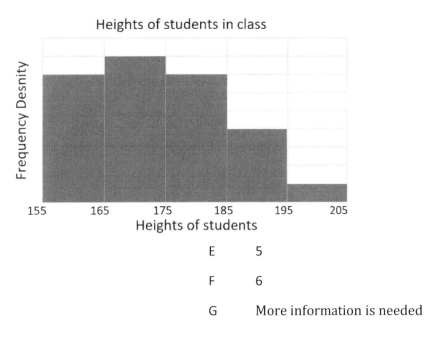

A   1

B   2

C   3

D   4

E   5

F   6

G   More information is needed

297. Angles AOB, BOC, and COD are all $\frac{\pi}{2}$. O is the centre of the circle, and its radius is 4cm. ABCD is a square. What is the area of the shaded region in this diagram?

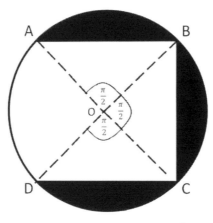

A $12\pi - 24$

B $12\pi + 24$

C $4\pi - 3$

D $4\pi + 3$

E   8

F 8π

G   More information is needed

298. AO = OD = 4cm. BA = CD = 4cm. BC is an arc of the circle, which has a centre of O. What is the area of the shaded region?

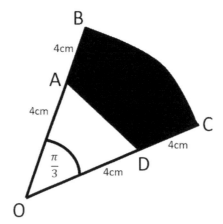

A $24 + 8\sqrt{3}$

B 24

C $\frac{32\pi}{3} - 4\sqrt{3}$

D $\frac{32\pi}{3} + 4\sqrt{3}$

E   More information is needed

299. BC is an arc of a circle, which has a centre of O. The ratio of the lengths of OA: OB is 1: 2. What is the area of the shaded region?

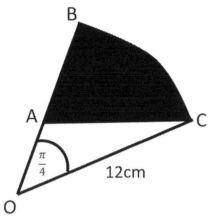

A 36π

B $18\pi - 12\sqrt{2}$

C $18\pi + 12\sqrt{2}$

D $24\pi - 6\sqrt{2}$

E $24\pi + 24\sqrt{2}$

F   More information is needed

300. BDEG is a rectangle. ABHG is a kite. AGB is a sector of a circle. BHG is a sector of a circle. FG = BC = 4cm. CH = HF = 3cm. AB = AG = 6cm. Angle BHG is $\frac{\pi}{3}$, and angle BAG is $\frac{2\pi}{3}$. What is the area of the shaded region?

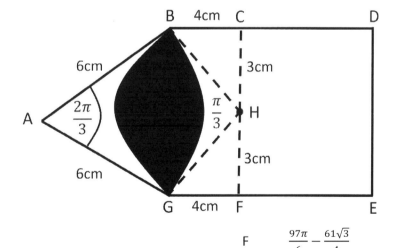

A $\frac{11\pi}{2} + \frac{35\pi}{2}$

B $\frac{11\pi}{2} - \frac{35\pi}{2}$

C $\frac{75\pi}{8} - \frac{36\sqrt{2}}{4}$

D $\frac{75\pi}{8} + \frac{36\sqrt{2}}{4}$

E $\frac{97\pi}{6} + \frac{61\sqrt{3}}{4}$

F $\frac{97\pi}{6} - \frac{61\sqrt{3}}{4}$

Table of Answers

1	B
2	A
3	C
4	D
5	A
6	B
7	A
8	C
9	B
10	A
11	C
12	A
13	B
14	D
15	A
16	D
17	C
18	B
19	A
20	D
21	B
22	B
23	B
24	C
25	D
26	A
27	A
28	A
29	C
30	B

31	C
32	B
33	D
34	A
35	D
36	D
37	B
38	A
39	A
40	D
41	D
42	C
43	B
44	B
45	C
46	D
47	A
48	A
49	D
50	B
51	B
52	D
53	A
54	A
55	C
56	B
57	D
58	D
59	D
60	A

61	A
62	D
63	A
64	A
65	C
66	D
67	D
68	D
69	C
70	A
71	B
72	B
73	C
74	A
75	C
76	C
77	D
78	C
79	A
80	D
81	D
82	B
83	C
84	C
85	D
86	B
87	A
88	A
89	D
90	C

91	A
92	B
93	C
94	D
95	A
96	A
97	C
98	B
99	B
100	D
101	A
102	B
103	A
104	E
105	C
106	C
107	C
108	C
109	B
110	B
111	A
112	C
113	A
114	E
115	D
116	A
117	D
118	B
119	C
120	C

121	B
122	D
123	D
124	B
125	B
126	A
127	A
128	D
129	E
130	B
131	D
132	D
133	E
134	D
135	F
136	A
137	B
138	C
139	A
140	C
141	C
142	B
143	B
144	E
145	C
146	A
147	D
148	B
149	D
150	C

151	A	181	B	211	C	241	A	271	A
152	C	182	E	212	A	242	E	272	E
153	A	183	A	213	D	243	A	273	B
154	D	184	A	214	C	244	D	274	A
155	C	185	A	215	F	245	B	275	E
156	C	186	B	216	A	246	C	276	C
157	E	187	D	217	D	247	B	277	B
158	A	188	D	218	E	248	A	278	E
159	C	189	D	219	A	249	B	279	B
160	C	190	D	220	B	250	C	280	A
161	D	191	F	221	E	251	G	281	D
162	B	192	E	222	B	252	B	282	A
163	B	193	D	223	B	253	E	283	D
164	C	194	A	224	A	254	E	284	D
165	D	195	B	225	E	255	D	285	C
166	E	196	D	226	A	256	C	286	B
167	E	197	B	227	B	257	F	287	D
168	D	198	B	228	A	258	E	288	F
169	B	199	F	229	C	259	A	289	A
170	B	200	D	230	B	260	F	290	A
171	F	201	C	231	A	261	C	291	B
172	I	202	F	232	E	262	A	292	E
173	B	203	C	233	B	263	D	293	C
174	E	204	F	234	E	264	B	294	F
175	D	205	B	235	A	265	A	295	B
176	D	206	E	236	C	266	B	296	C
177	E	207	B	237	A	267	C	297	A
178	A	208	H	238	E	268	C	298	C
179	E	209	A	239	B	269	C	299	B
180	B	210	A	240	F	270	A	300	F

Worked Solutions

1. Answer: B

Complete the square for x and y to derive a form from which the radius can be found.

$$(x + 4)^2 - 16 + (y + 2)^2 - 4 - 29 = 0$$

$$(x + 4)^2 + (y + 2)^2 = 49$$

The equation of a circle $(x - a)^2 + (y - b)^2 = r^2$

Therefore, radius is equal to $\sqrt{49} = 7$

2. Answer: A

The gradient of the normal is the negative reciprocal of the gradient of the tangent. To find the gradient of the tangent we differentiate the curve and find the first derivative when $x = 2$.

$$y = 5x^3 - 12x^2 + 6x^{\frac{1}{2}}$$

$$y' = 15x^2 - 24x + 3x^{\frac{-1}{2}}$$

When $x = 2$, $y' = 12 + \frac{3}{\sqrt{2}} = \frac{(24 + 3\sqrt{2})}{2}$

Therefore, the gradient of the normal is equal to $-\frac{1}{\frac{(24 + 3\sqrt{2})}{2}} = \frac{-8 + \sqrt{2}}{93}$

3. Answer: C

The discriminant $b^2 - 4ac = 4 - 4(2)(-9) = 76$

If $b^2 - 4ac > 0$, then there are real distinct roots, and as $76 > 0$.

$\sqrt{76}$ is not a rational number, therefore, the solutions are real but not rational.

4. Answer: D

The expression $(1 + x + x^2)^3$ can be rewritten as $\left(1 + (x + x^2)\right)^3$. By creating an inner bracket, we can expand this as if it were a two-term bracket and apply the binomial theorem.

This can be expanded using the binomial expansion:

$$1 + 3(x + x^2) + 3(x + x^2)^2 + 1(x + x^2)^3$$

This can be fully expanded and then simplified to give:

$$x^6 + 3x^5 + 6x^4 + 7x^3 + 6x^2 + 3x + 1$$

Thus, the coefficient of $x^4 = 6$

5. Answer: A

We complete the square on the quadratic to get $(x + 7)^2 - 49 + \frac{11}{2} = (x + 7)^2 - \frac{87}{2}$

This means that $p = 7$ and $q = -\frac{87}{2}$.

6. Answer: B

Note: $(\sqrt{a} + \sqrt{b})(\sqrt{a} - \sqrt{b}) = a - b$

Taking $\frac{1}{\sqrt{1} + \sqrt{2}}$, we can rationalise the surd.

This gives us:

$$\frac{1}{\sqrt{1} + \sqrt{2}} \times \frac{\sqrt{1} - \sqrt{2}}{\sqrt{1} - \sqrt{2}}$$

Using the rule shown above $((\sqrt{a} + \sqrt{b})(\sqrt{a} - \sqrt{b}) = a - b)$, the denominator is $1 - 2 = -1$ and the numerator is $\sqrt{1} - \sqrt{2}$. Therefore, $\frac{1}{\sqrt{1} + \sqrt{2}} = \sqrt{2} - \sqrt{1} = \sqrt{2} - 1$

The second term $\frac{1}{\sqrt{2} + \sqrt{3}}$ becomes $\sqrt{3} - \sqrt{2}$ when we rationalise it.

The third term $\frac{1}{\sqrt{3} + \sqrt{4}}$ becomes $\sqrt{4} - \sqrt{3}$ when we rationalise it.

Therefore, we can spot a pattern:

$$\frac{1}{\sqrt{1} + \sqrt{2}} + \frac{1}{\sqrt{2} + \sqrt{3}} + \frac{1}{\sqrt{3} + \sqrt{4}} \ldots$$

$$= \sqrt{2} - \sqrt{1} + \sqrt{3} - \sqrt{2} + \sqrt{4} - \sqrt{3}$$

Every term is cancelled out by a term that occurs three places after it occurs. $\sqrt{2}$ cancels out, $\sqrt{3}$ cancels out and so on.

When we consider the series up to $\frac{1}{\sqrt{35} + \sqrt{36}}$, we notice that every term will cancel **except** the $-\sqrt{1}$ at the start and the $\sqrt{36}$ at the end.

Thus, we are left with $-1 + 6 = 5$.

7. Answer: A

This rearranges to $2x^2 - 6x - 36 < 0$.

If we factorise the quadratic, we find that the roots are $x = -3$ and $x = 6$.

We can find the values of x, where the inequality holds true, by plotting a quadratic. The values of x are when the curve is below the x axis, is when x is between the roots.

Therefore, $-3 < x < 6$.

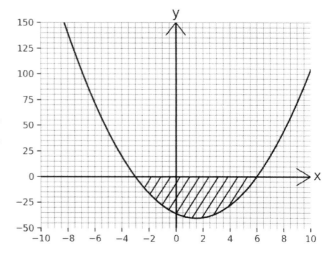

154

8. Answer: C

The first line $3y + 2x = 6$ can be rewritten as $y = -\frac{2}{3}x + 2$ and the second line $5y + 3x = 11$ can be rewritten as $y = -\frac{3}{5}x + \frac{11}{5}$.

The gradient of the line parallel to $3y + 2x = 6$ has the same gradient, which is $-\frac{2}{3}$.

The gradient of the line perpendicular to $5y + 3x = 11$ is the negative reciprocal, which is $-\frac{1}{-\frac{3}{5}} = \frac{5}{3}$.

Therefore, the product is $-\frac{10}{9}$.

9. Answer: B

This uses the remainder theorem. Therefore, substitute in the value $x = 2$, into the polynomial given $f(x) = x^3 - 5x^2 + 4x + 3$.

This gives $2^3 - 5(2^2) + 4(2) + 3 = -1$.

Alternatively, this question can be solved by using polynomial long division, however, this takes longer and it is not recommended given the time pressure in the exam.

10. Answer: A

We can draw a tree diagram to represent the different outcomes that occurred in the first two picks out of the bag.

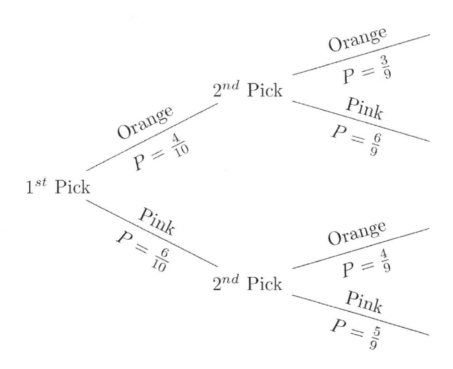

Briefly summarising it:

1st Pick:

Either $\frac{4}{10}$ chance of picking an orange marble and a $\frac{6}{10}$ chance of picking a pink marble.

2nd Pick:

If you picked orange in the first pick: a $\frac{3}{9}$ chance of picking an orange marble again or a $\frac{6}{9}$ chance of picking a pink marble.

If you picked pink in the first pick: a $\frac{4}{9}$ chance of picking an orange marble or a $\frac{5}{9}$ chance of picking a pink marble again.

You can find the probability totals by following through each branch in the tree diagram.

Now we need to find the probability that we picked two orange marbles in our first two picks (which in turn also finds the probability we picked one of each marble colour given we know we picked at least one orange marble). This can be found from the tree diagram using the formula:

$$P(A \text{ given } B) = \frac{P(A \cap B)}{P(B)}$$

$$P(orange, orange \text{ given at least one orange}) = \frac{\frac{12}{90}}{\frac{12}{90} + \frac{24}{90} + \frac{24}{90}} = \frac{1}{5}$$

Therefore, the probability of the first two picks being orange and then orange is $\frac{1}{5}$ and the probability of having picked one pink and one orange is $\frac{4}{5}$ (given the fact we had picked at least one of orange).

This allows us to draw a second tree diagram to find out what happens for our third pick; however, it is simple to logically consider it without spending time drawing a tree diagram.

There is a $\frac{1}{5}$ chance we picked orange and orange, and if this happened then there are only two orange marbles remaining in the bag, hence the probability of picking a third orange marble on the third pick is $\frac{2}{8}$

There is a $\frac{4}{5}$ chance we picked one orange and one pink marble, and if this happened then there are three orange marbles remaining in the bag, hence the probability of picking an orange marble on the third pick is $\frac{3}{8}$

Thus, the overall probability of picking an orange marble on the third pick is:

$$\frac{1}{5} \times \frac{2}{8} + \frac{4}{5} \times \frac{3}{8} = \frac{7}{20}$$

11. Answer: C

Use the idea that $8 = 2^3$, also $(2^a)^b = 2^{ab}$ and finally $\frac{2^a}{2^b} = 2^{a-b}$. The steps are shown below:

$$\frac{8^x}{2^y} = \frac{2^{3x}}{2^y} = 2^{3x-y}$$

We are told that $3x - y = 15$

Therefore, $\frac{8^x}{2^y} = 2^{15}$

12. Answer: A

$$\left(\sqrt{3}\right)^m = \frac{3^{2x}}{81^y}$$

Use the idea that $(3^a)^b = 3^{ab}$:

$$3^{\frac{1}{2}m} = \frac{3^{2x}}{3^{4y}}$$

$$3^{\frac{1}{2}m} = 3^{2x-4y}$$

$$\frac{1}{2}m = 2x - 4y$$

$$m = 4x - 8y$$

13. Answer: B

Take logarithms of both sides:

$$\log(a^{5x}b^{2x}c^x d^{-3x}) = \log(4)$$

Expand out into multiple logarithms using the rule that $\log(a) + \log(b) = \log(ab)$. Then bring down the power x as $\log(a)^b = b\log(a)$.

$$\log(a^{5x}) + \log(b^{2x}) + \log(c^x) + \log d^{-3x} = \log(4)$$

$$x\log(a^5) + x\log(b^2) + x\log(c) + x\log(d^{-3}) = \log(4)$$

Factorise out the x and then rearrange to make x the subject of the equation.

$$x[\log(a^5) + \log(b^2) + \log(c) + \log(d^{-3})] = \log(4)$$

$$x = \frac{\log(4)}{\log(a^5) + \log(b^2) + \log(c) + \log(d^{-3})}$$

Apply the rule that $\log(a) + \log(b) = \log(ab)$, to simplify the expression.

$$x = \frac{\log(4)}{\log\left(\frac{a^5 b^2 c}{d^3}\right)}$$

14. Answer: D

Change the expression $3^{x+2} \times 9^{\frac{3}{2}x} = 27^{27}$, such that all terms have a base of 3.

$$3^{x+2} \times 3^{2\times\frac{3}{2}x} = 3^{3\times27}$$

$$3^{x+2} \times 3^{3x} = 3^{81}$$

$$x + 3x + 2 = 81$$

$$4x + 2 = 81 \quad \therefore x = \frac{79}{4}$$

15. Answer: A

$$\frac{x}{x-10} > \frac{1}{2}$$

$$\frac{x}{x-10} - \frac{1}{2} > 0$$

$$\frac{x+10}{2(x-10)} > 0$$

$$\frac{x+10}{x-10} > 0$$

Consider what happens to this fraction as x varies over different values. For it to be greater than 0, then $x < -10$ or $x > 10$.

16. Answer: D

Let the roots of the equation be α and β. If they differ by $\frac{14}{3}$, this means that $\alpha - \beta = \frac{14}{3}$

Use the rules that for a quadratic equation $(ax^2 + bx + c)$ with roots α and β, $\alpha + \beta = -\frac{b}{a}$ and $\alpha\beta = \frac{c}{a}$.

$$\alpha + \left(\alpha - \frac{14}{3}\right) = \frac{10}{3}$$

$$2\alpha = 8$$

$$\alpha = 4$$

Hence, substitute $\alpha = 4$ into the expression: $\alpha\left(\alpha - \frac{14}{3}\right) = -\frac{k}{3}$, which is derived using the rule that $\alpha\beta = \frac{c}{a}$.

$4\left(4 - \frac{14}{3}\right) = -\frac{k}{3}$ ∴ Solving for k, we find that $k = 8$

17. Answer: C

For $(3^x)^2 - 13(3^x) = -40$, let $a = 3^x$, to form a new quadratic equation.

$$a^2 - 13a + 40 = 0$$

Solve this quadratic through factorisation to find solutions in a.

$$a^2 - 13a + 40 = (a-8)(a-5) = 0$$

Therefore, $a = 8$ and $a = 5$

When you reverse the substitution, we find that:

$3^x = 8$ and $3^x = 5$

Taking logarithms of both sides: $\qquad x = \frac{\log 8}{\log 3}$ and $x = \frac{\log 5}{\log 3}$

The sum of these values is $\qquad \frac{\log 8 + \log 5}{\log 3} = \frac{\log 40}{\log 3}$.

158

18. Answer: B

First, we complete the square on $y = f(x)$.

$$2x^2 - 4x + 8 = 2[x^2 - 2x + 4] = 2[(x-1)^2 - 1 + 4] = 2(x-1)^2 + 6$$

This means that the minimum point for $y = f(x)$ is $(1,6)$

The translation $f(x-2)$ shifts the curve $y = f(x)$ two units to the right.

This increases the x value of the minimum point by 2.

The minimum point of $f(x-2)$ is $(3,6)$.

19. Answer: A

First, we complete the square on $y = f(x)$.

$$-3x^2 + 5x + 8 = -3\left[x^2 - \frac{5}{3}x - \frac{8}{3}\right] = -3\left[\left(x - \frac{5}{6}\right)^2 - \frac{25}{36} - \frac{8}{3}\right] = -3\left(x - \frac{5}{6}\right)^2 + \frac{121}{12}$$

This means that the maximum point for $y = f(x)$ is $(\frac{5}{6}, \frac{121}{12})$

The translation $-4f(x+1)$ shifts the curve $y = f(x)$ one unit to the left in the x direction, stretches it by factor 4 in the y direction and finally, the negative will reflect the curve in the x axis.

This decreases the x value of the maximum point by 1, you multiply the y value in the maximum point by -4.

The minimum point of $-4f(x+1)$ is $(-\frac{1}{6}, -\frac{121}{3})$.

20. Answer: D

Input in the first few values to try and spot a pattern:

$a_1 = 3$ $a_2 = 5$ $a_3 = \frac{5}{3}$ $a_4 = \frac{1}{3}$ $a_5 = \frac{1}{5}$ $a_6 = \frac{3}{5}$

$a_7 = 3$ $a_8 = 5$

Therefore, the sequence repeats with a period of 6.

To find a_{2020}, we divide $\frac{2020}{6}$, which is 336 remainder 4. This means that our value is the 4th term in the sequence which is $\frac{1}{3}$.

21. Answer: B

You substitute in low values of x, such as $x = -1, 1, 2, -2, 3, -3$, into the polynomial and record which values have a remainder of 0, hence are factors.

You will find that $x = 3$ and $x = -2$ are both factors of the polynomial.

Use polynomial long division or compare coefficient to divide $2x^3 - x^2 - 13x - 6$ by $(x - 3)$.

This will give you the polynomial $2x^2 + 5x + 2$.

Then you can further factorise this quadratic to give $(x + 2)(2x + 1)$

Therefore, $2x^3 - x^2 - 13x - 6 = (x - 3)(x + 2)(2x + 1)$

It has three roots: $3, -2 \; and \; -\frac{1}{2}$

22. Answer: B

If you have to maximise a trigonometric function, begin with the simple form and see what the maximum and minimum possible answers or bounds are.

$$(4\cos^2(11x - 4) + 2)^3 .$$

- $\cos(11x - 4)$ is between -1 and 1 as this is the standard linear bracket cos expression
- When square the expression, $(\cos(11x - 4))^2$, the range is between 0 and 1 as you square the previous range of -1 and 1.
- When the expression is multiplied by 4, then it becomes $4(\cos(11x - 4))^2$, the range is between 0 and 4 as you multiply the previous range 0 and 1 by 4
- When you add 2, the expression $4(\cos(11x - 4))^2 + 2$, the range is between 2 and 6 as you add 2 from the previous range 0 and 4.
- When you cube this, the expression is $(4\cos^2(11x - 4) + 2)^3$, and the range is 8 and 216 as you square the previous range 2 to 6.

Therefore, the maximum value that the expression can take is 216.

23. Answer: B

To find the number of stationary points, we have to differentiate the function.

This gives $y' = -9x^2 - 14x + 1$.

Stationary points are when the first derivative is equal to 0, hence $f'(x) = 0$.

$$-9x^2 - 14x + 1 = 0$$

The discriminant of this quadratic is $14^2 - 4(-9)(1) = 232$

As $b^2 - 4ac > 0$, there are two distinct roots.

160

24. Answer: C

Change the expression to have all the terms with 2^x as the base.

$$(2^x)^2 - 8(2^x) - m = 0$$

To have one or more solutions, the discriminant has to be greater than or equal to 0.

Therefore, $8^2 - 4(1)(-m) \geq 0$.

$$64 + 4m \geq 0$$

$$4m \geq -64$$

$$m \geq -16$$

25. Answer: D

$$\frac{2x}{x+6} = \frac{3x-4}{2x}$$

$$4x^2 = 3x^2 + 14x - 24$$

$$x^2 - 14x + 24 = 0$$

This factorises to give $x^2 - 14x + 24 = (x - 12)(x - 2) = 0$

Therefore, $x = 12$ or $x = 2$

The sum of the possible values is $12 + 2 = 14$

26. Answer: A

Use the remainder theorem to form two simultaneous equations.

When $f(x)$ is divided by $(x - 1)$, the remainder is 12, therefore substitute 1 into the polynomial and the result is 12.

$$1 + a + b + 3 = 12$$

$$a + b = 8$$

When $f(x)$ is divided by $(x + 2)$, the remainder is 12, therefore substitute -2 into the polynomial and the result is 12.

$$-32 + 16a - 8b + 12 = 12$$

$$16a - 8b = 32$$

$$16a - 8b = 32$$

$$a + b = 8$$

$$a = 8 - b$$

$$16(8 - b) - 8b = 32$$

$$b = 4 \text{ and } a = 4$$

Therefore, the product of $a \times b = 4 \times 4 = 16$

27. Answer: A

The sum of an arithmetic progression is given by the expression $\frac{n}{2}(2a + (n-1)d)$

Therefore, the sum of the first 20 terms is $\frac{20}{2}(2a + (20-1)d)$

This is equal to 350: $10(2a + 19d) = 350$

$$2a + 19d = 35$$

Secondly, the sum of the next 15 terms is the sum of the first 35 terms minus the sum of the first 20 terms. $\frac{35}{2}(2a + (35-1)d) - \frac{20}{2}(2a + (20-1)d)$

This is equal to 3150:

$$\frac{35}{2}(2a + 34d) - 350 = 3150$$

$$2a + 34d = 200$$

We can solve both equations simultaneously to find the common difference.

$$2a + 19d = 35$$

$$2a + 34d = 200$$

$$35 - 19d = 200 - 34d$$

$$15d = 165$$

$$d = 11$$

28. Answer: A

The width is equal to $\frac{\sqrt{150}}{3 + 2\sqrt{3}}$

This needs to be rationalised, which will give:

$$\frac{\sqrt{150}}{3 + 2\sqrt{3}} = \frac{\sqrt{150}}{3 + 2\sqrt{3}} \times \frac{3 - 2\sqrt{3}}{3 - 2\sqrt{3}} = -5\sqrt{6} + 10\sqrt{2}$$

Therefore, the perimeter equals:

$$2W + 2L = 3 + 2\sqrt{3} + 3 + 2\sqrt{3} - 5\sqrt{6} + 10\sqrt{2} - 5\sqrt{6} + 10\sqrt{2}$$

This is equal to:

$$6 + 4\sqrt{3} - 10\sqrt{6} + 20\sqrt{2}$$

29. Answer: C

First cross multiply to make it a single fraction.

$$\frac{5}{1} + \frac{6\sqrt{2} - 5\sqrt{3}}{\sqrt{3} - \sqrt{2}} = \frac{5(\sqrt{3} - \sqrt{2}) + 1(6\sqrt{2} - 5\sqrt{3})}{\sqrt{3} - \sqrt{2}}$$

Expand and simplify.

$$= \frac{5\sqrt{3} - 5\sqrt{2} + 6\sqrt{2} - 5\sqrt{3}}{\sqrt{3} - \sqrt{2}}$$

$$= \frac{\sqrt{2}}{\sqrt{3} - \sqrt{2}}$$

Use surd rules to rationalise the denominator, hence you multiply the numerator and the denominator by $\sqrt{3} + \sqrt{2}$

$$\frac{\sqrt{2}}{\sqrt{3} - \sqrt{2}} \times \frac{\sqrt{3} + \sqrt{2}}{\sqrt{3} + \sqrt{2}} = \frac{\sqrt{6} + 2}{3 - 2} = 2 + \sqrt{6}$$

30. Answer: B

First, we complete the square on $y = f(x)$.

$$4x^2 + 6x + 9 = 4\left[x^2 + \frac{6}{4}x + \frac{9}{4}\right] = 4\left[\left(x + \frac{6}{8}\right)^2 - \frac{36}{64} + \frac{9}{4}\right] = 4\left(x + \frac{6}{8}\right)^2 + \frac{27}{4}$$

This means that the minimum point for $y = f(x)$ is $(\frac{-6}{8}, \frac{27}{4})$

The translation $11f(2x + 3)$ shifts the curve $y = f(x)$ three units to the left in the x direction, stretches it by factor $\frac{1}{2}$ in the x direction and by factor 11 in the y direction.

This decreases the x value of the original minimum point by 3 then you divide it by 2. You multiply the y value in the original minimum point by 11.

The minimum point of $11f(2x + 3)$ is $(-\frac{15}{8}, \frac{297}{4})$.

31. Answer: C

The initial 681 pizzas will provide 681 new pizzas to eat. After they have been consumed, the leftovers of every 9 pizzas makes a new pizza. Therefore, there are $\frac{681}{9}$ more pizzas, which is $75\ remainder\ 6$. Then, after the 75 pizzas have been eaten, there are $\frac{75}{9}$ new pizzas that can be made from the leftovers. This is equal to 8 remainder 3 pizzas. Notice, that the sum of the remainders to give 9 $6 + 3 = 9$, therefore, there is one more pizza that can be made.

Overall, we have $681 + 75 + 8 + 1 = 765$

NB: Some of you may have used a geometric series $\frac{a}{1-r} = \frac{681}{1 - \frac{1}{9}} = 766.125$ This is an incorrect answer because the geometric series is infinite, yet at some point, the leftovers from the pizzas do not make a whole pizza. The geometric series will keep adding even decimal pizzas, but the question specifically wants **full** pizzas.

32. Answer: B

$$\frac{1}{a} + \frac{1}{b} = \frac{1}{6}$$

$$\frac{a+b}{ab} = \frac{1}{6}$$

$$6a + 6b = ab$$

$$ab - 6a - 6b = 0$$

Notice that this can be factorised in an unusual manner:

$$(a-6)(b-6) = 36$$

This requires the product of two numbers $a - 6$ and $b - 6$ to give 36.

The list of solutions that are factors of 36.

$(a-6)$	$(b-6)$	$(a-6)(b-6)$
1	36	36
2	18	36
3	12	36
4	9	36
6	6	36
9	4	36
12	3	36
18	2	36
36	1	36

Therefore, we can see that the largest value a can take is when $(a - 6) = 36$, hence $a = 42$. When $a - 6 = 36$, this means that $b - 6 = 1$, therefore, $b = 7$. This means that the sum of a and b is:

$$42 + 7 = 49$$

33. Answer: D

The distance between two points is found through the length of the line connecting them, which also applies for three-dimensional points.

$$\sqrt{((3-6)^2 + (1-3)^2 + (5-6)^2} = \sqrt{(9+4+1)} = \sqrt{14}$$

34. Answer: A

The probability of getting at most two tails is $1 - P(3\ tails)$.

This is equal to $1 - \left(\frac{1}{2}\right)^3 = \frac{7}{8}$

35. Answer: D

This is the binomial distribution with $X \sim B(\frac{1}{2}, 20)$

$$P(X = 5) = 20C5 \times 0.5^5 \times 0.5^{15}$$

As $20C5 = 20C15$, this is the same as $P(X = 5) = 20C15 \times 0.5^5 \times 0.5^{15}$

36. Answer: D

This is the binomial distribution with $X \sim B(\frac{1}{5}, 30)$

$$P(X = 11) = 30C11 \times 0.2^{11} \times 0.8^{19}$$

As $30C11 = 30C19$, this is the same as $P(X = 5) = 30C19 \times \left(\frac{1}{5}\right)^{11} \times \left(\frac{4}{5}\right)^{19}$

37. Answer: B

Use the remainder theorem to form simultaneous equations.

When $f(x)$ is divided by $(x - 2)$, the remainder is -24, therefore substitute 2 into the polynomial and the result is -24.

$$16 - 16 + 4p + 2q + r = -24$$

$$4p + 2q + r = -24$$

When $f(x)$ is divided by $(x + 4)$, the remainder is 240, therefore substitute -4 into the polynomial and the result is 240.

$$256 + 128 + 16p - 4q + r = 240$$

$$16p - 4q + r = -144$$

When $f(x)$ is divided by $(x + 1)$, the remainder is 0, therefore substitute -1 into the polynomial and the result is 0.

$$3 + p - q + r = 0$$

$$p - q + r = -3$$

Solving these three equations simultaneously:

$$4p + 2q + r = -24$$

$$16p - 4q + r = -144$$

$$p - q + r = -3$$

Equation 1: $16p + 8q + 4r = -96$ Equation 2 is: $16p - 4q + r = -144$

Equation 3 becomes: $16p - 16q + 16r = -48$

Subtracting equation 2 from equation 1 we get: $12q + 3r = 48$ Subtracting equation 3 from equation 2 we get: $12q - 15r = -96$ Solving these we find that: $q = 2$ $r = 8$

Substituting these results into equation 1, we get: $p = -9$ $q = 2$ $r = 8 \therefore pqr = -144$

38. Answer: A

This is a permutation question. The word has 12 letters and therefore if all letters were different there are $12P12 = 12!$ Ways or rearranging the word.

However, the letter o is repeated 4 times and the letter a is repeated 2 times.

Therefore, you divide 12! by the factorial of these numbers To find the number of different permutations and to remove repeats.

$$\frac{12!}{4! \times 2!}$$

39. Answer: A

There are 5 matches, each with 3 options for the results. This is equal to $3 \times 3 \times 3 \times 3 \times 3$, as each match has 3 possible outcomes.

Therefore, there are 3^5 outcomes, which is 243.

40. Answer: D

The information in the question will let us set up the expression below:

$$\frac{4}{1-r} = 6$$

Hence $r = \frac{1}{3}$

The fourth term in the geometric sequence is ar^3

$$4 \left(\frac{1}{3}\right)^3 = \frac{4}{27}$$

41. Answer: D

To solve the simultaneous equations $y = x$ and $x^2 - 4x + 4 + y^2 - 20y - 100 = 18$, we perform a substitution:

$$x^2 - 4x + 4 + x^2 - 20x - 100 = 18$$

This simplifies to give $2x^2 - 24x - 114$

The discriminant of this equation is 1488 $(b^2 - 4ac = 24^2 - 4(2)(-96))$

As the discriminant is greater than 0, there are two solutions to the equation, and they meet at two points.

42. Answer: C

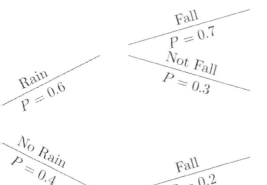

You can draw a tree diagram to represent the information:

$P(Rainy\ given\ that\ I\ did\ not\ fall\ over)$
$$= \frac{P(rainy\ and\ did\ not\ fall\ over)}{P(fell\ over)}$$

$$= \frac{0.6 \times 0.3}{(0.6 \times 0.3) + (0.4 \times 0.8)}$$

$$= \frac{9}{25}$$

43. Answer: B

$$y = \log_{10}\left(\frac{1}{3x^2 + 17x - 56}\right)$$

$$y = \log_{10}\left(\frac{1}{(3x - 7)(x + 8)}\right)$$

Therefore, the curve is undefined when $x = \frac{7}{3}$ or $x = -8$, as at both of these values we would need to compute $\frac{1}{0} =$ undefined. Therefore, there are asymptotes when $x = \frac{7}{3}$ or $x = -8$, which gives us $a\ and\ b$.

To find the roots for $y = \log_{10}\left(\frac{1}{3x^2 + 17x - 56}\right)$

$$0 = \log_{10}\left(\frac{1}{3x^2 + 17x - 56}\right)$$

$$10^0 = \frac{1}{3x^2 + 17x - 56}$$

$$1 = \frac{1}{3x^2 + 17x - 56}$$

$$1 = 3x^2 + 17x - 56$$

$$3x^2 + 17x - 57 = 0$$

Apply the quadratic formula: $\frac{-b \pm \sqrt{b^2 - 4ac}}{2a}$

This gives $x = \frac{-17 \pm \sqrt{973}}{6}$, which gives $c\ and\ d\ \therefore$.The product is: $\frac{7}{3} \times -8 \times \frac{-17 + \sqrt{973}}{6} \times \frac{-17 - \sqrt{973}}{6}$

This requires numerous steps for simplification to reach the final answer: $= \frac{1064}{3}$

44. Answer: B

Use the remainder theorem to form simultaneous equations.

When $f(x)$ is divided by $(x - 1)$, the remainder is 3, therefore substitute 1 into the polynomial and the result is 3.

$$a + b + c = 3$$

When $f(x)$ is divided by $(x - 2)$, the remainder is 12, therefore substitute 2 into the polynomial and the result is 12.

$$4a + 2b + c = 12$$

When $f(x)$ is divided by $(x + 2)$, the remainder is 0, therefore substitute -2 into the polynomial and the result is 0.

$$4a - 2b + c = 0$$

Solving these three equations simultaneously:

$$a + b + c = 3$$

$$4a + 2b + c = 12$$

$$4a - 2b + c = 0$$

If we subtract equation 3 from equation 2, we find that:

$$4b = 12$$

Hence, $b = 3$. If we substitute this into equation 1, we find that:

$a + c = 0$ and that $a = -c$. This can be used in equation 2, to find a and c:

$$4a + 6 - a = 12$$

Therefore, $a = 2$ and $c = -2$. Thus, $a = 2, b = 3$ and $c = -2$. This means that $a - b + c = -3$

45. Answer: C

You can convert the numbers from standard form into their full form and then perform the subtraction.

$$3.86 \times 10^6 = 3860000$$

$$4.55 \times 10^7 = 45500000$$

The subtraction of these numbers gives: $41640000 = 4.164 \times 10^7$

46. Answer: D

Any quadratic can be written in the general form, where (p, q) is the minimum point: $y = a(x - p)^2 + q$

We can then substitute in the minimum point into this equation.

$$y = a(x - 1.5)^2 - 1.5$$

$$3 = a(3 - 1.5)^2 - 1.5$$

$$a = 2$$

Therefore, $y = 2(x - 1.5)^2 - 1.5$. This simplifies to $y = 2x^2 - 6x + 3$

47. Answer: A

First, if we apply the binomial expansion to expand $(2x + 5)^4$:

$$(2x + 5)^4 = 16x^4 + 160x^3 + 600x^2 + 1000x + 625$$

Therefore, we now expand $(1 + x)(16x^4 + 160x^3 + 600x^2 + 1000x + 625)$. This gives:

$$16x^5 + 176x^4 + 760x^3 + 1600x^2 + 1625x + 625$$

Therefore, the coefficient of $x^3 = 760$

48. Answer: A

First, if we apply the binomial expansion to expand $\left(2x + \dfrac{1}{x}\right)^6$:

$$\left(2x + \frac{1}{x}\right)^6 = 64x^6 + 192x^4 + 240x^2 + 160 + \frac{60}{x^2} + \frac{12}{x^4} + \frac{1}{x^6}$$

Then, we apply the binomial expansion to expand $(3 + 2x)^2 = 9 + 12x + 4x^2$

Therefore, we now expand $(9 + 12x + 4x^2)(64x^6 + 192x^4 + 240x^2 + 160 + \frac{60}{x^2} + \frac{12}{x^4} + \frac{1}{x^6})$.

This gives: $256x^8 + 768x^7 + 1344x^6 + 2304x^5 + 2688x^4 + 2880x^3$ ... $\therefore$ the coefficient of $x^3 = 2880$

49. Answer: D

The sum of an arithmetic sequence is $\dfrac{n}{2}(2a + (n-1)d)$

$$\frac{4}{2}(2a + 3d) = \frac{12}{2}(2a + 11d)$$

$$\therefore 6a + 33d = 2a + 3d$$

$$4a = -30d$$

50. Answer: B

The logarithm of a number less than the base will give an answer less than 1, hence $\log_{11} 7$, is less than 1, but $\log_2 7$ is greater than 1.

$$(3^{-3} + 3^{-2})^{-1} = \left(\frac{1}{27} + \frac{1}{9}\right)^{-1} = \frac{4}{27}^{-1} = \frac{27}{4}$$

$$\frac{5}{10(\sqrt{2} - 1)^2} = \frac{1}{2(2 - 2\sqrt{2} + 1)} = \frac{1}{6 - 4\sqrt{2}}$$

This can be rationalised to give: $\dfrac{1}{6 - 4\sqrt{2}} \times \dfrac{6 + 4\sqrt{2}}{6 + 4\sqrt{2}} = \dfrac{6 + 4\sqrt{2}}{36 - 32} = \dfrac{6 + 4\sqrt{2}}{4}$

We can tell that the numerator is larger than the denominator and as they are both positive numbers, this is also greater than 1. Therefore, there is only one value that is less than 1, which is B.

51. Answer: B

As the common ratio must be the same in a geometric sequence:

$$\frac{2p - 4}{p - 3} = \frac{4p - 3}{2p - 4}$$

Hence, $(2p - 4)^2 = (p - 3)(4p - 3)$

$$4p^2 - 16p + 16 = 4p^2 - 15p + 9$$

$$p = 7$$

This means that the common ratio is $\frac{2p-4}{p-3} = \frac{2(7)-4}{7-3} = 2.5$

The sum of the first 3 terms in this sequence is: $\left(\frac{a\left(1-2.5^3\right)}{1-2.5}\right)$

$$a = 7 - 3 = 4$$

$$\left(\frac{4(1 - 2.5^3)}{1 - 2.5}\right) = 39$$

Alternatively, find the first three terms by substituting in $p = 7$ into the expression given in the question: $(7 - 3), (14 - 4) \ and \ (28 - 3)$, and then find the sum, which is equal to 39.

52. Answer: D

The expression $(1 + 4x + x^2)^4$ can be rewritten as $\left(1 + (4x + x^2)\right)^4$. By creating an inner bracket, we can expand this as if it were a two-term bracket and apply the binomial theorem.

This can be expanded using the binomial expansion:

$$1 + 4(4x + x^2) + 6(4x + x^2)^2 + 4(4x + x^2)^4 + (4x + x^2)^4$$

This can be fully expanded and then simplified to give:

$$5x^8 + 80x^7 + 480x^6 + 1280x^5 + 1286x^4 + 48x^3 + 100x^2 + 16x + 1$$

Thus, the coefficient of $x^2 = 100$

170

53. Answer: A

If we let $2^x = a$

Then:

$$5(2^{3x}) + 14(2^{2x}) + 7(2^x) - 2 = 0$$

$$5a^3 + 14a^2 + 7a - 2 = 0$$

You substitute in low values of a, such as $a = -1, 1, 2, -2, 3, -3$, into the polynomial and record which values have a remainder of 0, hence are factors.

You will find that $a = -1$ and $a = -2$ are both factors of the polynomial.

You can use polynomial long division to divide the cubic $(5a^3 + 14a^2 + 7a - 2)$ by $(a + 1)$. Eventually, you find that the overall cubic will factorise to give:

$$(5a - 1)(a + 1)(a + 2) = 0$$

Therefore, $a = \frac{1}{5}, a = -1$ and $a = -2$

Remember, $a = 2^x$

$2^x > 0$, if we consider the graph of 2^x or any exponential, we notice that it is always greater than 0. Therefore, we can discount the solutions $2^x = -1$ or $2^x = -2$ as they are impossible.

We are left with $2^x = \frac{1}{5}$

$$x = \log\frac{\frac{1}{5}}{\log 2} = \log\frac{5^{-1}}{\log 2}$$
$$= -\frac{\log 5}{\log 2}$$

54. Answer: A

$$\frac{1}{a} + \frac{1}{b} = \frac{1}{c}$$

$$\frac{a + b}{ab} = \frac{1}{c}$$

$$ab = ca + cb$$

$$ab - ca = cb$$

$$a(b - c) = cb$$

$$a = \frac{cb}{b - c}$$

55. Answer: C

$$17\left(1 - \frac{1}{17^2}\right)^{\frac{1}{2}}$$

$$= (17^2)^{\frac{1}{2}}\left(1 - \frac{1}{17^2}\right)^{\frac{1}{2}}$$

$$= (17^2 - 1)^{1/2}$$

$$= \sqrt{288}$$

$$= \sqrt{144}\sqrt{2} = 12\sqrt{2}$$

56. Answer: B

The volume of both the sphere and the circular film (cylinder shape) is equal, as we assume that no paint is lost in the fall. Therefore, we recall the volume of a sphere is $\frac{4}{3}\pi r^3$ and the volume of a cylinder is $\pi r^2 h$. Remember to change the diameter of the sphere given as 5mm to the radius (5/2) and to change all the units into mm to start (15cm radius is 150mm)

$\frac{4}{3}\pi\left(\frac{5}{2}\right)^3 = \pi(150)^2 h$. Therefore, $h = \frac{\frac{4}{3}\times\left(\frac{5}{2}\right)^3}{150^2} = \frac{1}{1080}$. The thickness is $\frac{1}{1080}\,mm$

57. Answer: D

The sum to infinity of a geometric series is $\frac{a}{1-r}$. This is equal to:

$$\frac{q}{1-q} = 4q$$

$$q = 4q - 4q^2$$

$$4q^2 - 3q = 0$$

Therefore, $q = \frac{3}{4}$ or $q = 0$.

The question states that $q \neq 0$, therefore the answer is $q = \frac{3}{4}$ only.

58. Answer: D

$$0.\dot{5}\dot{4} = 0.54 + 0.0054 + 0.000054 \ldots$$

$$a = 0.54 \ and \ r = \frac{1}{100}$$

Therefore, the sum to infinity is $\frac{a}{1-r}$

$$= \frac{0.54}{1 - \frac{1}{100}}$$

$$= \frac{0.54}{\frac{99}{100}}$$

$$= \frac{54}{99}$$

$$= \frac{6}{11}$$

59. Answer: D

$$0.6\dot{3}\dot{6} = 0.6 + 0.036 + 0.00036 + 0.0000036 \ldots$$

$$0.6\dot{3}\dot{6} = 0.6 + (0.036 + 0.00036 + 0.0000036 \ldots)$$

This is 0.6 an infinite geometric series with $a = 0.036 \ and \ r = \frac{1}{100}$

Therefore, the sum to infinity is $\frac{a}{1-r}$

$$= \frac{0.036}{1 - \frac{1}{100}}$$

$$= \frac{0.036}{\frac{99}{100}}$$

$$= \frac{3.6}{99}$$

$$= \frac{36}{990}$$

$$= \frac{2}{55}$$

Hence, $0.6\dot{3}\dot{6} = 0.6 + \frac{2}{55}$

$$= \frac{7}{11}$$

60. Answer: A

Considering the equilateral triangle, using Pythagoras's theorem, we can find the height of the triangle.

$$\sqrt{x^2 - \left(\frac{x}{2}\right)^2} = \sqrt{x^2 - \frac{x^2}{4}} = \sqrt{\frac{3}{4}x^2} = \frac{\sqrt{3}}{2}x$$

The area of the equilateral triangle is $\frac{1}{2} \times base \times height = \frac{1}{2} \times \frac{\sqrt{3}}{2}x \times x$

The volume of the prism is $\frac{1}{2} \times \frac{\sqrt{3}}{2}x \times x \times l$, as the volume of any prism, is cross-sectional area multiplied by the length.

We are told that the volume is 250.

$$\frac{1}{2} \times \frac{\sqrt{3}}{2}x \times x \times l = 250$$

$$l = \frac{1000}{\sqrt{3}x^2} = \frac{1000\sqrt{3}}{3x^2}$$

$$Surface\ Area = 2 \times the\ area\ of\ the\ equilateral\ triangle$$

$$+ area\ of\ the\ rectangular\ base\ of\ the\ prism$$

$$+ 2 \times the\ area\ of\ the\ side\ rectangles$$

This is written as $2 \times \frac{1}{2} \times \frac{\sqrt{3}}{2}x^2 + 3xl$

$$surface\ area = \frac{\sqrt{3}}{2}x^2 + 3xl = \frac{\sqrt{3}}{2}x^2 + 3x(\frac{1000\sqrt{3}}{3x^2})$$

$$surface\ area = \frac{\sqrt{3}}{2}x^2 + (\frac{1000\sqrt{3}}{x})$$

$$Let\ the\ surface\ area = f(x)$$

$$f'(x) = \sqrt{3}x - \frac{1000\sqrt{3}}{x^2}$$

For the maximum area, the first derivative is equal to 0, $f'(x) = 0$

$$\sqrt{3}x - \frac{1000\sqrt{3}}{x^2} = 0$$

As $x \neq 0$, we can multiply the whole equation by x^2 and divide by $\sqrt{3}$:

$$x^3 - 1000 = 0$$

Therefore, $x = 10$

Find the second derivative and show that $f''(x) < 0$, when $x = 10$, hence it is a maximum point.

This can be substituted back into the main surface area equation to find the maximum area.

$$surface\ area = \frac{\sqrt{3}}{2}x^2 + \left(\frac{1000\sqrt{3}}{x}\right) = \frac{\sqrt{3}}{2}(100) + \left(\frac{1000\sqrt{3}}{10}\right)$$

Therefore, the maximum surface area is $50\sqrt{3} + 100\sqrt{3} = 150\sqrt{3}$

61. Answer: A

Firstly, we arrange the expression to derive a cubic inequality.

$$x^3 - 5x > 2x^2 - 6$$

$$x^3 - 2x^2 - 5x + 6 > 0$$

Now, pretend that we are solving the following equation:

$$x^3 - 2x^2 - 5x + 6 = 0$$

Substitute in low values of x into the cubic, to try and factorise it and make it equal 0.

Try the values $x = -1, 1, 2, -2, 3, -3$, (after you find one factor you can use polynomial long division to break down the cubic and then solve the remaining quadratic, instead of trying many different values).

We find that it is divisible by $1, -2$ and 3.

This means that the cubic factorises to give:

$$(x - 1)(x + 2)(x - 3) = 0$$

Then, we revert back to inequality form:

$$(x - 1)(x + 2)(x - 3) > 0$$

This graph can be sketched, or a table of values can be found to find what happens to the function for different values of x.

The graph shows, that the function is greater than 0 and above the x axis when:

$-2 < x < 1$ or $x > 3$

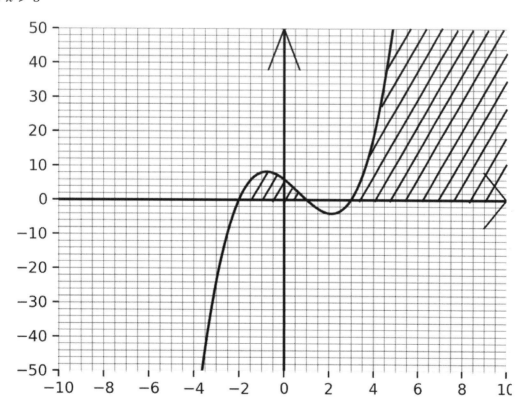

62. Answer: D

Firstly, we arrange the expression to derive a cubic inequality.

$$x^3 - 4x^2 > 7x - 10$$

$$x^3 - 4x^2 - 7x + 10 > 0$$

Now, pretend that we are solving the following equation:

$$x^3 - 4x^2 - 7x + 10 = 0$$

Substitute in low values of x into the cubic, to try and factorise it.

Try the values $x = -1, 1, 2, -2, 3, -3, 4, -4, 5, -5$ (after you find one factor you can use polynomial long division to break down the cubic and then solve the remaining quadratic, instead of trying many different values).

We find that it is divisible by $1, -2$ and 5.

This means that the cubic factorises to give: $(x - 1)(x + 2)(x - 5) = 0$

Reverting to inequality form: $(x - 1)(x + 2)(x - 5) > 0$

This graph can be sketched, or a table of values can be found to find what happens to the function for different values of x.

The graph shows that the function is greater than 0 and above the x axis when:

$-2 < x < 1$ or $x > 5$

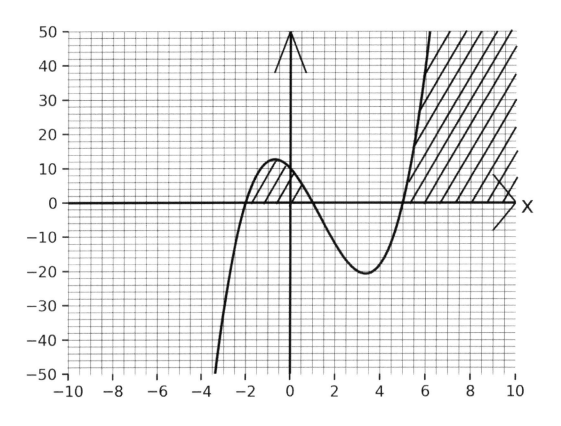

176

63. Answer: A

We cannot multiply both sides of an inequality by a negative without changing the sign. As $(x-3)$ is a variable we do not know if it is negative or not, hence, multiply both sides by $(x-3)^2$, which is always positive.

Hence, $(x-3)x(x-2) > \frac{1}{2}(x-3)^2$

$$x(x-3)(x-2) - \frac{1}{2}(x-3)^2 > 0$$

$$\frac{2x^3 - 11x^2 + 18x - 9}{2} > 0$$

$$2x^3 - 11x^2 + 18x - 9 > 0$$

Now, pretend that we are solving the following equation:

$$2x^3 - 11x^2 + 18x - 9 = 0$$

Substitute in low values of x into the cubic, To try and factorise it.

Try the values $x = -1, 1, 2, -2, 3, -3, \frac{3}{2}, -\frac{3}{2}$ (after you find one factor you can use polynomial long division to break down the cubic and then solve the remaining quadratic, instead of trying many different values).

We find that it is divisible by $1, \frac{3}{2}$ and 3.

This means that the cubic factorises to give:

$$(x-1)(2x-3)(x-3) = 0$$

Reverting to inequality form:

$$(x-1)(2x-3)(x-3) > 0$$

This graph can be sketched, or a table of values can be found to find what happens to the function for different values of x.

The graph shows, that the function is greater than 0 and above the x axis when:

$1 < x < \frac{3}{2}$ or $x > 3$

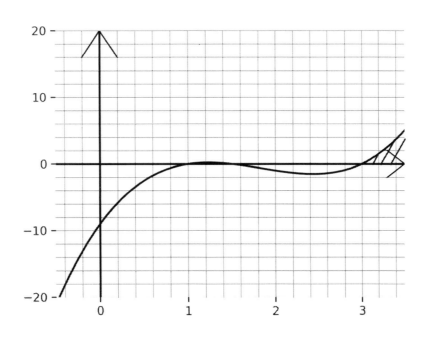

177

64. Answer: A

If the points are collinear, this means that the gradients of the line between the points are the same.

$$\frac{4-q}{2-p} = \frac{7-q}{4-p} = \frac{7-4}{4-2}$$

Therefore, all the gradients are equal to $\frac{3}{2}$

$$\frac{4-q}{2-p} = \frac{3}{2}$$

$$8 - 2q = 6 - 3p$$

$$-2q + 3p = -2$$

$$3p - 2q = -2$$

65. Answer: C

We need to find the perpendicular bisector of the line joining the centres.

The first circle equation can be rewritten so we can find the centre and radius:

$$x^2 - 4x + y^2 - 6y - 15 = 0$$

$$(x-2)^2 + (y-3)^2 = 28$$

Therefore, it has centre $(2,3)$

The second equation is a circle with centre $(5,-3)$

The midpoint of the two centres is $(\frac{7}{2}, 0)$ and the gradient of the line joining the centres is $\frac{6}{-3} = -2$.

Therefore, the locus of points equidistant between the centres has gradient $\frac{1}{2}$ and passes through the point $(\frac{7}{2}, 0)$.

$$y = \frac{1}{2}x + c$$

$$0 = \frac{7}{4} + c$$

$$c = -\frac{7}{4}$$

Thus, the line is $y = \frac{1}{2}x - \frac{7}{4}$, which is the same as $4y = 2x - 7$ and $4y - 2x = -7$

66. Answer: D

$$y = x^3$$

$$y = x^3 + 4$$

$$y = -5 \times [\left(\frac{1}{3}x\right)^3 + 4]$$

$$y = -5 \times \left[\left(\frac{1}{3}x\right)^3 + 4\right] - 6$$

$$y = -\frac{5}{27}x^3 - 26 \quad \therefore \quad 27y = -5x^3 - 702$$

67. Answer: D

$CBAD$ – you perform a horizontal shift inside brackets first (there is none), then a vertical shift (C), then a horizontal stretch inside the brackets (B), then a vertical stretch outside the brackets (A) and finally a vertical shift outside the brackets (D).

68. Answer: D

If the diameter is between $(3,5)$ and $(7,7)$, then the midpoint is $\left(\frac{3+7}{2}, \frac{5+7}{2}\right) = (5,6)$

The radius is half of the length of the diameter which is:

$$\frac{\sqrt{((7-3)^2 + (7-5)^2}}{2} = \sqrt{5}$$

$$\therefore (x-5)^2 + (y-6)^2 = 5$$

$$x^2 - 10x + 25 + y^2 - 12y + 36 = 5$$

$$x^2 - 10x + y^2 - 12y + 61 = 5$$

69. Answer: C

To find whether they are increasing or decreasing, we have to differentiate the equation and if the derivative is greater than 0 in the given range, then it is increasing and if it is less than 0 then it is decreasing.

$$p(x) = 5x - \frac{1}{x}$$

$$p'(x) = 5 + \frac{1}{x^2}$$

5 is a positive number, x^2 is always positive, therefore $\frac{1}{x^2}$ is always positive. Hence, the overall expression $5 + \frac{1}{x^2}$ is always positive and the function $p(x)$ is increasing for all values of x.

$$q(x) = x^5 + 6x^3$$

$$q'(x) = 5x^4 + 18x^2$$

x^4 is always positive, therefore $5x^4$ is always positive. x^2 is always positive, therefore $18x^2$ is always positive. Hence, the overall expression $5x^4 + 18x^2$ is always positive and the function $q(x)$ is increasing for all values of x.

This means that both $q(x)$ and $p(x)$ are increasing for all values of x.

70. Answer: A

$$3x^2 + y^2 = 36 + xy$$

$$x = y - 3$$

$$y = x + 3$$

$$3x^2 + (x + 3)^2 = 36 + x(x + 3)$$

$$3x^2 + x^2 + 6x + 9 = 36 + x^2 + 3x$$

$$3x^2 + 3x - 27 = 0$$

Apply the quadratic formula $\frac{-b \pm \sqrt{b^2 - 4ac}}{2a}$, which will solve to give:

$$x = \frac{(-1 + \sqrt{37})}{2}$$

$$x = \frac{(-1 - \sqrt{37})}{2}$$

$$y = x + 3$$

$x = \frac{(-1+\sqrt{37})}{2}$ $y = \frac{5+\sqrt{37}}{2}$

$x = \frac{(-1-\sqrt{37})}{2}$ $y = \frac{5-\sqrt{37}}{2}$

71. Answer: B

Rewrite the question using a single base (3):

$$27^x - 9^x = -9 + 3^{x+2}$$

$$3^{3x} - 3^{2x} = -9 + 9(3^x)$$

$$a = 3^x$$

$$a^3 - a^2 - 9a + 9 = 0$$

Substitute in low values of x into the cubic, To try and factorise it.

Try the values $a = -1, 1, 2, -2, 3, -3$ (after you find one factor you can use polynomial long division to break down the cubic and then solve the remaining quadratic, instead of trying many different values).

We find that it is divisible by $1, -3$ and 3.

This means that the cubic factorises to give:

$$(a - 1)(a + 3)(a - 3) = 0$$

$$\therefore 3^x = 1, -3, 3$$

3^x is always greater than 0, therefore, $3^x = -3$ is not a solution. This means that there are two solutions, that $x = 1$ and $x = 0$.

72. Answer: B

For p to be the largest possible value, then $(\log_8 q)^2$ must be the smallest possible value (which allows $9(\log_8 p)^2 = 1$.

As a square number is always greater than 0, for $(\log_8 q)^2$ to be the smallest possible value:

$$(\log_8 q)^2 = 0$$

$$\log_8 q = 0$$

$$q = 1$$

$$9(\log_8 p)^2 = 1$$

$$(\log_8 p)^2 = \frac{1}{9}$$

$$\log_8 p = \frac{1}{3}$$

Note, that $\log_8 p \neq \frac{-1}{3}$ as p is a positive number.

$$p = 8^{\frac{1}{3}} = 2$$

Therefore, $pq = 2$

73. Answer: C

$$4x^4 = (2x - p)^2$$

$$(2x^2)^2 = (2x - p)^2$$

Take square roots of both sides, both note that as the LHS is squared, you have to account for both possible (positive and negative) versions of the expression.

$$2x^2 = 2x - p$$

$$2x^2 = p - 2x$$

We also have 2 other possibilities $-2x^2 = 2x - p$ and $-2x^2 = p - 2x$, however, when rearranged these gives the same equations as the two shown above.

The discriminant of both equations must be greater than 0.

$$2x^2 - 2x + p = 0$$

$$4 - 4(2)(p) > 0$$

$$4 - 8p > 0 \therefore p < \frac{1}{2}$$

$$2x^2 + 2x - p = 0$$

$$4 - 4(2)(-p) > 0$$

$$4 + 8p > 0 \therefore p > -\frac{1}{2}$$

$$-\frac{1}{2} < p < \frac{1}{2}$$

74. Answer: A

$$6x^3 - 5x^2 - 17x + 6 = 0$$

Substitute in low values of x into the cubic, To try and factorise it.

Try the values $a = -1, 1, 2, -2, 3, -3$ (after you find one factor you can use polynomial long division to break down the cubic and then solve the remaining quadratic, instead of trying many different values).

We find it is divisible by $x = 2$.

Use polynomial long division to divide the cubic $6x^3 - 5x^2 - 17x + 6$ by $(x - 2)$.

This gives $6x^2 + 7x - 3$

This quadratic can be factorised to give: $(3x - 1)(2x + 3)$

This means that the cubic factorises to give:

$$(x - 2)(3x - 1)(2x + 3) = 0$$

$$\therefore x = 2, x = \frac{1}{3}, x = -\frac{3}{2}$$

75. Answer: C

The number of solutions is the number of times that the graph crosses the x axis. Therefore, it is easiest to find the values for which the graph has 4 real solutions by sketching it. To sketch:

First, we differentiate the equation $\frac{6}{4}x^4 - 8x^3 + 9x^2 + q$, To find the turning points.

$$6x^3 - 24x^2 + 18x = 0$$

$$6x(x^2 - 4x + 3) = 0$$

$$6x(x - 3)(x - 1) = 0$$

Therefore, there are turning points, when $x = 0, 1, 3$

Given the shape of a positive quartic, these turning points be a minimum, then a maximum and then a minimum. For us to have 4 real solutions, both our minimum points must be below the x axis and the maximum point must be above the x axis.

$$y(0) = q$$

$$y(1) = \frac{5}{2} + q$$

$$y(3) = -\frac{27}{2} + q$$

Hence, we need:

$$q < 0$$

$$\frac{5}{2} + q > 0 \qquad q > -\frac{5}{2}$$

$$-\frac{27}{2} + q < 0 \qquad q < \frac{27}{2}$$

We need all of the answers to be true, therefore, $-\frac{5}{2} < q < 0$

76. Answer: C

$$\frac{1}{4}(3x^3 + 9) - 5$$

$$= \frac{1}{4}\left(3(x^3 + 3)\right) - 5$$

$$\frac{3}{4}(x^3 + 3) - 5$$

By creating an inner bracket, we can clearly see the transformations that apply.

Using the rule $Af(Bx + C) + D$ is transformed in the order $CBAD$, we find the correct answer:

Vertical shift upwards by 3, stretch by a factor of $\frac{3}{4}$ in the y axis, vertical shift by -5

77. Answer: D

We need to notice the binomial expansion pattern. As the first term is x^4, we know the binomial will be a bracket to the fourth power. As the last term is $81y^4$, we can guess that the binomial includes a $3y$ term $(as\ (3y)^4 = 81y^4)$.

Therefore, $x^4 + 12x^3y + 54x^2y^2 + 108xy^3 + 81y^4 = (x + 3y)^4$

78. Answer: C

$$\log_{4x-4}(x^4 + 2x^3 - 3x^2) = 1$$

Therefore,

$$(4x - 4)^1 = x^4 + 2x^3 - 3x^2$$

$$4x - 4 = x^4 + 2x^3 - 3x^2$$

$$x^4 + 2x^3 - 3x^2 - 4x + 4 = 0$$

Substitute in low values of x into the quartic, To try and factorise it.

Try the values $a = -1, 1, 2, -2, 3, -3$ (after you find one factor you can use polynomial long division to break down the cubic and then solve the remaining quadratic, instead of trying many different values).

We find it is divisible by $x = 1\ and\ x = -2$, as the quartic factorises to give $(x - 1)^2(x + 2)^2$

When we substitute both values, $x = 1$ and $x = -2$, we find that they are both unusable and false.

1 is false as you cannot have a logarithm with a base of 0, as this is undefined (you cannot raise 0 to the power of anything).

-2 is false as when you substitute -2 into $x^4 + 2x^3 - 3x^2$, you get -12. You cannot have a logarithm of a negative number.

Therefore, there are 0 solutions.

79. Answer: A

This is a compound interest calculation: 100×1.05^4

$$100 \times 1.05 = 105$$
$$105 \times 1.05 = 110.25$$
$$110.25 \times 1.05 = 115.7625$$
$$115.7625 \times 1.05 = 121.55$$

Therefore, the answer is £121.55

80. Answer: D

$A \propto \frac{1}{B^4}$

If B is increased by 50%, then we are dealing with a 1.5 multiplier:

$$A' \propto \frac{1}{(1.5B)^4} = \frac{1}{1.5^4 B^4}$$

Thus, we need to find $1.05^4 = 5.0625$

$$A' \propto \frac{1}{5.0625} \times \frac{1}{B^4}$$
$$A' \propto \frac{1}{5.0625} \times A$$

$\frac{1}{5.0625}$ is roughly equal to $\frac{1}{5} = 0.2$. Therefore, it is slightly less than 0.2 (around 0.1975).

Therefore, the percentage change in A is around an 80% decrease as it is multiplied by a 0.19 multiplier.

81. Answer: D

The minute hand moves 360 degrees in 60 minutes. This means that it moves 6 degrees per minute. The hour hand moves 30 degrees in 60 minutes. This means that it moves 0.5 degrees per minute. As they are both moving in the same direction, the expression for the relative speed between them is 5.5 degrees per minute.

The total number of minutes in 24 hours is 60×24. Therefore, the total distance (in terms of degrees) travelled by the hands in a relative sense (at 5.5 degrees per minute) is: $(60 \times 24) \times 5.5$.

If we consider the number of full circles this is, given that a circle has 360 degrees:

$$\frac{(60 \times 24) \times 5.5}{360} = 22$$

Each full circle contains 2 right angles, once when the right angle that the minute hand makes is "in front" of the hour hand and a second time when the minute hand has travelled round and the angle made is "behind" the hour hand.

Therefore, a full circle has 2 right angles, and in 24 hours the relative speeds show that 22 full circles are made. Hence, there are $22 \times 2 = 44$ right angles.

82. Answer: B

There are 15 options and you are choosing 11, therefore there are $15C11$ different teams.

But we also have nationality requirements, and for the specific ways to form a team with 5 Brazilian, 3 English and 3 Spanish players, there are smaller combinations we need to consider. The final calculation is as follows:

$$\frac{7C5 \times 4C3 \times 4C3}{15C11}$$

Now expand out the combinations into factorial notation:

$$\frac{\frac{7!}{5!\,2!} \times \frac{4!}{3!\,1!} \times \frac{4!}{3!\,1!}}{\frac{15!}{11!\,4!}}$$

We can cancel a lot of terms out and simplify (e.g., $\frac{7!}{5!} = \frac{7\times6\times5!}{5!} = 7 \times 6, \, and \, 4C3 = 4 \, etc \dots$)

$$\frac{\frac{7 \times 6}{2} \times 4 \times 4}{\frac{15 \times 14 \times 13 \times 12}{4 \times 3 \times 2 \times 1}}$$

We can further cancel out as many terms as possible, and this gives the final answer

$$\frac{16}{65}$$

83. Answer: C

We can have a ring with any numbers of beads (1, 2, 3 or 3) and a ring that has a ruby on the left and then a sapphire bead on the right is different to a ring with a sapphire on the left and a ruby on the right. Therefore, we use the permutations function.

If we only used 1 bead on the ring, there are $4P1$ different rings possible.

If we used 2 beads on the ring, there are $4P2$ different rings possible.

If we used 3 beads on the ring, there are $4P3$ different rings possible.

If we used 4 beads on the ring, there are $4P4$ different rings possible.

The sum of all these options is the number of rings possible:

$$4P1 + 4P2 + 4P3 + 4P4 = 64$$

84. Answer: C

There are 5! ways to seat the family if there are no restrictions.

If the parents do not want to sit next to each other, this is $5! -$ combinations when the parents always sit together. This is an easier scenario to consider.

To find the number of combinations where the parents do sit next to each other:

Suppose a parent sits in the first seat, then there are 2 options for people who can sit in the first seat. Then there is only 1 option (the other parent) who can sit in the second seat. For the third seat, there are 3 options (any child) who can sit there, followed by 2 options in the 4th seat (either of the other two children) and 1 option for the last seat (the last child).

Hence,

$$2 - 1 - 3 - 2 - 1$$

This is $2 \times 1 \times 3 \times 2 \times 1 = 12$ combinations.

However, the parent pair do not have to sit in the first two seats, and they can sit in the first two seats, or the 2nd and 3rd seat or the 3rd and 4th seat or finally in the 4th or 5th seats. Therefore, there are $12 \times 4 = 48$ options.

Therefore, our answer for the number of combinations where the parents do not sit next to each other is $120 - 48 = 72$

85. Answer: D

On each burrito, you can have 1, 2, 3, 4, 5, 6, 7, **or** 8 toppings. The order of toppings does not matter as a burrito with rice first and then salsa is the same as a burrito with salsa first and then rice. Therefore, we use combinations.

Focusing on toppings firstly, there are $8C0$ ways of making a burrito with no toppings, $8C1$ ways of making a burrito with one topping, and so on to reach $8C8$ ways to make a burrito with all 8 toppings.

Therefore, the number of different combinations of burritos when we just consider the toppings is:

$$8C0 + 8C1 + 8C2 + 8C3 + 8C4 + 8C5 + 8C6 + 8C7 + 8C8$$

Use the factorial notation to find the value of each one:

$$1 + 8 + 28 + 56 + 70 + 56 + 28 + 8 + 1 = 256$$

However, we also have 5 types of wraps, hence we multiply $256 \times 5 = 1280$

Therefore, there are 1280 possible burrito options.

86. Answer: B

For $y = ab^x$

$$\log y = \log a + x \log b$$

If we compare this to the format $y = mx + c$

$\log y = \log a + x \log b$, directly links to it, where $m = \log b \ and \log a = c$.

Therefore, if we plot $\log y$ to x, it is a straight line with a linear relationship.

None of the other graphs will provide a linear relationship when we plot $x \ to \log y$.

87. Answer: A

We can either take a white or black ball out of box A.

If we take a white ball out of box A:

$$P(White\ from\ A) = \frac{x}{x+y}$$

The probability of taking a black ball from box B, after taking a white ball from box A is:

$$\frac{x}{x+y} \times \frac{x}{x+y+1}$$

If we take a black ball out of box A:

$$P(Black\ from\ A) = \frac{y}{x+y}$$

The probability of taking a black ball from box B, after taking a black ball from box A is:

$$\frac{y}{x+y} \times \frac{x+1}{x+y+1}$$

The sum of these probabilities is our answer:

$$\frac{x}{x+y} \times \frac{x}{x+y+1} + \frac{y}{x+y} \times \frac{x+1}{x+y+1}$$

$$= \frac{x^2 + y(x+1)}{(x+y)(x+y+1)}$$

88. Answer: A

Using logarithm rules, we can rewrite the expression in a simple form:

$$(x - 2y)^2 = xy$$

$$x^2 - 4xy + 4y^2 = xy$$

$$x^2 - 5xy + 4y^2 = 0$$

$$(x - y)(x - 4y) = 0$$

$$\therefore x - y = 0$$

$$x = y \therefore \frac{x}{y} = 1$$

OR

$$x - 4y = 0$$

$$x = 4y \therefore \frac{x}{y} = 4$$

Therefore $\frac{x}{y} = 1\ or\ 4$

89. Answer: D

Use the information given to form two simultaneous equations, applying a range of different logarithm rules ($a\ln(b) = \ln(b^a)$ and $\ln(a) + \ln(b) = \ln(ab)$):

$$u_5 = 2\ln p + 4\ln q = \ln(1296)$$

Therefore,

$$\ln(p^2 q^4) = \ln(1296)$$
$$p^2 q^4 = 1296$$

Forming our second equation:

$$u_7 = 2\ln p + 6\ln q = \ln(11664)$$

Therefore,

$$\ln(p^2 q^6) = \ln(11664)$$
$$p^2 q^6 = 11664$$

Therefore, we now have two equations we can simultaneously solve:

$$p^2 q^4 = 1296$$
$$p^2 q^6 = 11664$$

If we divide the second equation by the first, we get:

$$q^2 = \frac{11664}{1296} = 9$$
$$q = 3$$

Substituting this into the first equation, we can find p. *Note, q cannot equal -3 as it is a positive integer.*

$$81p^2 = 1296$$
$$p^2 = 16$$
$$p = 4$$

Note, p cannot equal -4 as it is a positive integer.

Thus, $p = 4$ and $q = 3$.

90. Answer: C

Recall that the sum of a geometric series to infinity is $\frac{a}{1-r}$, where a is the first term and r is the common ratio.

$$a + ar + ar^2 + ar^3 \dots$$

$$\frac{a}{1-r} = 6$$

Our second series is formed by squaring the terms in the first series:

$$a^2 + a^2r^2 + a^2r^4 + a^2r^6 \dots$$

This is a second geometric series with first term a^2 and common difference r^2

Therefore, the sum to infinity is:

$$\frac{a^2}{1-r^2} = 30$$

$$a^2 = 30 - 30r^2$$

The first sequence shows that $a = 6 - 6r$

Hence, from the first sequence: $a^2 = (6-6r)^2 = 36 - 72r + 36r^2$

$$30 - 30r^2 = 36 - 72r + 36r^2$$

$$66r^2 - 72r + 6 = 0$$

$$11r^2 - 12r + 1 = 0$$

$$(11r - 1)(r - 1) = 0$$

Therefore, $r = 1$ or $r = \frac{1}{11}$

A convergent geometric series has to have the magnitude of r strictly less than 1, therefore we discount the solution $r = 1$.

91. Answer: A

For the term x^6, we need to cube the term $3x^2$. Therefore, the full term will be:

$$5C3 \times p^2 \times (3x^2)^3 = 1215x^6$$

$$10p^2(27x^6) = 1215x^6$$

$$270p^2 = 1215$$

$$p^2 = \frac{9}{2}$$

$$p = \pm\sqrt{\frac{9}{2}}$$

$$\text{In the question } p < 0 \text{ is stated } \therefore \ p = -\sqrt{\frac{9}{2}} = -\frac{3\sqrt{2}}{2}$$

92. Answer: B

Using logarithm rules, $a\ln(b) = \ln(b^a) \; and \; \ln(a) + \ln(b) = \ln(ab)$, we can simplify both equations.

$$\log_2 xy^3 = 2$$

$$\log_3 \frac{1}{x} \times \frac{1}{y^4} = -2$$

As $\log_a b = c \; can \; be \; written \; as \; a^c = b$:

$$xy^3 = 4$$

$$\frac{1}{xy^4} = \frac{1}{9}$$

Hence, we have two more simple simultaneous equations to solve:

$$xy^3 = 4$$

$$xy^4 = 9$$

$$\therefore y = \frac{9}{4}$$

Substituting this into the first equation,

$$x = \frac{4}{\left(\frac{9}{4}\right)^3} = \frac{256}{729}$$

$\therefore \; x = \frac{256}{729}$ and $y = \frac{9}{4}$

93. Answer: C

Firstly, if we assume the first inequality is instead an equation, to find our critical values:

$$-2x^2 + 5x + 7 \leq 0$$

$$-2x^2 + 5x + 7 = 0$$

$$-(2x - 7)(x + 1) = 0$$

Hence, $x = \frac{7}{2}$ and $x = -1$ are critical values. $\therefore$ If we sketch a quadratic, for the curve to be less than zero, as the quadratic is $\cap$ shaped (negative x^2 coefficient), the region is $x \leq -1 \; and \; x \geq \frac{7}{2}$.

For the second inequality, again we assume it is instead an equation, To find our critical values:

$$x^2 - 9x + 18 \geq 0$$

$$x^2 - 9x + 18 = 0$$

$$(x - 6)(x - 3) = 0$$

Hence, $x = 6$ and $x = 3$ are critical values.

If we sketch a quadratic, for the curve to be greater than zero, as the quadratic is U shaped (positive x^2 coefficient), the region is $x \leq 3 \; and \; x \geq 6$. $\therefore$ The overall critical region is: $x \leq -1 \; and \; x \geq 6$

94. Answer: D

Firstly, complete the Venn diagram. You let the centre value equal x. Then football and rugby (but not cricket) is $27 - x$, football and cricket (but not rugby) is $15 - x$ and cricket and rugby (but not football) is $12 - x$. The sum of all the values in this Venn diagram is 100. Therefore, solve to find x. This will give $x = 2$.

The completed Venn Diagram looks as follows:

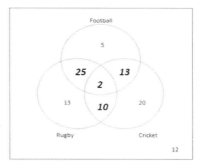

If one student is chosen at random from the 100 students, and then a second student is chosen from the remaining students, what is the probability that the first student plays football and the second student plays rugby but not cricket.

We have to split the first part of the question (picking a football player) into two scenarios:

Case 1 is that the first student plays football and rugby but not cricket.

Case 2 is that the first student players either football only, football and cricket only, or football, cricket and rugby.

The sum of case 1 and case 2 will consider all possible football players and will have no overlap

Using case 1 to find the probability that the second student plays rugby but not cricket. This is the probability of case 1 multiplied by the probability that given case 1 was chosen, the second person plays rugby but not cricket.

- o P(Case 1) is the 25 people who play football and rugby but not cricket divided by 100.
- o P(Rugby but not cricket given case 1) is the 13 who play rugby only plus the 24 remaining people who play rugby and football only (13+24=37) divided by 99.

$$= \frac{25}{100} \times \frac{37}{99} = \frac{37}{396}$$

Using case 2 to find the probability that the second student plays rugby but not cricket. This is the probability of case 2 multiplied by the probability that given case 2 was chosen, the second person plays rugby but not cricket.

- o P(Case 2) is the 2 people who play all 3, plus the 5 people who play football only and the 13 people who play football and cricket (2+5+13=20) divided by 100.
- o P(Rugby but not cricket given case 2) is the 13 who play rugby only plus the 25 people who play rugby and football only (13+25=38) divided by 99.

$$= \frac{20}{100} \times \frac{38}{99} = \frac{38}{495}$$

The sum of these probabilities is the final answer.

$$\frac{37}{396} + \frac{38}{495} = \frac{337}{1980}$$

95. Answer: A

$$\int_1^2 x^2(\sqrt{x} + x^3 - 4x + 1)$$

$$= \int_1^2 (x^{\frac{5}{2}} + x^5 - 4x^3 + x^2)$$

$$= (\frac{2}{7}x^{\frac{7}{2}} + \frac{1}{6}x^6 - x^4 + \frac{1}{3}x^3)_1^2$$

$$= \frac{2}{7}(2)^{\frac{7}{2}} + \frac{1}{6}(2)^6 - (2)^4 + \frac{1}{3}(2)^3 - (\frac{2}{7}(1)^{\frac{7}{2}} + \frac{1}{6}(1)^6 - (1)^4 + \frac{1}{3}(1)^3)$$

$$= \frac{2}{7}(8)(\sqrt{2}) + \frac{32}{3} - 16 + \frac{8}{3} - \frac{2}{7} - \frac{1}{6} + 1 - \frac{1}{3}$$

$$= \frac{16}{7}\sqrt{2} - \frac{103}{42}$$

96. Answer: A

Let $x = $ *the vertical side of the rectangle base*

Perimeter$= 2x + 2r + \pi r = 60$

$$2x = 60 - 2r - \pi r$$

$$x = \frac{60 - 2r - \pi r}{2}$$

The area is equal to $\frac{\pi r^2}{2}$ *(semi circle area on the top)* $+ 2xr$ *(rectangular base area)*

$$Area = \frac{\pi r^2}{2} + 2r(\frac{60 - 2r - \pi r}{2})$$

$$Area = \frac{\pi r^2}{2} + r(60 - 2r - \pi r)$$

$$Area = \frac{\pi r^2}{2} + 60r - 2r^2 - \pi r^2$$

$$Area = 60r - 2r^2 - \frac{1}{2}\pi r^2$$

To find the maximum area, we differentiate the expression and equate the first derivative to 0. This will give us the radius, which we can substitute into the area expression to find the maximum value.

Let $60r - 2r^2 - \frac{1}{2}\pi r^2 = f(r)$

$$f'(r) = 60 - 4r - \pi r$$

$$f'(r) = 0$$

$$r = \frac{60}{4 + \pi}$$

Therefore, the area is equal to:

$$Area = 60r - 2r^2 - \frac{1}{2}\pi r^2$$

$$\max Area = 60(\frac{60}{4 + \pi}) - 2\left(\frac{60}{4 + \pi}\right)^2 - \frac{1}{2}\pi \left(\frac{60}{4 + \pi}\right)^2$$

$$\max Area = \frac{3600}{4 + \pi} - (\frac{2}{1} + \frac{\pi}{2})(\frac{3600}{(4 + \pi)^2})$$

$$\max Area = \frac{3600}{4 + \pi} - \left(\frac{4 + \pi}{2}\right)\left(\frac{3600}{(4 + \pi)^2}\right)$$

$$\max Area = \frac{3600}{4 + \pi} - (\frac{1800}{4 + \pi})$$

$$\max Area = \frac{1800}{4 + \pi}$$

97. Answer: C

Using logarithm rules, $a \ln(b) = \ln(b^a)$ and $\ln(a) + \ln(b) = \ln(ab)$, we can simplify the equation.

$$\log_2 19x + 30 = \log_2 x^3$$

Therefore, $19x + 30 = x^3$

$$x^3 - 19x - 30 = 0$$

Substitute in low values of x into the cubic, To try and factorise it and make it equal 0.

Try the values $x = -1, 1, 2, -2, 3, -3$, (after you find one factor you can use polynomial long division to break down the cubic and then solve the remaining quadratic, instead of trying many different values).

We notice that $x = -2$, is a factor of the cubic, and we can use polynomial long division to break it down into a quadratic.

$$\frac{x^3 - 19x - 30}{x + 2} = x^2 - 2x - 15$$

This quadratic factorises to give: $(x + 3)(x - 5)$.

Therefore, the whole cubic simplifies to give:

$$x^3 - 19x - 30 = (x + 3)(x - 5)(x + 2) = 0$$

Thus,

$$x = 5, -2, -3$$

However, when we substitute -2 or -3 into the logarithm $\log_2 x$ or $\log_2(19x + 30)$ we get negative answers. You cannot have the logarithm of a negative number, thus, $x = 5$ is the only solution.

98. Answer: B

The mean of a set of 15 numbers if 66 and when a number y is removed from the set, the mean reduces to reach 60.

The total of the 15 numbers is $15 \times 66 = 990$

The total of the remaining 14 numbers is $14 \times 60 = 840$

y is the difference between these totals, therefore,

$$y = 990 - 840 = 150$$

The mean weight of a group of 20 teenagers was 62kg and when two teenagers left the group, whose weights were 65kg and 59kg, the mean fell to xkg.

The total weight of the 20 teenagers was $62 \times 20 = 1240$

The lower total weight after two teenagers leave the group is: $1240 - 65 - 59 = 1116$

The new mean is $\frac{1116}{18} = 62$

Therefore, $x = 62$

The product $xy = 9300$

99. Answer: B

Assuming the actual radii are $1, 2, 4$ respectively for the three circles.

The area of the inner circle: $\pi(1)^2 = \pi$

The area of the middle segment: $\pi(2)^2 - \pi(1)^2 = 3\pi$ *as the area of the middle section is the whole middle circle minus the inner circle.*

The area of the outer segment: $\pi(4)^2 - \pi(2)^2 = 12\pi$ *as the area of the outer section is the whole outer circle minus the middle area + the inner circle.*

Thus, the relative areas are in the ratio: $1 : 3 : 12$

100. Answer: D

There is a $\frac{1}{65}$ chance of taking a double-headed coin

There is a $\frac{64}{65}$ chance of taking a standard coin

Steps: Firstly, find the probability of getting 6 heads after randomly choosing a coin from this bag. Then find the probability of us having chosen a double-headed coin (given that we got 6 heads). Finally, find the probability of flipping a tail next throw.

Scenario 1: Choosing the double-headed coin and getting 6 heads: $\frac{1}{65} \times 1^6 = \frac{1}{65}$

Scenario 2: Choosing the standard coin and getting 6 heads: $\frac{64}{65} \times \left(\frac{1}{2}\right)^6 = \frac{64}{65} \times \frac{1}{64} = \frac{1}{65}$

Thus, $P(6\ heads\ after\ randomly\ picking\ a\ coin\ from\ this\ bag) = \frac{1}{65} + \frac{1}{65} = \frac{2}{65}$

$$Recall: P(A\ given\ B) = \frac{P(A \cap B)}{P(B)}$$

$$P(double\ headed\ given\ 6\ heads\ were\ tossed\ in\ a\ row) = \frac{\frac{1}{65}}{\frac{2}{65}} = \frac{1}{2}$$

Therefore, there is $\frac{1}{2}$ a chance we have a double-headed coin and $\frac{1}{2}$ a chance it is standard.

If we flip it again the probability of tails:

Double-headed and tails have probability 0

Standard and tails have probability $\frac{1}{2}$.

$$P(double\ headed) = \frac{1}{2}$$

$$P(standard) = \frac{1}{2}$$

Hence, $P(tails) = \frac{1}{2} \times 0 + \frac{1}{2} \times \frac{1}{2} = \frac{1}{4}$

Therefore $P(tails) = \frac{1}{4}$

101. Answer: A

The formula for an equilateral triangle is $\frac{\sqrt{3}}{4}a^2$, where a is the side length. This is derived by splitting one of the sides to arrive at a right-angled triangle with unknown height, $\frac{a}{2}$ side length and a hypotenuse of a. Therefore using $\frac{a}{2}$ as our adjacent angle and our known angle of 60°. We can use either the tan or the cos functions to calculate the height of $\frac{a\sqrt{3}}{2}$. Then using the area of a triangle formula, we can obtain the general formula for an equilateral triangle.

$$\left(\frac{1}{2} \times base \times height\right) = \frac{1}{2} \times a \times \frac{a\sqrt{3}}{2} = \frac{\sqrt{3}}{4}a^2$$

Substituting $\frac{3}{2}x$ into the general formula provides the output $\frac{9x^2\sqrt{3}}{16}$, wherein $\sqrt{3}$ is expressed as $3^{0.5}$ in the original question.

102. Answer: B

If the diagonal of the lawn is 39 metres and the ratio of sides is 12:5, we can either spot the Pythagorean triple or calculate the sides using Pythagoras. $(12x)^2 + (5x)^2 = (39)^2$, which results to $x = 3$, providing side lengths of 36m and 15m. The second part of the question introduces a path which wraps around the entire lawn. This means we need to add 2m to either side of the lawn creating side lengths of 40m and 19m. Now we can calculate the total area of the lawn and the path combined, $40 \times 19 = 760$ metres^2.

103. Answer: A

A square-based pyramid ABCDE exists, where E is the top vertex and ABCD form the square base. By using triangle BDE/ACE we can calculate the height, the triangles are the exact same, but we will use ACE notation for this worked solution. We have been told this is a unit shape, meaning all sides lengths are equal to 1. Therefore, we can calculate length AC using Pythagoras: $AB^2 + BC^2 = AC^2$, in which AC is $\sqrt{2}$. We can now calculate the height of triangle ACE to calculate the height of the pyramid, to this we can form a right-angled triangle with base $\frac{1}{2}AC$, hypotenuse AE wherein the missing side is the height. By applying Pythagoras again in the form: $\left(\frac{1}{2}AC\right)^2 + h^2 = AE^2$ we can calculate h. Remember AE is also a unit length side!

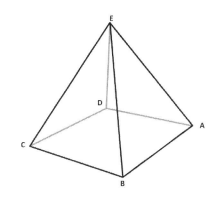

$\left(\frac{\sqrt{2}}{2}\right)^2 + h^2 = 1^2$, which can be rearranged to $h^2 = 1 - \frac{2}{4}$, yielding an answer for h of $\frac{\sqrt{2}}{2}$.

104. Answer: E

The two equations are, $y = 3\tan 2x$ and $y = x$. The modifier of 3 on the first equation is a red-herring and would not affect the number of interceptions as it stretches the already asymptotic graph further in the $y - axis$. Therefore, we can simplify our outlook to $y = \tan 2x$ and $y = x$, the modifier of 2 can be interpreted as a doubling of the domain of the function so we can further simplify our outlook to $y = \tan x$ and $y = x$ with a domain of $0 \leq x \leq 4\pi$. These graphs can be sketched and observed for the four intercepts, the first and most tricky of which is at the origin.

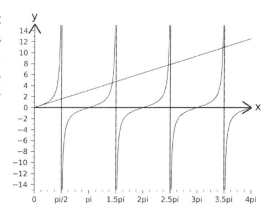

105. Answer: C

$$\log_3(2 - 3x) = \log_9(6x^2 - 19x + 2)$$

$$** \log_9(2 - 3x)^2 = \log_9(6x^2 - 19x + 2)$$

$$4 - 12x + 9x^2 = 6x^2 - 19x + 2$$

$$3x^2 + 7x + 2 = 0$$

$$(3x + 1)(x + 2) = 0$$

$$x = -2 \text{ or } x = -\frac{1}{3}$$

**This step can be seen when $y = 9^x$, and $\log_3 y = 2x$ & $\log_9 y = x \therefore \log_3 y = \log_9 y^2$

106. Answer: C

$$27^x - 3^{x+2} = 0$$

$$3^{3x} - 3^2 \times 3^x = 0$$

$$3^{3x} - 9 \times 3^x = 0$$

$$Let \ 3^x = y$$

$$y^3 - 9y = 0$$

$$y(y^2 - 9) = 0$$

$$y(y - 3)(y + 3) = 0$$

$$y = 0 \ or \ y = 3 \ or \ y = -3$$

$$3^x \neq 0 \ or \ 3^x = 3 \ or \ 3^x \neq -3$$

$$x = 1$$

107. Answer: C

$$\cos x + \sin x \tan x = \sqrt{2}$$

$$\cos x + \frac{\sin^2 x}{\cos x} = \sqrt{2}$$

$$\cos^2 x + (1 - \cos^2 x) = \sqrt{2} \cos x$$

$$1 = \sqrt{2} \cos x$$

$$\cos x = \frac{1}{\sqrt{2}}$$

Therefore, within the available values $x = \frac{\pi}{4}$.

197

108. Answer: C

By creating a table of values, we can see the changing values of each graph. In this case, we only need values from 0 to 4 to accurately pass judgement.

x	1. $y = 3x$	2. $y = 2^x$	1<2?
0	0	1	Y
1	3	2	N
2	6	4	N
3	9	8	N
4	12	16	Y

By reading this table, we can see initially the second graph is higher. However, whenever they switch positions, we know there has been an intersection. We see this switch twice as indicated by the third column of the table; therefore, we can conclude the lines intersect twice.

109. Answer: B

$$\frac{x^3 + 2}{2x}$$

$$\frac{x^2}{2} + x^{-1}$$

Differentiating once:

$$x - x^{-2}$$

Differentiating twice:

$$1 + 2x^{-3}$$

$$1 + \frac{2}{x^3}$$

110. Answer: B

Here, we are given a function in terms of volume and time. A single differentiation yields $\frac{dV}{dt}$, a function which expresses the change in Volume. If we further differentiate to $\frac{d^2V}{dt^2}$, this will allow us to calculate the maximum rate of change of Volume.

$$V = 2t + 2t^2 - \frac{t^3}{3}$$

$$\frac{dV}{dt} = 2 + 4t - t^2$$

$$\frac{d^2V}{dt^2} = 4 - 2t$$

$$\frac{d^2V}{dt^2} = 0 \text{ at maximum of } \frac{dV}{dt} \therefore 4 - 2t = 0 \therefore t = 2$$

111. Answer: A

$$2 \log_2(x + 15) - \log_2 x = 6$$

$$\log_2(x + 15)^2 - \log_2 x = 6$$

$$\log_2 \frac{(x + 15)^2}{x} = 6$$

$$\frac{(x + 15)^2}{x} = 2^6$$

$$x^2 + 30x + 225 = 64x$$

$$x^2 - 34x + 225 = 0$$

$$(x - 25)(x - 9) = 0$$

$$\therefore x = 25 \ or \ x = 9$$

112. Answer: C

$e^x, \cos x, \ln x, \sin x, \log x$ are the five functions. We can immediately rule out $\log x$ and $\ln x$ as these take values below the $x - axis$ in the given range. After being presented the options of $e^x, \sin x,$ and $\cos x$ we can immediately choose e^x as the minimum value of e^x in the given range is 1 (at $x = 0$) and this is the maximum value of the other functions in any given range.

113. Answer: A

$$\sin^4(x) - \cos^4(x)$$

$$\sin^2 x \left(1 - \cos^2 x\right) - \cos^2 x \left(1 - \sin^2 x\right)$$

$$\sin^2 x - \sin^2 x \cos^2 x - \cos^2 x + \cos^2 x \sin^2 x$$

$$\sin^2 x - \cos^2 x$$

114. Answer: E

$$\log(3x - 2) + \log(x + 2) = \log(15x + 16)$$

$$\log[(3x - 2)(x + 2)] = \log(15x + 16)$$

$$3x^2 + 4x - 4 = 15x + 16$$

$$3x^2 - 11x - 20 = 0$$

$$(3x + 4)(x - 5) = 0$$

$$\therefore x = -\frac{4}{3} \ or \ x = 5$$

$$\text{But } x \neq -\frac{4}{3} \text{ as this is not within the domain of} \log(3x - 2)$$

199

115. Answer: D

The product of two perpendicular gradients is always -1. We can use this mathematical fact to create the following equation:

$$(\alpha + 2)(\alpha) = -1$$
$$\alpha^2 - 2\alpha + 1 = 0$$
$$(\alpha - 1)^2 = 0$$
$$\therefore \alpha = 1$$

116. Answer: A

$$f(x) = \frac{(x+1)(2x-4)}{2x}$$
$$f(x) = \frac{x^2 - x - 2}{x}$$
$$f(x) = x - 1 - 2x^{-1}$$
$$f'(x) = 1 + 2x^{-2}$$
$$f'(2) = 1 + \frac{2}{4} = \frac{6}{4} = \frac{3}{2}$$

117. Answer: D

$$f(x) = 3x(3 - 2x) \therefore -\frac{a}{12}f(x+a) = -\frac{a}{12}\left[3(x+a)(3 - 2(x+a))\right] = -\frac{1}{3} \times 3(x+4)(3 - 2x - 8)$$
$$= -(x+4)(-2x-5) = (x+4)(2x+5)$$

Therefore, the roots of this equation are $x = -4$ and $x = -\frac{5}{2}$. The question states to integrate between bounds of the origin and the integer root ($x = -4$), and the equation $-\frac{a}{4}f(x+a)$ which is $3(x+4)(2x+5)$ using the above calculations.

$$3\int_{-4}^{0}(x+4)(2x+5) = 3\int_{-4}^{0}(2x^2 + 13x + 20) = 3\left[\frac{2}{3}x^3 + \frac{13}{2}x^2 + 20x\right]_{-4}^{0}$$
$$= 3[0] - 3\left[\frac{2}{3}(-4)^3 + \frac{13}{2}(-4)^2 + 20(-4)\right] = -3\left[\frac{2}{3}(-64) + \frac{13}{2}(16) - 80\right] = -3\left[-\frac{128}{3} + 104 - 80\right]$$
$$= -3\left[-\frac{128}{3} + 24\right] = 128 - 72 = 56$$

118. Answer: B

We use a standard permutation calculation to work out the possible calculations giving us $11!$ (this is the same as $11P0$ on the calculator). Then to remove duplicates we divide through by $3!\,4!\,4!$ we do this because not all the tops are of different colours. Presenting us with Option B, $\frac{11!}{3!4!4!}$.

119. Answer: C

We can eliminate option B as the functions have completely different ranges due to the change in the sign after the 1. Option D can be eliminated too as this represented the same graph but shifted in the x direction by $\frac{\pi}{2}$ to the right. Option A presents two similar graphs, they are actually $\frac{\pi}{2}$ away from each other in the $x - axis$. Option C is a variation of the general rule $\cos A = \sin\left(\frac{\pi}{2} - A\right)$, where A has been replaced by $2x$ and an additional π has been added to the input for both functions.

120. Answer: C

To calculate the derivative, using the simplest method, we must get y on one side without any other components.

$$\frac{1}{24}x = \frac{y^{\frac{1}{3}}}{12} - \frac{1}{6}$$

$$\frac{1}{2}x = y^{\frac{1}{3}} - 2$$

$$\frac{1}{2}x + 2 = y^{\frac{1}{3}}$$

$$\left(\frac{1}{2}x + 2\right)^3 = y$$

$$y = \frac{1}{8}x^3 + \frac{3}{2}x^2 + 6x + 8$$

$$\frac{dy}{dx} = \frac{3}{8}x^2 + 3x + 6$$

$$\frac{d^2y}{dx^2} = \frac{3}{4}x + 3$$

$$\frac{d^3y}{dx^3} = \frac{3}{4}$$

121. Answer: B

If we take (3.2) as the first term of the question and evaluate, we can obtain: $\frac{3^2 \times 2}{2(3-2)}$ which simplifies to 9. Now we can tackle the second term of the question (3.9), $\frac{3^2 \times 9}{2(3-9)}$, which calculates to $\frac{81}{-12}$ simplifying to our answer of $-\frac{27}{4}$.

122. Answer: D

We need to calculate the area of each shape. The triangle can be calculated using the formula $\frac{1}{2} ab \sin C$ and the rectangle using $base \times height$. For the triangle, the area we calculate is: $\frac{1}{2} \times 4n \times 6n \times \sin(150°) = 6n^2$, the rectangle's areas is $(n+1)(5n-2) = 5n^2 + 3n - 2$. We have been told these areas are equivalent, therefore, we can set up the equation:

$$6n^2 = 5n^2 + 3n - 2$$

$$n^2 - 3n + 2 = 0$$

$$(n-2)(n-1) = 0$$

$$\therefore n = 2 \; and \; n = 1$$

The question states n is an even integer $\therefore \; n = 2$

123. Answer: D

$$V = \frac{11}{9} \gamma l^4 \text{ where } \left(\gamma = \frac{9}{2} \right)$$

Rate of change of V is found by differentiating with respect to length

$$\frac{dV}{dl} = \frac{44}{9} l^3 \gamma \; \therefore \frac{dV}{dl} = \frac{44}{9} l^3 \left(\frac{9}{2} \right)$$

$$\frac{dV}{dl} = 22l^3$$

$$\text{When } l = 2, \frac{dV}{dl} = 22(8) = 176$$

124. Answer: B

A standard Cosine rule question using the formula $a^2 = b^2 + c^2 - 2bc \cos A$, where $a = x, b = \sqrt{27}, c = \sqrt{12} \; and \; A = 60°$. Substituting these values creates a solvable equation of, $x^2 = 27 + 12 - 2 \times \sqrt{27} \times \sqrt{12} \times \frac{1}{2}$. Simplifying to $x^2 = 39 - 18 = 21, \therefore x = \sqrt{21}$.

125. Answer: B

The minimum value of $a - b$ is found when $a = 10 \; \& \; b = 60$, yielding $a - b = -50$. The maximum value of $a - b$ is found when $a = 40 \; \& \; b = 30$, yielding $a - b = 10$.

126. Answer: A

Simplifying $\frac{3^{2x}}{27^y} = \frac{3^{2x}}{3^{3y}} = 3^{2x-3y}$. If we look at rearranging the linear equation to $2x = 3y - 1$ and then to $2x - 3y = -1$. This is the same as the power on the simplified equation and can be substituted to yield $3^{-1} = \frac{1}{3}$.

127. Answer: A

$$f(x) = (x^2 + 4x - 6)^2$$

$$f(x) = x^4 + 8x^3 + 4x^2 - 48x + 36$$

$$f'(x) = 4x^3 + 24x^2 + 8x - 48$$

$$f'(-1) = -4 + 24 - 8 - 48 = -36$$

128. Answer: D

$$\log_{\frac{1}{2}}\left[\log_8\left(\frac{x^2 - 2x}{x - 3}\right)\right] = 0$$

$$\log_8\left(\frac{x^2 - 2x}{x - 3}\right) = 1$$

$$\frac{x^2 - 2x}{x - 3} = 8$$

$$x^2 - 2x = 8x - 24$$

$$x^2 - 10x - 24 = 0$$

$$(x + 2)(x - 12) = 0$$

$$x = 12 \text{ and } x \neq -2 \text{ as the domain of } \log_8\left(\frac{x^2 - 2x}{x - 3}\right) \text{ would not be satisfied}$$

129. Answer: E

The y stretch factor of 13 is irrelevant here. So looking solely at $\tan 9x$, in the range given, is the same as looking at $\tan x$ in range $9 \times$ the size i.e. $0 \leq x \leq \frac{9\pi}{2}$. Here, we can sketch the $\tan x$ graph and see that it crosses the $x - axis$ five times at coordinates $(0,0)$ $(\pi, 0)$ $(2\pi, 0)$ $(3\pi, 0)$ $(4\pi, 0)$.

130. Answer: B

$$f(x) = x^3 + 2x$$

$$f'(x) = 3x^2 + 2$$

$$f'(1) = 5$$

$$\frac{-1}{f'(1)} = -\frac{1}{5}$$

131. Answer: D

$$\log(3x - 1) = \log 16 - \log(3x + 1)$$

$$\log(3x - 1) = \log\frac{16}{3x + 1}$$

$$(3x - 1)(3x + 1) = 16$$

$$9x^2 - 1 = 16$$

$$9x^2 = 17$$

$$x^2 = \frac{17}{9}$$

$$x = \frac{\sqrt{17}}{3}$$

132. Answer: D

$$\sqrt{\frac{1}{1 + \tan^2 x}} = 1$$

$$\frac{1}{1 + \tan^2 x} = 1$$

$$1 = 1 + \tan^2 x$$

$$\tan^2 x = 0$$

$$\tan x = 0$$

$$x = 0$$

133. Answer: E

$$\lim_{x \to 0} \left(\frac{x^2 - 1}{x - 1} + 2\right)$$

$$\lim_{x \to 0} \left(\frac{(x - 1)(x + 1)}{x - 1} + 2\right)$$

$$\lim_{x \to 0} ([x + 1] + 2)$$

$$\lim_{x \to 0} (x + 3)$$

$$0 + 3 = 3$$

134. Answer: D

The equation is outlined in form $Ae^{Bx} + C$, we are told the asymptote lies at $y = -9$, therefore we can calculate $C = -9$ as the asymptote for any function of Ae^{Bx} lies at $y = 0$. Therefore we must translate the graph down by 9 units. We are also given the coordinate $(0, -6)$ if we substitute into the equation of $y = Ae^{Bx} - 9$ we get $-6 = Ae^{B \times 0} - 9$ which simplifies to $3 = Ae^0$. Therefore $A = 3$. Now using the last coordinate of $(3, -4)$ we can solve the equation for B. Our equation is now $y = 3e^{Bx} - 9$.

$$-4 = 3e^{3B} - 9$$

$$\frac{5}{3} = e^{3B}$$

$$\left(\frac{5}{3}\right)^{\frac{1}{3}} = e^B$$

$$\ln\left[\left(\frac{5}{3}\right)^{\frac{1}{3}}\right] = B$$

$$B = \frac{1}{3}\ln\left(\frac{5}{3}\right)$$

135. Answer: F

$$AC^2 = AB^2 + BC^2 \quad \therefore AC^2 = 40 \quad \therefore AC = 2\sqrt{10}$$

$$Area\ of\ ACD = \frac{1}{2} \times AC \times CD$$

$$\frac{1}{2} \times 2\sqrt{10} \times 3 = 3\sqrt{10}\ \text{units}^2$$

136. Answer: A

$$\sin A \equiv \cos(90° - A)$$

$$\therefore \text{if } \sin A = 0.8 \text{ then } \cos(90° - A) = 0.8 = \frac{4}{5}$$

137. Answer: B

Note: This question has many methods, we have opted for this method although all are equally correct.

We can observe from the ratios that the original number of counters is a multiple of 7 and the final number of counters is a multiple of 5. A simple equation we can set up is $\frac{7x-10}{5}$ and we know this should give no remainder. We can remove the $-\frac{10}{5}$ component as this is already a multiple of 5 and will not influence our value for x. The first integer which satisfies $\frac{7x}{5}$ is $x = 5$, using this we can calculate the original number of counters $7 \times 5 = 35$ of these we want the green counters which represent $\frac{3}{7}$ of the population i.e. $\frac{3}{7} \times 35 = 15$.

138. Answer: C

Factors of prime p are p and 1. $p^3 = p \times p \times p$ ∴ factors include p, 1 & p^3.

139. Answer: A

$$Area \text{ of cone} = \frac{1}{3}\pi r^2 h$$

$$Area \text{ of cylinder} = \pi r^2 h$$

$$r = \frac{20}{2} = 10cm \ \& \ h = 10cm \ \therefore r = h$$

$Vol.$ of two cones and one cylinder of equal height and radius $= \frac{5}{3}\pi r^2 h = \frac{5}{3} \times 3 \times 10^3 = 5000$

Now given that the containers are 80% full, $5000 \times 0.8 = 4000cm^3$

140. Answer: C

Area of sheet metal required is the sum of two square faces and three rectangular faces. Square face is x^2, rectangular face is xy, ∴ total area of sheet metal is $2x^2 + 3xy$.

$2x^2 + 3xy = 54$, $V = x^2 y$, to eliminate the y variable from the volume calculation we can rearrange the first equation. $54 - 2x^2 = 3xy$ ∴ $\frac{54-2x^2}{3x} = y$. This can be substituted into the volume equation. $V = x^2\left(\frac{54-2x^2}{3x}\right)$. By differentiating this with respect to height (x) we can calculate the maximum volume the pool can have.

$$V = x^2\left(\frac{54-2x^2}{3x}\right)$$

$$V = \frac{54x - 2x^3}{3}$$

$$V = 18x - \frac{2}{3}x^3$$

$$\frac{dV}{dx} = 18 - 2x^2$$

When the rate of change of volume is equal to 0, then we are at either a maximum or a minimum.

$$18 - 2x^2 = 0$$

$$x^2 = 9$$

$$x = \pm 3$$

$$x \neq -3 \ \therefore x = 3$$

$$\text{When } x = 3, V = 18(3) - \frac{2}{3}(3^3) = 54 - 18 = 36$$

141. Answer: C

The digits must BEGIN and END in 3. Such digits are limited to: $33, 303, 313, 323, 333, 343, 353,$ $363, 373, 383$ and 393. A total of eleven such numbers exist in the given range.

142. Answer: B

Using the Cosine rule, we can calculate x. The Cosine rule is $a^2 = b^2 + c^2 - 2bc \cos A$, where $a = x, b = 15, c = \sqrt{50}$ and $A = 45°$. $x^2 = 225 + 50 - 2(\sqrt{50})(15) \cos 45°$ which simplifies to $x^2 = 125$, which can again be simplified to $x = 5\sqrt{5}$.

143. Answer: B

The sum of the numbers previously was $6 \times 8 = 48$, the new sum of the numbers is $6 \times 11 = 66$. The total change in the value is $+18$ if the new value is 6 the old value must satisfy $6 - (old) = 18 \therefore$ the old number must be -12.

144. Answer: E

$$x^3 + y^3 = 0$$
$$y^3 = -x^3$$
$$y = -x$$
$$\frac{dy}{dx} = -1, \text{for all values of } x$$

145. Answer: C

The probability of picking two blue gloves: $\frac{1}{3} \times \frac{1}{6}$

The probability of picking two green gloves: $\frac{1}{3} \times \frac{1}{6}$

The probability of picking two black gloves: $\frac{1}{3} \times \frac{1}{6}$

Sum of these independent probabilities: $3 \times \frac{1}{3} \times \frac{1}{6} = \frac{1}{6}$

146. Answer: A

$$f(x) = x^\pi$$
$$f'(x) = \pi x^{\pi-1}$$
$$f'(1) = \pi(1)^{\pi-1} = \pi$$

147. Answer: D

$$y = 5x - 7 + \frac{2\sqrt{x} + 3}{x}$$

$$y = 5x - 7 + 2x^{-0.5} + 3x^{-1}$$

$$\frac{dy}{dx} = 5 - x^{-\frac{3}{2}} - 3x^{-2}$$

$$5 - (4)^{-\frac{3}{2}} - 3x^{-2}$$

$$5 - \frac{1}{8} - \frac{3}{16} = 5 - \frac{5}{16} = \frac{80 - 5}{16} = \frac{75}{16}$$

148. Answer: B

$$y = e^{-x}$$

$$\frac{dy}{dx} = -e^{-x}$$

$$\text{When } x = -1, \frac{dy}{dx} = -e$$

$$\therefore \text{ perpendicular gradient is } \frac{1}{e}$$

$$\text{Using formula } (y - y_1) = m(x - x_1)$$

$$y - e = \frac{1}{e}(x + 1)$$

$$y = \frac{x}{e} + \frac{1}{e} + e$$

149. Answer: D

$$f(x) = \frac{1}{2} e^{0.01x} \ln(x)$$

$$\text{When } f(x) = 0 \text{ function crosses } x - axis$$

$$0 = \frac{1}{2} e^{0.01x} \ln(x)$$

$$0 = e^{0.01x} \ln(x)$$

$$e^{0.01x} \neq 0 \text{ as the range of } e^{0.01x} \text{ is numbers above 0}$$

$$\therefore \ln(x) = 0, x = 1$$

150. Answer: C

$$y = 2x^2 + 3\left(\frac{x}{2} - 3\right)^2$$

$$y = 2x^2 + 3\left(\frac{x^2}{4} - 3x + 9\right)$$

$$y = 2x^2 + \left(\frac{3x^2}{4} - 9x + 27\right)$$

$$y = \frac{11}{4}x^2 - 9x + 27$$

$$\frac{dy}{dx} = \frac{11}{2}x - 9$$

$$\frac{dy}{dx} = \frac{11x - 18}{2}$$

$$\frac{dx}{dy} = \frac{2}{11x - 18}$$

$$\text{When } x = -1, \frac{dx}{dy} = \frac{2}{-29} = -\frac{2}{29}$$

151. Answer: A

$$f(x) = 5x^3 + \frac{7}{2}x^2 - 2x + 6$$

$$f'(x) = 15x^2 + 7x - 2$$

$$f'(x) = 0 \text{ at } x - \text{intercepts}$$

$$15x^2 + 7x - 2 = 0$$

$$(5x - 1)(3x + 2) = 0$$

$$\therefore x = \frac{1}{5} \text{ or } x = -\frac{2}{3} \quad \therefore \text{ positive } x - \text{intercept is} \frac{1}{5}$$

152. Answer: C

$$f(x) = x^3 - 61x + \frac{32}{3} - (14x + 1)(x - 3)$$

$$f(x) = x^3 - 61x + \frac{32}{3} - (14x^2 - 41x - 3)$$

$$f(x) = x^3 - 61x + \frac{32}{3} - 14x^2 + 41x + 3$$

$$f(x) = x^3 - 14x^2 - 20x + \frac{41}{3}$$

$$f'(x) = 3x^2 - 28x - 20$$

When $f'(x) = 0$ then the direction of $f(x)$ has changed, or in other words a stationary point

$$3x^2 - 28x - 20 = 0$$

$$(3x + 2)(x - 10) = 0$$

$$x = -\frac{2}{3} \text{ and } x = 10$$

The question asks for a positive value of x $\therefore$ $x \neq -\frac{2}{3}$

$$\therefore x = 10$$

153. Answer: A

$$(x + 1)^2 = 4$$

$$x + 1 = \pm 2 \therefore x = -1 \pm 2 \therefore x = -3 \text{ or } x = 1$$

$$(x - 1)^2 = 16$$

$$x - 1 = \pm 4 \therefore x = 1 \pm 4 \therefore x = -3 \text{ or } x = 5$$

The value of x which satisfies both equations is $x = -3$

154. Answer: D

We first equate $f(x)$ and $g(x)$ to calculate bounds within which to integrate.

$$\frac{1}{2}x^2 - \frac{9}{2}x + 11 = x^2 - 9x + 11$$

$$0 = \frac{1}{2}x^2 - \frac{9}{2}x$$

$$\frac{1}{2}x(x-9) = 0 \ \therefore x = 0 \text{ and } x = 9$$

Then we integrate each curve and find the difference in the area within bounds of $x = 0$ and $x = 9$.

$$\left| \int_0^9 f(x)\,dx - \int_0^9 g(x)dx \right|$$

$$\int_0^9 g(x) - f(x)\,dx$$

$$\int_0^9 \left(\frac{1}{2}x^2 - \frac{9}{2}x \right) dx$$

$$\left[\frac{x^3}{6} - \frac{9x^2}{4} \right]_0^9 = \left[\frac{729}{6} - \frac{729}{4} \right] - [0] = \frac{2(729)}{12} - \frac{3(729)}{12} = -\frac{729}{12} = -\frac{243}{4}$$

Given we are calculating an area, the value is $\frac{243}{4}$

155. Answer: C

First, we look at the range $10 - 20$, in which we find that 12 to 19 satisfy the conditions (8)

Then, we look at the range $21 - 30$, in which we find that 23 to 29 satisfy the conditions (7)

Then, we look at the range $31 - 40$, in which we find that 34 to 39 satisfy the conditions (6)

Then, we look at the range $41 - 50$, in which we find that 45 to 49 satisfy the conditions (5)

Then, we look at the range $51 - 60$, in which we find that 56 to 59 satisfy the conditions (4)

Then, we look at the range $61 - 70$, in which we find that 67 to 69 satisfy the conditions (3)

Then, we look at the range $71 - 80$, in which we find that 78 and 79 satisfy the conditions (2)

Then, we look at the range $81 - 90$, in which we find that 89 satisfies the conditions (1)

Then, we look at the range $91 - 99$, in which we find that no values satisfy the conditions (0)

$$8 + 7 + 6 + 5 + 4 + 3 + 2 + 1 = 36$$

156. Answer: C

We will approach this problem as you would any surd simplification question. Therefore, $i^2 = \left(\sqrt{-1}\right)^2 = -1$

$$\frac{3-i}{2+4i} \times \frac{2-4i}{2-4i}$$

$$\frac{6-2i-12i+4i^2}{4-16i^2}$$

$$\frac{6-14i+(-4)}{4-(-16)}$$

$$\frac{2-14i}{20}$$

$$\frac{1}{10}-\frac{7}{10}i$$

$$\therefore a = \frac{1}{10}$$

157. Answer: E

$$\log[\log(x)] + \log[\log(x^3 - 2)] = 0$$

$$\log[\log(x) \times \log(x^3 - 2)] = 0$$

$$\log(x) \times \log(x^3 - 2) = 0$$

Equation is satisfied when one of the components is equal to 0

$$\therefore \log(x) = 0 \ or \ \log(x^3 - 2) = 0$$

$$x = 1 \ or \ x^3 = 3$$

Given x is an integer, $x = 1$

Substituting $x = 1$ into the original equation yields component $\log[\log(1)]$ which is not possible

This is not possible as $\log 1 = 0$ and $\log 0 =$ undefined

158. Answer: A

If the $Area$ of the square is 36, then side length must be 6. The diagonal of the square is equal to the diameter of the larger circle, therefore splitting the square in two from opposing vertices creates an isosceles right-angle triangle with side length 6, $\therefore$ using $a^2 + b^2 = c^2$, we can calculate the diagonal. $6^2 + 6^2 = D^2 \therefore D = 6\sqrt{2}$. The perimeter of the shaded area is equal to $\frac{1}{4}$ of the circumference of the circle + one side length of the square. $\therefore \frac{1}{4}\pi D + 6 = \frac{6\sqrt{2}}{4}\pi + 6 = \frac{3\sqrt{2}}{2}\pi + 6$

159. Answer: C

$$-\frac{x}{2} + 9 = 16, -\frac{x}{2} = 7, x = -14$$

$$2x^2 - 2 = 16, 2x^2 = 18, x^2 = 9, x = \pm 3, x \neq -3 \text{(not in domain)}$$

$$\therefore x = -14 \text{ or } x = 3$$

$$-14 \times 3 = -42$$

160. Answer: C

The gradient function is the derivative function of the original from which the gradient can be calculated at certain values of the x variable. $\therefore$ if $f(x) = 2x^4 + 2x - 1$, then the gradient function is the derivative $f'(x) = 8x^3 + 2$.

161. Answer: D

$$y = \frac{1}{4}x^4 + \frac{1}{3}x^3 + \frac{1}{2}x^2$$

$$\frac{dy}{dx} = x^3 + x^2 + x$$

$$\frac{d^2y}{dx^2} = 3x^2 + 2x + 1$$

$$\therefore \text{ when } x = 1, 3 + 2 + 1 = 6$$

162. Answer: B

$$\frac{1}{3}\cos x = \frac{1}{2}\sin x$$

$$\frac{2}{3} = \tan x$$

This is only satisfied once in the interval

163. Answer: B

Given $a^3 = b^2$, we need to calculate what is equivalent to $b\sqrt{a}$. All the options are given in b, $\therefore$ we must use substitution

to solve. Using $a^3 = b^2$ we can calculate $a = b^{\frac{2}{3}}$ and $\therefore \sqrt{a} = \sqrt{b^{\frac{2}{3}}} = b^{\frac{1}{3}}, \therefore b \times b^{\frac{1}{3}} = b^{\frac{4}{3}}$.

164. Answer: C

$$\sin x = \frac{1}{\cos\left(x - \frac{\pi}{2}\right)}$$

$$\sin x = \frac{1}{\sin x} \quad \therefore \quad \sin^2 x = 1 \quad \therefore \quad \sin(x) = \pm 1$$

$$\therefore \text{ in given domain } \left(\frac{\pi}{2}, 1\right) \& \left(\frac{3\pi}{2}, -1\right) \quad \therefore \quad 2 \text{ intersections}$$

165. Answer: D

If there on average 90 customers per hour and each spends 0.2 of an hour, then the average number of customers is a product of these: $90 \times \frac{1}{5} = 18$

166. Answer: E

We are using the Cosine rule, $a^2 = b^2 + c^2 - 2bc \cos A$. For the given question, $a = x, b = 7, c = \sqrt{12}$ and $A = 30°$. Therefore, we can set up equation $x = \sqrt{49 + 12 - 2(7)(\sqrt{12}) \cos 30°}$, which can be simplified to $x = \sqrt{61 - 2(7)(2\sqrt{3})\left(\frac{\sqrt{3}}{2}\right)}$, further simplified to $x = \sqrt{61 - 42} = \sqrt{19}$.

167. Answer: E

$$\text{Let an integer be } n, \therefore n^2 = \text{square of integer}, \therefore \text{square of integer} - \text{integer} = n^2 - n$$

$$\text{We can write this as } n(n-1), \text{the product of two consecutive integers}$$

168. Answer: D

We can calculate the probability of the rule being abolished by multiplying the probability each student has of being elected by the probability each student has of abolishing the rule. This can be thought of as a probability tree where we aim to collate the total probability of a certain outcome being met regardless of path.

For α the probability they are selected and abolish the rule is $0.4 \times 0.6 = 0.24$

For β the probability they are selected and abolish the rule is $0.25 \times 0.5 = 0.125$

For γ the probability they are selected and abolish the rule is $(1 - 0.4 - 0.25) \times 0.1 = 0.035$

$\therefore$ The sum of these probabilities gives us the probability of the rule being abolished $0.24 + 0.125 + 0.035 = 0.4$

169. Answer: B

The question lays out the following, $x = \frac{m+9}{2}, y = \frac{2m+15}{2}, z = \frac{3m+18}{2}$, we need to calculate the average of x, y, and z. As with any average question, the calculation will be the sum divided by the number of values, $\frac{x+y+z}{3} = \frac{\frac{m+9}{2} + \frac{2m+15}{2} + \frac{3m+18}{2}}{3} = \frac{\frac{6m+42}{2}}{3} = \frac{3m+21}{3} = m + 7$

170. Answer: B

$$h(x) = \frac{e^3}{(x^2 + 1)^{-1}}$$

$$h(x) = e^3(x^2 + 1) = x^2 e^3 + e^3$$

$$h'(x) = 2xe^3$$

$$\therefore h'(2) = 4e^3$$

214

171. Answer: F

$$\log_{7\sqrt{7}}(x - 4) = \frac{2}{3} - \log_{7\sqrt{7}}(x - 10)$$

$$\log_{7\sqrt{7}}(x - 4) + \log_{7\sqrt{7}}(x - 10) = \frac{2}{3}$$

$$\log_{7\sqrt{7}}(x - 4)(x - 10) = \frac{2}{3}$$

$$x^2 - 14x + 40 = 7$$

$$x^2 - 14x + 33 = 0$$

$$(x - 3)(x - 11) = 0$$

$$x = 3 \text{ and } x = 11$$

$$(2^x)^x = 4^{6 - \frac{x}{2}}$$

$$2^{x^2} = 2^{2\left(6 - \frac{x}{2}\right)}$$

$$x^2 = 12 - x$$

$$x^2 + x - 12 = 0$$

$$(x + 4)(x - 3) = 0$$

$$x = -4 \text{ and } x = 3$$

$\therefore$ The only overlapping solution is $x = 3$, however, when substituting $x = 3$

into the original equation, $\log_{7\sqrt{7}}(x - 4)$ is no longer a defined value $\therefore$ no solutions

172. Answer: I

$$\tan\theta = \cos\theta + 3\tan\theta - \frac{2}{\cos\theta}$$

$$\frac{\sin\theta}{\cos\theta} = \cos\theta + \frac{3\sin\theta}{\cos\theta} - \frac{2}{\cos\theta}$$

$$\sin\theta = \cos^2\theta + 3\sin\theta - 2$$

$$-2\sin\theta + 2 = (1 - \sin^2\theta)$$

$$\sin^2\theta - 2\sin\theta + 1 = 0$$

$$(\sin\theta - 1)^2 = 0$$

$$\sin\theta = 1$$

$$\theta = 90°$$

BUT when this value is tested, $\tan 90°$ does not have a value, $\therefore$ no solutions

173. Answer: B

$$\cfrac{1}{\cfrac{1}{x+2}+\cfrac{1}{x+3}}$$

$$\cfrac{1}{\cfrac{x+3+x+2}{(x+2)(x+3)}}$$

$$\cfrac{1}{\cfrac{2x+5}{(x+2)(x+3)}}$$

$$\frac{(x+2)(x+3)}{2x+5}$$

$$\frac{x^2+5x+6}{2x+5}$$

174. Answer: E

Original price is x, after the first discount $x \times 0.8 = 0.8x$, after the second discount $0.8x \times 0.7 = 0.56x$, i.e. 44% off the original price.

175. Answer: D

$$\tan\theta = \frac{opposite}{adjacent}, \therefore a = \text{opposite}, b = \text{adjacent}$$

$$\tan^{-1}\left(\frac{a}{b}\right) = \theta, \cos\theta = \frac{adjacent}{hypotenuse}$$

$\therefore$ using information about the hypotenuse from the question and the adjacent from above

$$\cos\theta = \frac{b}{\sqrt{a^2+b^2}}$$

176. Answer: D

$$(10)^{\log(x-2)} = 100$$

$$(10)^{\log(x-2)} = 10^2$$

$$\log(x-2) = 2$$

$$x-2 = 100$$

$$x = 102$$

177. Answer: E

Due to the limited range of values m can take, it is easier to count values of m which satisfy this equation. The mathematical method is as follows. $m + 7 < 9 \rightarrow m < 2$. We also know due to the domain of a square root function $m + 7 \geq 0$ $\therefore$ values which m can take include $m = -7, -6, -5, -4, -3, -2, -1, 0, 1$. We are also told m is an even integer, which leaves $-6, -4, -2$ and 0 for possible values of m.

178. Answer: A

$$8^{\log_2(\log_8 x)}$$

$$2^{3\log_2(\log_8 x)}$$

$$\left[2^{\log_2(\log_8 x)}\right]^3$$

Apply rule $a^{\log_a b} = b$

$$(\log_8 x)^3$$

179. Answer: E

$$f(x) = \frac{(3x+2)^2}{x^{0.5}}$$

$$f(x) = \frac{9x^2 + 12x + 4}{x^{0.5}}$$

$$f(x) = 9x^{\frac{3}{2}} + 12x^{0.5} + 4x^{-0.5}$$

$$f'(1) = 9 + 12 + 4 = 25$$

180. Answer: B

Given $\int_{11}^{0} f(x)\, dx = 19.2$, the value of $\int_{0}^{11} f(x)\, dx = -19.2$ and the value of $\int_{0}^{11} 2\, dx = 22$

$$\int_{0}^{11} [f(x)+2]\, dx = \int_{0}^{11} f(x)\, dx + \int_{0}^{11} 2\, dx = -19.2 + 22 = 2.8$$

181. Answer: B

$$f(x) = \frac{\left(3 - 4\sqrt{x}\right)^2}{\sqrt{x}}$$

$$f(x) = (9 - 24x^{0.5} + 16x)(x^{-0.5})$$

$$f(x) = 9x^{-0.5} - 24 + 16x^{0.5}$$

$$f'(x) = -\frac{9}{2}x^{-1.5} + 8x^{-0.5}$$

$$f'(9) = -\frac{9}{2}(9)^{-1.5} + 8(9)^{-0.5} = -\frac{9}{2}\left(\frac{1}{27}\right) + 8\left(\frac{1}{3}\right) = -\frac{1}{6} + \frac{8}{3} = \frac{5}{2}$$

182. Answer: E

Using the Sine rule we can set up the following equation, $\frac{\sin 60°}{\sqrt{12}} = \frac{\sin x°}{2}$, which simplifies to $\frac{2 \times \frac{\sqrt{3}}{2}}{2\sqrt{3}} = \sin x°$, further simplifying to $\frac{1}{2} = \sin x°$, which gives $x = 30°$, or as it is written in the answer $\frac{\pi}{6}$.

183. Answer: A

This question is considering when does e^x approach the value of 0. The greater the negative value of x the closer the value of e^x is to 0, $\therefore$ the answer is as $x \to -\infty$.

184. Answer: A

For a quadratic expression to be positive for all real values of x, the minimum point must lie above the $x - axis$. We know this graph is a graph with positive x^2 coefficient $\therefore$ we just need to ensure that no part of the graph intersects with the $x - axis$ or in other words the discriminant is negative.

$$b^2 - 4ac < 0$$
$$(4 + \alpha)^2 - 4(1)(4 - 2\alpha) < 0$$
$$16 + 8\alpha + \alpha^2 - 16 + 8\alpha < 0$$
$$\alpha^2 + 16\alpha < 0$$
$$\alpha(\alpha + 16) < 0$$
$$-16 < \alpha < 0$$

185. Answer: A

$$\log_{\frac{1}{x}}(216) = 3$$
$$\left(\frac{1}{x}\right)^3 = 216$$
$$\left(\frac{1}{x}\right)^3 = 6^3$$
$$\frac{1}{x} = 6 \quad \therefore x = \frac{1}{6}$$

186. Answer: B

We have two components which multiply to 0. $\therefore$ at least one component is equal to zero. So we are presented with the following options $a = 4$ $b = anything$ or $a = anything$ $b = -6$ or $a = 4$ & $b = -6$. If we take the first option for $a^2 + b^2$ and let $b = 0$, we can calculate our minimum value of $4^2 + 0^2 = 16$.

187. Answer: D

$$\lim_{x \to 3} \frac{x^2 - 9}{x - 3}$$
$$\lim_{x \to 3} \frac{(x - 3)(x + 3)}{x - 3}$$
$$\lim_{x \to 3}(x + 3)$$

$(3) + 3 = 6$

188. Answer: D

The easiest way to spot the value of x here is to look at the value of $\frac{24x^2}{ax}$ which is $-4x \therefore a = -6$

189. Answer: D

$$2\sin^2 x + 2 = 7\cos x$$

$$2(1 - \cos^2 x) + 2 = 7\cos x$$

$$2 - 2\cos^2 x + 2 = 7\cos x$$

$$2\cos^2 x + 7\cos x - 4 = 0$$

$$(2\cos x - 1)(\cos x + 4) = 0$$

$$\cos x = \frac{1}{2} \text{ as } \cos x \neq -4$$

$$x = \frac{\pi}{3}$$

190. Answer: D

By calculating the derivative and setting it equal to 0, we can calculate the value of x at which the minimum value of the function is found. $y = e^{-x} + 2e^x \therefore \frac{dy}{dx} = -e^{-x} + 2e^x, \frac{dy}{dx} = 0$ at the minimum point as gradient is zero at the turning point of a graph. $0 = -e^{-x} + 2e^x$, which is simplified to $e^{-x} = 2e^x$ and further to $\frac{1}{2} = e^{2x}$. After applying natural logarithms to both sides, $\ln\left(\frac{1}{2}\right) = 2x \rightarrow \ln 2^{-1} = 2x \rightarrow -\ln 2 = 2x \rightarrow -\frac{1}{2}\ln 2 = x \rightarrow -\frac{1}{2}\log_e 2 = x$

191. Answer: F

$$P(B|A) = \frac{P(A \cap B)}{P(A)} = \frac{2}{3}$$

$$P(A|B) = \frac{P(A \cap B)}{P(B)} = \frac{1}{3}$$

$$P(A'|B') = \frac{P(A' \cap B')}{P(B')} = \frac{5}{6}$$

Arranging the first equation: $P(A \cap B) = \frac{2}{3}P(A)$

Arranging the second equation: $P(A \cap B) = \frac{1}{3}P(B)$

Equating the two of these, $2P(A) = P(B)$.

Letting $P(A \cap B) = x$, $P(A) = \frac{3}{2}x$, $P(B) = 3x$

Using this we can calculate $P(A \cup B) = P(A) + P(B) - P(A \cap B) = \frac{3}{2}x + 3x - x = \frac{7}{2}x$

We can also calculate the value of $P(A' \cap B')$ as $1 - \frac{7}{2}x$

The area of $P(B') = 1 - P(B) = 1 - 3x$

$$\therefore \text{ Using } P(A'|B') \text{ we get } \frac{1 - \frac{7}{2}x}{1 - 3x} = \frac{5}{6}$$

$$6 - 21x = 5 - 15x$$

$$1 = 6x \therefore x = \frac{1}{6}$$

Using this we can calculate $P(B)$ which we calculated to be $3x$, therefore $P(B) = 3 \times \frac{1}{6} = \frac{1}{2}$

This is not an available option, $\therefore$ we pick **F**.

192. Answer: E

If $f(3) = 0$, then $(x - 3)$ is a factor of the polynomial. Therefore by inspection, we can factorise $x^3 - 10x^2 - 23x + 132 = (x - 3)(x^2 - 7x - 44) = (x - 3)(x + 4)(x - 11)$ $\therefore$ the other positive root is $x = 11$

193. Answer: D

$$xy = 2$$

$$y = 2x^{-1}$$

$$\frac{dy}{dx} = -2x^{-2}$$

$$\frac{d^2y}{dx^2} = 4x^{-3} \therefore \text{ if } x = 2 \text{ then } 4x^{-3} = 4(2)^{-3} = 4\left(\frac{1}{8}\right) = \frac{1}{2}$$

194. Answer: A

$$\text{At the } y - \text{intercept}, x = 0 \therefore \text{ we can simplify.}$$

$$y = \cos\left(\frac{\pi}{3} + 32x\right)$$

$$y = \cos\left(\frac{\pi}{3}\right)$$

$$y = \frac{1}{2}$$

195. Answer: B

As $x \to -\infty$ the significance of non$-x^2$ values reduce, we can ignore the $x^0 and \ x^1$ values. Leaving us

$$\left(\frac{x^2}{4x^2}\right)^3 \to \left(\frac{1}{4}\right)^3 \to \frac{1}{64}$$

196. Answer: D

Let Amy $= b + 2$ and Bill $= b$, using these initial assumptions, we can calculate the ages of Amy and Bill. The information we are given tells us that Amy$^2 - 36 =$ Bill^2, we can set up the following equation: $(b + 2)^2 - 36 = b^2$, simplifying to $b^2 + 4b + 4 - 36 - b^2 = 0$ further simplifying to $4b = 32 \to b = 8$. The question asks the sum of their ages in 3 years, $(b + 2 + 3) + (b + 3) = 2b + 8 = 24$

197. Answer: B

A is the 'standard' drawing of a polynomial power 5 (i.e. a polynomial power 7 with two roots which are repeated) in which you would see four changes in direction resulting in two local minima and two local maxima (as these always must come in pairs for an odd polynomial).

B can be eliminated using some principles. We know that for an odd polynomial the graph will begin in one quadrant and end in the opposite quadrant, i.e. top left to bottom right or bottom left to top right. Therefore, when sketching it is easy to see there is no such possible combination that allows for three changes in direction.

C is alike to a cubic and is found when there are only two sets of repeated roots.

D is easy to envision when considering $a = 1$ and $b, c, d, e, f, g, h = 0$

198. Answer: B

$$f(x) = (x^3 + 2x)(\sqrt{x})$$

$$f(x) = x^{\frac{7}{2}} + 2x^{\frac{3}{2}}$$

$$f'(x) = \frac{7}{2}x^{\frac{5}{2}} + 3x^{\frac{1}{2}}$$

$$f''(x) = \frac{35}{4}x^{\frac{3}{2}} + \frac{3}{2}x^{-\frac{1}{2}}$$

Gradient of a function e.g. $f''(x)$ is found by differentiating it and substituting the $x-$value for which the gradient is to be found, $\therefore$ we need to calculate $f'''(x)$.

$$f'''(x) = \frac{105}{8}x^{\frac{1}{2}} - \frac{3}{4}x^{-\frac{3}{2}}$$

$$f'''(4) = \frac{105}{8}(2) - \frac{3}{4}\left(\frac{1}{8}\right) = \frac{105}{4} - \frac{3}{32} = \frac{837}{32}$$

199. Answer: F

The coefficient of x in the expansion of $(1 + x)^n$ is $\binom{n}{1} = n$, so the coefficient of x in this whole expression is $0 + 2 + 4 + 6 + \cdots + 78 + 80 = 2(1 + 2 + 3 + \cdots 39 + 40) = 2 \times \frac{1}{2}(40)(41)$ using the formula for the sum of the first n positive integers, $\frac{1}{2}n(n + 1)$. This gives $40 \times 41 = 1640$.

200. Answer: D

Using the Sine rule, we can set up the following equation, $\frac{x}{\sin 45°} = \frac{3\sqrt{2}}{\sin 30°}$, which can be simplified to $x = \frac{3\sqrt{2}\sin 45°}{\sin 30°} = \frac{3\sqrt{2} \times \frac{\sqrt{2}}{2}}{\frac{1}{2}} = \frac{3}{\frac{1}{2}} = 6$

201. Answer: C

$$\int_1^4 \left(2x^3 + ax^{-\frac{1}{2}} + 5\right) dx = \frac{301}{2}$$

$$\left[\frac{2}{4}x^4 + 2ax^{\frac{1}{2}} + 5x\right]_1^4 = \frac{301}{2}$$

$$\frac{2}{4}(4)^4 + 2a(4)^{\frac{1}{2}} + 5(4) - \left(\frac{2}{4}(1)^4 + 2a(1)^{\frac{1}{2}} + 5(1)\right) = \frac{301}{2}$$

$$128 + 4a + 20 - \frac{1}{2} - 2a - 5 = \frac{301}{2}$$

$$2a = 8$$

$$a = 4$$

222

202. Answer: F

$$\int_{-1}^{1} (x^3 - ax^{-3})\, dx$$

$$\left[\frac{1}{4}x^4 + \frac{1}{2}ax^{-2}\right]_{-1}^{1}$$

$$\frac{1}{4} + \frac{1}{2}a - \frac{1}{4} - \frac{1}{2}a$$

$$= 0$$

Therefore, as there is no a term in the final answer, the minimum value is 0 for all real values of a.

203. Answer: C

$$\int_{-2}^{4} (4x - 2b^2)\, dx$$

$$[2x^2 - 2b^2 x]_{-2}^{4}$$

$$32 - 8b^2 - (8 + 4b^2)$$

$$24 - 12b^2$$

To find the maximum value of $24 - 12b^2$, we can differentiate it and equate the first derivative to 0

$$-24b = 0$$

$$b = 0$$

To check the answer, we can find the second derivative, which is -24, as $-24 < 0$, this value is shown to be the maximum possible value.

$\therefore$, the maximum value occurs when $b = 0$.

204. Answer: F

$$\int_{-2}^{2} (2x - 3)\, dx - \int_{-2}^{2} (x + 1)^2\, dx$$

$$[x^2 - 3x]_{-2}^{2} - \int_{-2}^{2} x^2 + 2x + 1\, dx$$

$$[x^2 - 3x]_{-2}^{2} - \left[\frac{1}{3}x^3 + x^2 + x\right]_{-2}^{2}$$

$$4 - 6 - (4 + 6) - \left[\frac{8}{3} + 4 + 2 - \left(-\frac{8}{3} + 4 - 2\right)\right]$$

$$-12 - \left(\frac{26}{3} + \frac{2}{3}\right) = -\frac{64}{3}$$

205. Answer: B

$$\int_0^2 x^2 + 3x + 4\ dx$$

$$\left[\frac{1}{3}x^3 + \frac{3}{2}x^2 + 4x\right]_0^2$$

$$\frac{8}{3} + 6 + 8 - 0 - 0 - 0$$

$$= \frac{50}{3}$$

206. Answer: E

First, we need to find the meeting points of the two curves.

$$x^2 = 4x$$

$$x^2 - 4x = 0$$

$$x(x - 4) = 0$$

$x = 0$ or $x = 4$

By considering the shapes of the curves, we know the curve $y = 4x$ is above the curve $y = x^2$ in the range $x = 0$ to $x = 4$.

$\therefore$, we integrate:

$$\int_0^4 4x - x^2 dx$$

$$\left[2x^2 - \frac{1}{3}x^3\right]_0^4$$

$$32 - \frac{64}{3} - 0 + 0$$

$$= \frac{32}{3}$$

207. Answer: B

$$\int_1^a \frac{1}{2}x - \frac{1}{2}\, dx = \frac{49}{4}$$

$$\left[\frac{1}{4}x^2 - \frac{1}{2}x\right]_1^a = \frac{49}{4}$$

$$\frac{1}{4}a^2 - \frac{1}{2}a - \frac{1}{4} + \frac{1}{2} = \frac{49}{4}$$

$$\frac{1}{4}a^2 - \frac{1}{2}a - 12 = 0$$

$$a^2 - 2a - 48 = 0$$

$$(a - 8)(a + 6) = 0$$

$a = 8$ or $a = -6$

$a > 1$ as the bounds of the integral have the larger number as the upper bound.

Therefore, $a = 8$.

208. Answer: H

$$\int_1^5 x^2 + 3x + 10\, dx - \int_3^5 x^2 + 3x + 10\, dx$$

As they are both integrating the same function, and the ranges are continuous, we can subtract the integrals and solve a simpler integral:

$$\int_1^3 x^2 + 3x + 10\, dx$$

$$\left[\frac{1}{3}x^3 + \frac{3}{2}x^2 + 10x\right]_1^3$$

$$9 + \frac{27}{2} + 30 - \frac{1}{3} - \frac{3}{2} - 10$$

$$= \frac{122}{3}$$

209. Answer: A

The area of the shaded region is equal to the area of the triangle, plus the area of the "dip" below the x axis.

We need to find the height of the triangle, by finding the y coordinate of the intersection point between the curves.

$$x^2 - 1 = 2 - 2x$$

$$x^2 + 2x - 3 = 0$$

$x = 1$ or $x = -3$

When $x = -3$, $y = 8$

The area of the triangle is equal to $\frac{1}{2} \times base \times height$

$$\frac{1}{2} \times 4 \times 8$$

$$16$$

Secondly, we need to find the area of the "dip" of the curve $(x^2 - 1)$ below the axis. This is the same as the area between the line $y = 0$ and $y = x^2 - 1$. The bounds are between the roots of $y = x^2 - 1$, which are -1 and 1.

$$\int_{-1}^{1} 0 - (x^2 - 1)\, dx$$

$$\int_{-1}^{1} -(x^2 + 1)\, dx$$

$$\left[-\frac{1}{3}x^3 + x \right]_{-1}^{1}$$

$$-\frac{1}{3} + 1 - \frac{1}{3} + 1$$

$$= \frac{4}{3}$$

Therefore, the sum of both the areas is:

$$16 + \frac{4}{3} = \frac{52}{3}$$

Notice that, in the answers:

$$15 + \frac{7}{3} = 16 + \frac{4}{3} = \frac{52}{3}$$

210. Answer: A

$$\int_1^4 (4x - Z)\,dx = Z^2 - 2Z$$

$$[2x^2 - Zx]_1^4 = Z^2 - 2Z$$

$$32 - 4Z - 2 + Z = Z^2 - 2Z$$

$$Z^2 + Z - 30 = 0$$

$$(Z + 6)(Z - 5) = 0$$

$Z = 5$ or $Z = -6$

211. Answer: C

$$\int_1^k \frac{1}{\sqrt{x}}\,dx = 4$$

$$\int_1^k x^{-\frac{1}{2}}\,dx = 4$$

$$\left[2x^{\frac{1}{2}}\right]_1^k = 4$$

$$2k^{\frac{1}{2}} - 2 = 4$$

$$k^{\frac{1}{2}} = 3$$

$$k = 9$$

212. Answer: A

The function of the line is the integral of the gradient function.

$$\int x^2 + 12\,dx$$

$$\frac{1}{3}x^3 + 12x + c$$

The graph passes through the point $(3,28)$

$$\frac{1}{3}(3)^3 + 12(3) + c = 28$$

$$c = -17$$

$$y = \frac{1}{3}x^3 + 12x - 17$$

213. Answer: D

As the curve $y = 0.5x^2 + 8$, has been shifted 8 units upwards relative to $y = x^2$, we know that the area enclosed is underneath $y = 0.5x^2 + 8$ and above $y = x^2$.

We need to find the bounds to integrate between, which is the points of intersection between the two curves.

$$0.5x^2 + 8 = x^2$$

$$0.5x^2 = 8$$

$$x^2 = 16$$

$$x = \pm 4$$

$$\therefore \int_{-4}^{4} 0.5x^2 + 8 - x^2 \, dx$$

$$\int_{-4}^{4} -0.5x^2 + 8 \, dx$$

$$\left[-\frac{1}{6}x^3 + 8x \right]_{-4}^{4}$$

$$-\frac{4^3}{6} + 32 + \frac{(-4)^3}{6} + 32$$

$$= \frac{128}{3}$$

214. Answer: C

$$\int_{-1}^{1} (x)^5 \, dx$$

$$\left[\frac{1}{6}x^6 \right]_{-1}^{1}$$

$$\frac{1}{6} - \left(\frac{1}{6} \right)$$

$$= 0$$

215. Answer: F

The final term in the expression given is $\frac{3}{x^3}$. When $x = 0$, this term is undefined, as $\frac{3}{0}$ is undefined. The bounds of the integral are $-2 \; to \; 2$, hence $x = 0$ lies within the bounds. When integrated there are values for x which are undefined so the area "underneath" the curve at this point is incalculable.

This means that the answer is not possible to calculate given the information.

216. Answer: A

$$\frac{dy}{dx} = \frac{6x^2 + 3x^{\frac{1}{2}}}{x^{\frac{1}{2}}}$$

The equation of the original is the integral of the equation above.

$$\int \frac{6x^2 + 3x^{\frac{1}{2}}}{x^{\frac{1}{2}}} \, dx$$

$$\int 6x^{\frac{3}{2}} + 3 \, dx$$

$$\frac{12}{5}x^{\frac{5}{2}} + 3x + c$$

When $x = 4, y = 88.8$

$$\frac{12}{5}(4)^{\frac{5}{2}} + 3(4) + c = 88.8$$

$$c = 88.8 - 12 - \frac{384}{5}$$

$$c = 88.8 - 12 - 76.8$$

$$c = 0$$

$$y = \frac{12}{5}x^{\frac{5}{2}} + 3x$$

217. Answer: D

As both the upper and lower bounds are 1, both expressions will cancel out. Therefore, the solution for the integral is 0.

218. Answer: E

$$f(x) = (1 + x)^4 = x^4 + 4x^3 + 6x^2 + 4x + 1$$

$$\int_0^2 x^4 + 4x^3 + 6x^2 + 4x + 1 \, dx$$

$$\left[\frac{1}{5}x^5 + x^4 + 2x^3 + 2x^2 + x \right]_0^2$$

$$\frac{1}{5}(2)^5 + 2^4 + 2(2^3) + 2(2^2) + 2 - 0$$

$$= \frac{32}{5} + 16 + 16 + 8 + 2$$

$$= \frac{242}{5}$$

219. Answer: A

$$\int_b^5 \left(\frac{2}{\sqrt{x}}\right) dx = 4\sqrt{5} - 4$$

$$\int_b^5 \left(2x^{-\frac{1}{2}}\right) dx = 4\sqrt{5} - 4$$

$$\left[4x^{\frac{1}{2}}\right]_b^5 = 4\sqrt{5} - 4$$

$$4\sqrt{5} - 4\sqrt{b} = 4\sqrt{5} - 4$$

$$4\sqrt{b} = 4$$

$$b = 1$$

220. Answer: B

The negative quadratic $-x^2 - 4x$ is above the curve $x^2 + 4x$ between their points of intersection.

To find the area between them, we need to find their points of intersection.

$$-x^2 - 4x = x^2 + 4x$$

$$2x^2 + 8x = 0$$

$$2x(x + 4) = 0$$

$$x = 0 \ or \ x = -4$$

Therefore, the area bounded between the curves is,

$$\int_{-4}^0 -x^2 - 4x - x^2 - 4x \ dx$$

$$\int_{-4}^0 -2x^2 - 8x \ dx$$

$$\left[-\frac{2}{3}x^3 - 4x^2\right]_{-4}^0$$

$$0 - (-\frac{2}{3}(-4)^3 - 4(-4)^2)$$

$$-\frac{128}{3} + 64$$

$$= \frac{64}{3}$$

230

221. Answer: E

$$\int_1^2 (px^3 + qx^2)dx = \frac{29}{2}$$

$$\left[\frac{p}{4}x^4 + \frac{q}{3}x^3\right]_1^2 = \frac{29}{2}$$

$$\frac{p}{4}(2^4) + \frac{q}{3}(2)^3 - \frac{p}{4} - \frac{q}{3} = \frac{29}{2}$$

$$4p + \frac{8}{3}q - \frac{p}{4} - \frac{q}{3} = \frac{29}{2}$$

$$\frac{15}{4}p + \frac{7}{3}q = \frac{29}{2}$$

$$\int_{-1}^1 (qx^2 - px)dx = 2$$

$$\left[\frac{q}{3}x^3 - \frac{p}{2}x^2\right]_{-1}^1 = 2$$

$$\frac{q}{3} - \frac{p}{2} + \frac{q}{3} + \frac{p}{2} = 2$$

$$\frac{2q}{3} = 2$$

$$q = 3$$

$$\frac{15}{4}p + 7 = \frac{29}{2}$$

$$\frac{15}{4}p = \frac{15}{2}$$

$$p = 2$$

Therefore, $p = 2$ and $q = 3$

222. Answer: B

$$\int_1^2 (2x^2 + B)dx = -B^2 + \frac{32}{3}$$

$$\left[\frac{2}{3}x^3 + Bx\right]_1^2 = -B^2 + \frac{32}{3}$$

$$\frac{2}{3}(2)^3 + 2B - \frac{2}{3} - B = -B^2 + \frac{32}{3}$$

$$\frac{14}{3} + B = -B^2 + \frac{32}{3}$$

$$-B^2 - B + 6 = 0$$

$$(B + 3)(B - 2) = 0$$

$$B = -3 \text{ or } B = 2$$

223. Answer: B

As shown on the diagram in the question, between $x = 2$ and $x = 0$, the curve is above the x axis and the region bounded is under the curve and above the x axis. However, between $x = 0$ and $x = -2$, the curve is below the x axis and the region bounded is above the curve and under the x axis.

$$x(x+2)(2-x) = -x^3 + 4x$$

$$\int_0^2 -x^3 + 4x \, dx + \int_{-2}^0 0 - (-x^3 + 4x) \, dx$$

$$\left[-\frac{1}{4}x^4 + 2x^2 \right]_0^2 + \left[\frac{1}{4}x^4 - 2x^2 \right]_{-2}^0$$

$$\left(-\frac{1}{4}(2)^4 + 2(4) - 0 \right) + \left(0 - \left(\frac{1}{4}(-2)^4 - 2(4) \right) \right)$$

$$-4 + 8 - 4 + 8$$

$$= 8$$

224. Answer: A

$$\int_1^2 (x^2 + 5 + x^{-2}) \, dx$$

$$\left[\frac{1}{3}x^3 + 5x - \frac{1}{x} \right]_1^2$$

$$\frac{8}{3} + 10 - \frac{1}{2} - \frac{1}{3} - 5 + 1$$

$$= \frac{47}{6}$$

225. Answer: E

$$\int_{-5}^{-1} (x+4) + \int_{-1}^{-2} (x+4)$$

$$\left[\frac{1}{2}x^2 + 4x \right]_{-5}^{-1} + \left[\frac{1}{2}x^2 + 4x \right]_{-1}^{-2}$$

$$\left(\frac{1}{2} - 4 - \left(\frac{1}{2}(25) - 20 \right) \right) + \left(\frac{1}{2}(4) - 8 - \left(\frac{1}{2}(1) - 4 \right) \right)$$

$$4 - \frac{5}{2}$$

$$= \frac{3}{2}$$

226. Answer: A

$$f(x) = \frac{x^3 + x^2 - 10x + 8}{x - 2}$$

Using polynomial long division, or comparing of coefficients, we find that

$$x^3 + x^2 - 10x + 8 = (x - 1)(x + 4)(x - 2)$$

Therefore,

$$f(x) = (x - 1)(x + 4) = x^2 + 3x - 4$$

$f(x + 1)$, shifts the curve $f(x)$ 1 unit to the left.

The minimum point of $f(x)$ is found by completing the square:

$$\left(x + \frac{3}{2}\right)^2 - \frac{9}{4} - 4$$

$$\left(x + \frac{3}{2}\right)^2 - \frac{25}{4}$$

Therefore, the minimum of $f(x) = (-\frac{3}{2}, -\frac{25}{4})$

When shifted one unit to the left, this becomes:

$$(-2.5, -6.25)$$

227. Answer: B

The asymptotes of $\frac{1}{x+5}$, are at $x = -5$ and $y = 0$, as the function $\frac{1}{x}$ with asymptotes at $x = 0$ and $y = 0$ is shifted 5 units to the left.

The asymptotes of $\frac{1}{x+5} + 5$, are at $x = -5$ and $y = 5$, as the function $\frac{1}{x+5}$ with asymptotes at $x = -5$ and $y = 0$ is shifted 5 units up.

Therefore, $x = -5$ and $y = 5$

228. Answer: A

Use the rule that, for the function $f(x)$, that undergoes the transformation $Af(Bx + C) + D$, then the order you perform the transformations is $CBAD$.

The roots of $f(x)$ are $0, 4 \ and -2$.

C is 2.5 and B is $\frac{1}{2}$

Therefore, apply C first, which is a shift of 2.5 units leftwards, and then apply B, hence which is a stretch scale factor $\frac{1}{\frac{1}{2}} = 2$ along the x axis.

Therefore,

$$0 \to -2.5 \to -5$$

$$4 \to 1.5 \to 3$$

$$-2 \to -4.5 \to -9$$

Therefore, the new roots are:

$$(-9,0), (-5,0), (3,0)$$

229. Answer: C

The asymptote of $\log(x)$ is at $x = 0$

Both the transformations $2f(x) + 10$, affect the y coordinate of every point on $f(x)$ (stretch scale factor 2 in the y axis and a vertical shift 10 units upwards), therefore, there is no effect on the asymptote, $x = 0$.

The asymptote of $2f(x) + 10$ is also at $x = 0$.

230. Answer: B

$$0.5(0.5x^4 - 3) + 3$$

This can be expanded to give:

$$0.25x^4 - \frac{3}{2} + 3$$

$$0.25x^4 + \frac{3}{2}$$

Therefore, there is a stretch of scale factor $\frac{1}{4}$ in the y axis and a shift of 1.5 units upwards.

231. Answer: A

$$f(x) = (x+1)^3 - 9(x+1)$$
$$f(x) = (x+1)((x+1)^2 - 9)$$
$$f(x) = (x+1)(x^2 + 2x + 1 - 9)$$
$$f(x) = (x+1)(x^2 + 2x - 8)$$
$$f(x) = (x+1)(x+4)(x-2)$$

Therefore, the roots are at $-1, -4$ and 2.

As $1 \times 4 \times -2 = -8$, when $x = 0$, $y = -8$.

The coefficient of x^3 is positive as $1 \times 1 \times 1 = 1$, which is positive. Therefore, the curve takes the shape of a positive cubic equation.

Using these three details we can determine the curve's shape.

232. Answer: E

The roots of $f(x)$ are $x = 0$ and $x = 8$

Use the rule that, for the function $f(x)$, that undergoes the transformation $Af(Bx + C) + D$, then the order you perform the transformations is $CBAD$.

C is 5 and B is $\frac{4}{3}$.

Therefore, we apply C first and then B. There is a shift 5 units to the left, and then a stretch of scale factor $\frac{3}{4}$ in the x axis.

$$0 \to -5 \to -\frac{15}{4}$$

$$8 \to 3 \to \frac{9}{4}$$

Therefore, the roots of $f\left(\frac{4}{3}x + 5\right)$ are:

$$\left(\frac{-15}{4}, 0\right) and \left(\frac{9}{4}, 0\right)$$

233. Answer: B

If the equation has the form $fee = flat\ fee + days \times daily\ rate$

Using the two pieces of information given:

$$1365 = a + 5b$$

$$1374 = a + 8b$$

Therefore,

$$3b = 9$$

$$b = 3$$

$$1365 = a + 15$$

$$a = 1350$$

Therefore,

$$C = 3x + 1350$$

234. Answer: E

$$\frac{7 - 10}{k} = -\frac{3}{7}$$

$$-3k = -21$$

$$k = 7$$

235. Answer: A

$$x^2 + bx + 4$$

Complete the square to find an expression for the minimum point:

$$\left(x + \frac{b}{2}\right)^2 - \frac{b^2}{4} + 4$$

Therefore, $-\frac{b}{2} = -1$

$$b = 2$$

236

236. Answer: C

$$x^2 + 2x + k$$

Complete the square to find an expression for the minimum point:

$$(x + 1)^2 - 1 + k$$

Therefore, $-1 + k = 6.25$

$$k = 7.25$$

237. Answer: A

If it passes through the origin, then when $x = 0$, $y = 0$.

Therefore,

$$0 = \frac{1}{(0 + a)^4} - 9$$

$$9 = \frac{1}{a^4}$$

$$a^4 = \frac{1}{9}$$

$$a^2 = \pm\frac{1}{3}$$

$$a = \pm\frac{1}{\sqrt{3}}$$

238. Answer: E

First you move it 3 units to the right, therefore, x^2 becomes $(x - 3)^2$. Then it is vertically stretched by scale factor -3, therefore $(x - 3)^2$ becomes $-3(x - 3)^2$.

Therefore, the correct transformation is: $-3(x - 3)^2$

239. Answer: B

If $f(x) = ax^2 + bx + c$, then $f'(x) = 2ax + b$

$2ax + b = 0$, when $x = -3$

Therefore, $-6a + b = 0$.

The exact coordinate for $f'(x) = 0$, is $(-3,15)$, which lies on the curve, therefore:

$$15 = 9a - 3b + c$$

It also passes through the point $(2,10)$, therefore:

$$10 = 4a + 2b + c$$

They can all be solved simultaneously:

1. $\quad -6a + b = 0$

2. $\quad 15 = 9a - 3b + c$

3. $\quad 10 = 4a + 2b + c$

The first equation shows that: $6a = b$

Input this into the second and third equations:

$$15 = 9a - 3(6a) + c$$
$$10 = 4a + 2(6a) + c$$

This simplifies to give:

$$15 = -9a + c$$
$$10 = 16a + c$$

Hence,

$$5 = -25a$$
$$a = -\frac{1}{5}$$
$$c = 15 + 9a$$
$$c = \frac{66}{5}$$
$$b = 6a \therefore b = -\frac{6}{5}$$

Therefore, the final equation is:

$$-\frac{1}{5}x^2 - \frac{6}{5}x + \frac{66}{5}$$

240. Answer: F

A function is increasing when the first derivative is greater than 0.

Therefore, $f'(x) > 0$

$$f(x) = \frac{x^3}{3} - \frac{5x^2}{2} + 6x$$

$$f'(x) = x^2 - 5x + 6$$

$$x^2 - 5x + 6 > 0$$

By using the curve of $x^2 - 5x + 6 = (x - 3)(x - 2) = 0$

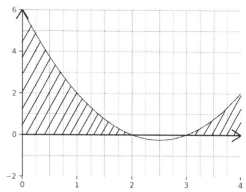

This shows that the area where the curve is greater than 0, is when $x < 2$ and $x > 3$.

241. Answer: A

$$f(x) = \frac{6}{x} + 2x - 41$$

A stationary point is when $f'(x) = 0$

$$f'(x) = -6x^{-2} + 2$$

$$-6x^{-2} + 2 = 0$$

$$\frac{6}{x^2} = 2$$

$$x^2 = 3$$

$$x = \pm\sqrt{3}$$

242. Answer: E

$$f(x) = \frac{x^4}{4} + \frac{2}{3}x^3 - \frac{x^2}{2} - 2x$$

A stationary point is when $f'(x) = 0$

$$f'(x) = x^3 + 2x^2 - x - 2$$

$$x^3 + 2x^2 - x - 2 = 0$$

If one root occurs at $x = -1$, this means that $(x + 1)$ is a factor of $x^3 + 2x^2 - x - 2$

Use polynomial long division or compare coefficient to divide the cubic $x^3 + 2x^2 - x - 2$ by the linear expression $(x + 1)$.

$$\frac{x^3 + 2x^2 - x - 2}{x + 1} = (x + 2)(x - 1)$$

Therefore, the three x coordinates of the stationary points are:

$$x = -1, x = -2 \text{ and } x = 1$$

243. Answer: A

A function is increasing when $f'(x) > 0$

$$f(x) = \frac{x^3}{3} + ax^2 - 6x$$

$$f'(x) = x^2 + 2ax - 6$$

The solution to $x^2 + 2ax - 6 > 0$ is $x > 2$ and $x < -3$.

For any positive quadratic, it is below the x axis between the two roots and above the x axis away from either root.

This suggests, that $x = 2$ and $x = -3$ are both roots of the equation $x^2 + 2ax - 6 = 0$

$$(x - 2)(x + 3) = x^2 + 2ax - 6$$

$$x^2 + x - 6 = x^2 + 2ax - 6$$

$$2a = 1$$

$$a = \frac{1}{2}$$

244. Answer: D

$$f(x) = ax^3 + bx^2 + cx + 5$$

$$f'(x) = 3ax^2 + 2bx + c$$

$f'(x) = 0$, when $x = 3$ and $x = -4$

$3ax^2 + 2bx + c = 0$, when $x = 3$ and $x = -4$

$$3a(9) + 2b(3) + c = 0$$

$$27a + 6b + c = 0$$

$$3a(16) + 2b(-4) + c = 0$$

$$48a - 8b + c = 0$$

$c = -12$, is given in the question

$$27a + 6b = 12$$

$$48a - 8b = 12$$

Solving these simultaneously, you find that:

$$a = \frac{1}{3}$$

$$b = \frac{1}{2}$$

245. Answer: B

If $f(x)$ passes through the point $(0,3)$, then $c = 3$

$$f(x) = ax^2 + bx + 3$$

$$f'(x) = 2ax + b$$

$2ax + b = 0$, when $x = -0.5 \therefore 2a(-0.5) + b = 0$

$$-a + b = 0$$

$$a = b$$

Also, $(-0.5, 2.25)$ lies on the curve, therefore:

$$a(-0.5)^2 - 0.5b + c = 2.25$$

$$0.25a - 0.5b + 3 = 2.25$$

$$a = b \therefore 0.25a - 0.5a + 3 = 2.25$$

$$a = 3$$

Therefore, $a = b = c = 3$

$$f(x) = 3x^2 + 3x + 3$$

246. Answer: C

The normal gradient is the negative reciprocal of the gradient of the tangent.

$$f(x) = x^2 + 2x$$

$$f'(x) = 2x + 2$$

When $x = 1$, $f'(x) = 4$

Therefore, the gradient of the normal is $-\frac{1}{4}$

The equation of the normal is $y = -\frac{1}{4}x + c$. It also passes through the point $(1,3)$

Therefore, $3 = -\frac{1}{4} + c$

$$c = \frac{13}{4}$$

$$y = -\frac{1}{4}x + \frac{13}{4}$$

It intersects the y axis when $x = 0$, therefore, at the point $\left(0, \frac{13}{4}\right)$

$$= (0, 3.25)$$

247. Answer: B

If $(x - 1)$ is a factor of $f(x)$, we can use polynomial long division or comparing coefficients to find the other roots.

$$\frac{x^3 + 3x^2 + 2x - 6}{x - 1} = x^2 + 4x + 6$$

Therefore,

$$f(x) = x^3 + 3x^2 + 2x - 6 = (x - 1)(x^2 + 4x + 6)$$

The discriminant of $x^2 + 4x + 6$, is $16 - 4(6) = -8$

$-8 < 0$, therefore, the quadratic has no real solutions.

This means that $f(x)$ only has one real root, at $x = 1$.

248. Answer: A

The tangent of $f(x)$ is found through the gradient function of $f(x)$

$$f(x) = x^2 + 3x + 5$$

$$f'(x) = 2x + 3$$

When $x = 0$, $f'(x) = 3$

Therefore, the tangent, which has form $y = mx + c$, is:

$$y = 3x + c$$

It passes through the point $(0,5)$.

$$c = 5$$

Therefore,

$$y = 3x + 5$$

This intersects the x axis when $y = 0$, $3x = -5$

$$x = -\frac{5}{3}$$

The coordinate is $\left(-\frac{5}{3}, 0\right)$

249. Answer: B

The point of intersection is found by equating both graphs.

$$e^x = 8e^{-x} - 2$$

$$e^{2x} = 8 - 2e^x$$

$$e^{2x} + 2e^x - 8 = 0$$

$$e^x = a$$

$$a^2 + 2a - 8 = 0$$

$$(a + 4)(a - 2) = 0$$

$$a = -4 \text{ or } a = 2$$

$e^x = -4$, which has no solutions as e^x is always greater than 0.

$$e^x = 2$$

$$x = \ln 2$$

When $x = \ln(2)$, $y = e^x = 2$

Therefore, the point of intersection is $(\ln(2), 2)$

250. Answer: C

$f(x)$ intersects the x axis when $f(x) = 0$

$$0 = \ln(x + 5) + \ln \left[(x - 2) + \frac{1}{x + 5}\right]$$

$$0 = \ln(x + 5) + \ln \left(\frac{((x - 2)(x + 5) + 1)}{x + 5}\right)$$

$$0 = \ln\big((x - 2)(x + 5) + 1\big)$$

$$0 = \ln (x^2 + 3x - 9)$$

$$e^0 = x^2 + 3x - 9$$

$$1 = x^2 + 3x - 9$$

$$x^2 + 3x - 10 = 0$$

$$(x + 5)(x - 2) = 0$$

$x = -5$ or $x = 2$

However, when $x = -5$, $\ln(x + 5) = \ln(0) = undefined$

Therefore, the only solution is $x = 2$.

The coordinate is $(2,0)$

251. Answer: G

All three rules are useful divisibility rules that you should learn. We included this question to introduce you to all three rules, which are all correct, and learning them will increase your mental maths speed greatly.

252. Answer: B

Without a calculator, the best way to solve this question is to try the solutions given, starting with A.

$$7^4 = 2401$$

$$14^4 = 38416$$

Therefore, without having to try any of the other numbers, we find that our answer is 14.

253. Answer: E

Without a calculator, the best way to solve this question is to try the solutions given, starting with A.

$$9^3 = 729$$

$$12^3 = 1728$$

We notice that we are still quite far away from 5832, therefore, we can skip a number and try 16.

$$16^3 = 4096$$

$$18^3 = 5832$$

Therefore, we find that our answer is 18.

254. Answer: E

We need to find the second- lowest common multiple of 3, 5 and 7.

As they are all prime numbers, there is no need to perform a prime factor decomposition, to find the LCM, which will therefore be $3 \times 5 \times 7$.

$$3 \times 5 \times 7 = 105$$

This is the first LCM; thus, the second LCM will be $105 \times 2 = 210$

255. Answer: D

To find the maximum length of cable that can remain unused, this must have meant he bought the maximum (upper) bound of wire and used the minimum (lower) bound of wire for each section of wiring.

The formula for the amount left over is:

$$Amount\ purchased - Amount\ used$$

The upper bound of 200m to the nearest metre is 200.5

The lower bound of 10m to the nearest half meter is 9.75

If he made 19 runs of wire, this means that the minimum length used is $19 \times 9.75 = 185.25$

$$200.5 - 185.25 = 15.25$$

256. Answer: C

The minimum number of small tanks needed must consider the "worst case scenario", where each tank has the minimum capacity and the large tank is filled to maximum capacity.

1000 litres to the nearest 100 litres is 1050 litres at the upper bound

110 litres to the nearest 10 litres is 105 litres at the lower bound.

Therefore, the minimum number of tanks needed is $\frac{1050}{105} = 10$

257. Answer: F

The maximum potential cost of distributing seeds will involve the maximum area of the field and the maximum cost of distributing seeds across the field.

The maximum length of the field is 45m, when rounding 40m to the nearest 10m. The maximum width of the field is 55m, when rounding 50m to the nearest 10m. Therefore, the maximum area possible is $55 \times 45 = 2475\text{m}^2$

The maximum cost per square metre is £25 when rounding £20 to the nearest ten pounds.

Therefore, the maximum cost for the whole field is $2475 \times £25 = £61875$

The minimum potential cost of distributing seeds will involve the minimum area of the field and the minimum cost of distributing seeds across the field.

The minimum length of the field is 35m, when rounding 40m to the nearest 10m. The minimum width of the field is 45m, when rounding 50m to the nearest 10m. Therefore, the minimum area possible is $45 \times 35 = 1575\text{m}^2$

The minimum cost per square metre is £15 when rounding £20 to the nearest ten pounds.

Therefore, the minimum cost for the whole field is $1575 \times £15 = £23625$

The difference between the maximum and minimum costs is $£61875 - £23625 = £38250$

258. Answer: E

If there is a total of n sweets to start, then A has $\frac{4}{11}n$ sweets and B has $\frac{7}{11}n$ sweets.

$\frac{4}{11}n - 6 + 2 : \frac{7}{11}n + 6 - 2$ is equivalent to $10 : 23$

$$\frac{\frac{4}{11}n - 4}{\frac{7}{11}n + 4} = \frac{10}{23}$$

$$\frac{92}{11}n - 92 = \frac{70}{11}n + 40$$

$$2n = 132$$

$$n = 66$$

$\frac{4}{11} \times 66 = 24$ sweets for A

$66 - 24 = 42$ sweets for B

Therefore, Person A = 24 & Person B = 42

246

259. Answer: A

$$a:b = 3:7 = \frac{3}{7}:1$$

$$b:c = 5:11 = 1:\frac{11}{5}$$

Therefore,

$$a:c = \frac{3}{7}:\frac{11}{5}$$

$$a:c = 15:77$$

$$c:a = 77:15$$

260. Answer: F

If there are n balls in the bag, that means that there are $\frac{2}{7}n$ red balls and $\frac{5}{7}n$ blue balls.

3 blue balls are removed, and 6 red balls are added, and the ratio of blue balls to red balls is

$(3x + 1):(4x + 2)$, *therefore, the ratio of red balls to blue balls is* $(4x + 2):(3x + 1)$

$$(\frac{2}{7}n + 6):(\frac{5}{7}n - 3) = (4x + 2):(3x + 1)$$

One possible solution, is where the ratios are exactly equal, therefore:

$$\frac{2}{7}n + 6 = 4x + 2$$

$$\frac{5}{7}n - 3 = 3x + 1$$

You can solve these simultaneously, to find that,

$n = 14$ and $x = 2$

Therefore, $x = 2$

261. Answer: C

$$x:y = 8:21 = \frac{8}{21}:1$$

$$y:z = 3:2 = 1:\frac{2}{3}$$

Therefore,

$$x:z = \frac{8}{21}:\frac{2}{3}$$

$$x:z = 24:42$$

$$x:z = 4:7$$

262. Answer: A

$$A = \frac{n^3 + n^2 + a}{n - a}$$

$$An - Aa = n^3 + n^2 + a$$

$$Aa + a = An - n^3 - n^2$$

$$a(A + 1) = n(A - n^2 - n)$$

$$a = \frac{n(A - n^2 - n)}{A + 1}$$

263. Answer: D

$$y = \sqrt[a]{\frac{2x + 1}{\sqrt{2w}}}$$

$$y^a = \frac{2x + 1}{\sqrt{2w}}$$

$$\sqrt{2w} = \frac{2x + 1}{y^a}$$

$$2w = \left(\frac{2x + 1}{y^a}\right)^2$$

$$w = \frac{\left(\frac{2x + 1}{y^a}\right)^2}{2}$$

264. Answer: B

$$C = 4\sqrt{\frac{2x}{\sqrt{2\sqrt{y}}}}$$

$$\frac{C}{4} = \sqrt{\frac{2x}{\sqrt{2\sqrt{y}}}}$$

$$\left(\frac{C}{4}\right)^2 = \frac{2x}{\sqrt{2\sqrt{y}}}$$

$$\frac{2x}{\frac{C^2}{16}} = \sqrt{2\sqrt{y}}$$

$$\frac{32x}{C^2} = \sqrt{2\sqrt{y}}$$

$$\left(\frac{32x}{C^2}\right)^2 = 2\sqrt{y}$$

$$\frac{1024x^2}{C^4} = 2\sqrt{y}$$

$$\frac{512x^2}{C^4} = \sqrt{y}$$

$$y = \frac{512^2 x^4}{C^8}$$

265. Answer: A

The graph of $y = \tan(2x)$ intersects the $x - axis$ at all values of x where x is a multiple of 90°.

If $x = 4410°$, tan $(2x)$ = tan(8820°) = tan (98(90)).

If $x = 4500°$, tan $(2x)$ = tan(9000°) = tan (100(90)).

The graph of $y = \tan(2x)$ has asymptotes at values of x where x is a multiple of 45°.

The point halfway between $x = 4410°$ & $x = 4500°$ is $x = 4455°$.

If $x = 4455°$, tan$(2x)$ = tan(8910) = tan (198(45)).

Therefore, the correct graph must have an asymptote at $x = 4455°$.

As the graph is $y = \tan(2x)$ and not $y = -\tan(2x)$, A is the correct option.

266. Answer: B

$\sin(30t)$ has a range between -1 and 1

$\sin(30t) + 4$ has a range between 3 and 5

This means that there are only two possible options which have a range shown between 3 and 5

For $\sin(t)$, the maximum point is when $t = 90$, therefore for $\sin(30t)$, the maximum point is when $t = \frac{90}{30} = 3$. Using this we can note that A is the correct curve, as the maximum point of 5 is at $x = 3$.

267. Answer: C

If you have a $\sin(x)$ and $\cos(x)$ graph on the same axis, you notice that they meet twice in 360 degrees.

The transformations of $\sin(15x) + 10$ and $\cos(15x) + 10$, has the same effect on both curves, shifting it up by 10 units and stretching it by scale factor $\frac{1}{15}$ in the x axis. If the curves meet twice in 360 degrees without being stretched horizontally, if there is a scale factor of $\frac{1}{15}$, this means that of $\sin(15x) + 10$ and $\cos(15x) + 10$ meet $2 \times 15 = 30$ times in 360 degrees.

However, the range of x is limited to between $0 \leq x \leq 24$. $\frac{360}{24} = 15$, therefore, our range is $\frac{1}{15}th$ the size of the full 360 degrees.

Thus, they meet $\frac{30}{15} = 2$ times in the specified range.

268. Answer: C

$$\frac{\frac{1}{b}}{\frac{1}{b} + 1} = b$$

$$\frac{1}{b} = b\left(\frac{1}{b} + 1\right)$$

$$\frac{1}{b} = 1 + b$$

$$1 = b + b^2$$

$$b^2 + b - 1 = 0$$

Using the quadratic formula:

$$x = \frac{-1 \pm \sqrt{1^2 - 4(1)(-1)}}{2(1)}$$

$$x = \frac{-1 \pm \sqrt{5}}{2}$$

269. Answer: C

Both halves of angle BAD are equal (rhombus properties):

$$5x + 3y = 25$$

Both halves of angle ADC are equal (rhombus properties):

$$20x + 5y = 65$$

Solve the equations simultaneously

$$20x + 12y = 100$$

$$20x + 5y = 65$$

$$7y = 35$$

$$y = 5$$

Therefore,

$$20x + 60 = 100$$

$$x = 2$$

Therefore, $x = 2$ and $y = 5$

270. Answer: A

The area scale factor between the similar triangles is $\frac{22.5}{10} = 2.25$

Therefore, the length scale factor between the similar triangles is $\sqrt{2.25} = 1.5$

$$\frac{x^2 - 4}{2(x - 2)} = 1.5$$

$$x^2 - 4 = 3x - 6$$

$$x^2 - 3x + 2 = 0$$

$$(x - 2)(x - 1) = 0$$

$x = 2$ or $x = 1$, however, when $x = 1$ the side length of A is $2(1 - 2) = -2$.

You cannot have a negative side length, therefore, $x = 2$ is the only solution.

271. Answer: A

If they are made from the same material, then their densities are both the same.

If the smaller statue is $\frac{3}{5}^{th}$ the height of the larger statue, then the length scale factor is $\frac{3}{5}$. Therefore, the volume scale factor is $\left(\frac{3}{5}\right)^3 = \frac{27}{125}$

For the large statue, if V is the volume of the larger sculpture, and D is the density of the larger sculpture (which is the same as the density of the smaller statue):

$$875 = V_{large} \times D$$

$$D = \frac{875}{V_{large}}$$

For the smaller statue, it has the same density D, therefore:

$$M_{small} = \frac{27}{125} V_{large} \times D$$

$$D = \frac{875}{V_{large}}$$

Therefore,

$$M_{small} = \frac{27}{125} V_{large} \times \frac{875}{V_{large}}$$

$$M_{small} = \frac{27}{125} \times 875$$

$$M_{small} = 189$$

272. Answer: E

The angle $(b + 18)$ is on a straight line, therefore, the other angle is $180 - (b + 18)$.

$2b$ and $180 - (b + 18)$ are both composite angles and therefore they sum to 180. This means that:

$$2b + 180 - b - 18 = 180$$

$$b = 18$$

The angles $2b$ and a are also on a straight line:

$$2b + a = 180$$

$$a + 36 = 180$$

$$a = 144$$

273. Answer: B

The sum of exterior angles is 360 degrees.

If there are n exterior angles, then $\left(\frac{n}{4} \times 24\right) + \left(\frac{n}{4} \times 32\right) + \left(\frac{n}{4} \times 12\right) + \left(\frac{n}{4} \times 4\right) = 360$

$$6n + 8n + 3n + n = 360$$

$$18n = 360$$

$$n = 20$$

274. Answer: A

The diagram suggests that this is a polygon with 10 sides, and the two parallel sides show that this must be true.

Therefore, as the sum of angles around a point is 360, this means that $10x = 360$.

$$x = 36$$

The triangles are all isosceles as it is a regular polygon.

$$y = \frac{180 - x}{2} = 72$$

Alternatively, using the formula for interior angles, $(n-2)180$, a 10-sided decagon has $8(180) = 1440$ degrees in total. As it is a regular polygon, each angle is $\frac{1440}{10} = 144$ degrees. Hence, $y = \frac{144}{2}$.

Overall, $x = 36$ and $y = 72$

$$x + y = 108$$

275. Answer: E

Composite angles add up to 180 degrees. Therefore, angle $ACE + CEF = 180$

$$102 + CEF = 180 \therefore CEF = 78$$

The angles in triangle DEF add up to 180 degrees. Therefore, angle EDF, is $180 - 50 - 78 = 52$

Secondly, opposite angles in a parallelogram are equal, therefore angle $AFE = 102$ degrees.

Thus, $AFD = 102 - 50 = 52$ degrees.

As the angles in a triangle add up to 180 degrees, this means that $ADF = 180 - 45 - 52 = 83$ degrees.

The angles on the straight line CDE add up to 180 degrees, and as BD bisects the angle CDA, this means angles $CDB = BDA = x$

$$CDB + BDA + ADF + EDF = 180$$

$$2x + 83 + 52 = 180$$

$$x = \frac{45}{2} = 22.5$$

$$CBD = 180 - 102 - 22.5 = 55.5$$

276. Answer: C

The triangle is isosceles, therefore, angle $GCD = CDG = 40$. As the angles in a triangle are equal to 180 degrees, angle $CGD = 180 - 80 = 100$.

The rule of composite angles means that in the parallelogram $DGEF$:

$$125 + DGF = 180$$

$$DGF = 55$$

The rule of composite angles means that in the parallelogram $ABCG$:

$$35 + AGC = 180$$

$$AGC = 145$$

The angles around the point G are equal to 360 degrees.

$$100 + 145 + 55 + x = 360$$

$$x = 60$$

277. Answer: B

If it is reflected in the line $y = 2$, the y coordinates of every point change. You find the vertical distance between the line $y = 2$ and the y coordinate of the point, then you double it and add it onto the coordinate. If it helps, visually sketch out the coordinate axis to reflect the points. After applying the first transformations the points become:

$$(3, -4) \rightarrow (3,8)$$

$$(1,0) \rightarrow (1,4)$$

$$(-2,0) \rightarrow (-2,4)$$

$$(-1, -4) \rightarrow (-1,8)$$

The translation by the vector, shifts every point one unit to the right, therefore, the final coordinates are:

$$(4,8)$$

$$(2,4)$$

$$(-1,4)$$

$$(0,8)$$

278. Answer: E

The point $(6,8)$ is one of the points on the triangle and it is also the point of rotation. Therefore, it remains unaffected by the rotation. The other two points essentially are reflected in the line $y = 8$, as there is one fixed point which is also the centre of rotation of 180 degrees. 180 degrees is half a turn so the other two points flip upwards.

Therefore, the new points after rotation are: $(4,12)$ $(8,12)$ $(6,8)$

These points are then reflected in the y axis which means that the x coordinates need to be multiplied by -1.

These points are then reflected in the x axis which means that the y coordinates need to be multiplied by -1.

$$(-4, -12) \qquad (-8, -12) \qquad (-6, -8)$$

279. Answer: B

Using the alternate segment circle theorem, we find that the angle next to a, CGD is 40 degrees.

As GE is the diameter of the circle, it meets the tangent GZ at 90 degrees.

Therefore,

$$a + 40 = 90$$

$$a = 50$$

If O is the centre of the circle, then OF and OG are both radii and therefore equal. This makes OGF an isosceles triangle. We know the angle in the middle is 80 degrees, therefore angles OGF and OFG are both $\frac{180-80}{2} = 50$ degrees, as there are 180 degrees in a triangle.

The tangent and the radius meet at 90 degrees, therefore $b + 50 = 90$

$$b = 40$$

$$a = 50 \ and \ b = 40$$

280. Answer: A

The angle at the centre of the circle is twice the angle at the circumference, therefore, angle BOC is $2 \times 58 = 116$ degrees.

If we draw a line OA, we can split the shape into two smaller isosceles triangles (as they both have sides that are radii), OAB and OAC.

Angle $AOB = 180 - (2 \times 39)$, as angles $OBA \ and \ OAB$ are both 39 degrees as OA and OB are radii.

$AOB = 102$ degrees

This means that as the angles around the point O add upto 360,

$$116 + 102 + AOC = 360$$

$$AOC = 142$$

As the triangle AOC is isosceles, the angle a is equal to:

$$\frac{180 - 142}{2} = 19$$

$$a = 19$$

If we join the line BC, we form a cyclic quadrilateral $ABCD$.

Recall from earlier, that angle BOC was 116 degrees. Triangle BOC is also isosceles as both OB and OC are radii.

Therefore, angle $OBC = \frac{180-116}{2} = 32$

The angle in the cyclic quadrilateral, $CBA = 32 + 39 = 71$ degrees.

Opposite angles in a cyclic quadrilateral add up to 180 degrees.

$$b + 71 = 180$$

$b = 109$

281. Answer: D

Small shed: £1000

Large shed:

The ratio of the respective lengths is $2:1$, the ratio of the areas is $4:1$ and the ratio of the volumes is $8:1$.

Therefore, the cost of bricks (which is proportional to the volume) is 8 times the cost of bricks for the small shed.

$$£800 \times 8 = £6400$$

Secondly, the cost of paint (which is proportional to the surface area) is 4 times the cost of paint for the small shed.

$$£200 \times 4 = £800$$

Therefore, the cost of the large shed is $£6400 + £800 = £7200$

The cost of the large and small shed combined is $£7200 + £1000 = £8200$

282. Answer: A

$(1,0)$, when reflected in the line $y = x$ becomes $(0,1)$

$(4,0)$, when reflected in the line $y = x$ becomes $(0,4)$

$(6,5)$, when reflected in the line $y = x$ becomes $(5,6)$

$(9,5)$, when reflected in the line $y = x$ becomes $(5,9)$

The translation $\binom{-5}{5}$ moves each point 5 to the left and 5 up. We subtract 5 from the x coordinate and add 5 to the y coordinate.

$(0,1)$ under the translation $\binom{-5}{5}$ becomes $(-5,6)$

$(0,4)$ under the translation $\binom{-5}{5}$ becomes $(-5,9)$

$(5,6)$ under the translation $\binom{-5}{5}$ becomes $(0,11)$

$(5,9)$ under the translation $\binom{-5}{5}$ becomes $(0,14)$

Therefore, the coordinates become: $(-5,6), (-5,9), (0,11), (0,14)$

283. Answer: D

The sum of the exterior angles in any polygon is 360. There are 12 exterior angles as there are 12 sides to the polygon.

$$360 - (12 \times 2) - (6 \times 4) = 312$$

The remaining 6 exterior angles sum to 312, and they are all the same

Therefore, their size is:

$$\frac{312}{6} = 52$$

284. Answer: D

When you multiply the terms of one sequence by the terms of a second sequence, the nth term of the sequence formed, is found by finding the product of the two n^{th} terms of the sequences used.

In other words, n^{th} term $S_3 = n^{th}$ term $S_1 \times n^{th}$ term S_2

n^{th} term S_1: $an^2 + bn + c$

Sequence: $10, 19, 32, 49, 70$

First difference: $9, 13, 17, 21$

Second difference: $4, 4, 4, 4$

a is half the second difference, which is $\frac{4}{2} = 2$

c is the 0th term which is $10 - 5 = 5$

Therefore, our n^{th} term is: $2n^2 + bn + 5$

When $n = 1$, $2 + b + 5 = 10$

$$b = 3$$

Therefore, our n^{th} term is $2n^2 + 3n + 5$

n^{th} term S_2: $an^2 + bn + c$

Sequence: $6, 7, 10, 15, 22$

First difference: $1, 3, 5, 7$

Second difference: $2, 2, 2, 2$

a is half the second difference, which is $\frac{2}{2} = 1$

c is the 0th term which is $6 - (-1) = 7$

Therefore, our n^{th} term is: $n^2 + bn + 7$

When $n = 1$, $1 + b + 7 = 6$

$$b = -2$$

Therefore, our n^{th} term is $n^2 - 2n + 7$

The nth term of S_3 is the product of our two n^{th} terms found:

$$(n^2 - 2n + 7)(2n^2 + 3n + 5) = 2n^4 - n^3 + 13n^2 + 11n + 35$$

285. Answer: C

n^{th} term in the form $an^2 + bn + c$

Sequence: $8, 8, 10, 14, 20$

First difference: $0, 2, 4, 6$

Second difference: $2, 2, 2, 2$

a is half the second difference, which is $\frac{2}{2} = 1$

c is the 0th term which is $8 - (-2) = 10$

Therefore, our n^{th} term is: $n^2 + bn + 10$

When $n = 1$, $1 + b + 10 = 8$

$$b = -3$$

Therefore, our n^{th} term is $n^2 - 3n + 10$

286. Answer: B

a is half the second difference, which is 1.

c is the 0th term which is 10.

Therefore, the nth term is in the form:

$$n^2 + bn + 10$$

Only the second options ii can fit this format, in the case where $b = -15.5$. For i and iii, $a = 2$, which is not true.

287. Answer: D

When you divide the terms of one sequence by the terms of a second sequence, the nth term of the sequence formed, is found by finding the division of the two n^{th} terms of the sequences used.

n^{th} term in the form $an^2 + bn + c$

Sequence: $24, 56, 100, 156, 224$

First difference: $32, 44, 56, 68$

Second difference: $12, 12, 12, 12$

a is half the second difference, which is $\frac{12}{2} = 6$

c is the 0th term which is $24 - 20 = 4$

Therefore, our n^{th} term is: $6n^2 + bn + 4$

When $n = 1, 6 + b + 4 = 24$

$$b = 14$$

Therefore, our n^{th} term is $6n^2 + 14n + 4$

The linear sequence has the nth term $2n + 4$

As we are dividing the terms between both sequences, we must divide the nth terms to find the nth term of the new sequence.

$$\frac{6n^2 + 14n + 4}{2n + 4} = 3n + 1$$

This can be found through either polynomial long division, or factorising $6n^2 + 14n + 4$, which gives $(2n + 4)(3n + 1)$.

Therefore, the nth term of $S_3 = 3n + 1$

288. Answer: F

$$3(n + 1)^2 + 6(n + 1) + 2 - (3n^2 + 6n + 2) = 57$$
$$3(n^2 + 2n + 1) + 6n + 6 + 2 - 3n^2 - 6n - 2 = 57$$
$$3n^2 + 6n + 3 + 6n + 6 + 2 - 3n^2 - 6n - 2 = 57$$
$$6n = 48$$
$$n = 8$$
$$n + 1 = 9$$

Therefore, terms 8 and 9.

289. Answer: A

If the ratio of the lengths is $4:2$, this means that the ratio of the area is $16:4$ and the ratio of the volume is $64:8$

As the cost of painting the dumbbells is proportional to the surface area, and that the cost of paint is £2 for the 5kg dumbbell, using the ratio $16:4$, it Is £8 for the large dumbbell.

As the cost of raw materials is proportional to the volume, and that the cost of raw materials is £5 for the 5kg dumbbell, using the ratio $64:8$, it Is £$\frac{64}{8} \times 5 = £40$ for the large dumbbell.

The difference in the cost of manufacturing is:

$$£40 + £8 - £5 - £2 = £41$$

290. Answer: A

A frustrum involves a large cone, that has the top part of it chopped off. The top part is henceforth called "smaller cone".

The ratio of the radii of the larger cone (30) to the smaller cone (20) is $\frac{30}{20} = 1.5$

Let x be the height of the smaller cone on top that is "chopped off".

The height of the larger cone is $12 + x$

The ratio: $\frac{12+x}{x} = \frac{3}{2}$

$$3x = 24 + 2x$$

$$x = 24$$

Therefore, the height of the smaller cone on top that is chopped off is $24cm$.

The height of the overall cone that the frustrum is from is: $24 + 12 = 36cm$

291. Answer: B

Use the rule for the subtraction of vectors:

1. $y - 4x = 6$

2. $y - 2x^2 - 3x = 5$

Equation 1 rearranges to give

$$y = 4x + 6$$

Equation 2 rearranges to give

$$y = 2x^2 + 3x + 5$$

You can equate equation 1 and 2:

$$4x + 6 = 2x^2 + 3x + 5$$

$$2x^2 - x - 1 = 0$$

This factorises to give:

$$(x - 1)(2x + 1)$$

Therefore,

$$x = 1$$

$$x = -\frac{1}{2}$$

$$y = 4x + 6$$

When $x = 1$, $y = 10$

When $x = -\frac{1}{2}$, $y = 4$

292. Answer: E

Use the rule for the addition of vectors:

$$2x + 2y - 2z = 8$$

$$x - 2y + 3z = -6$$

$$2x + 3y + z = 7$$

Subtract equation three from equation one:

$$-y - 3z = 1$$

$$y = -3z - 1$$

Equation two can be multiplied by 2, to give:

$$2x - 4y + 6z = -12$$

Subtract the new expression for equation two from equation one:

$$6y - 8z = 20$$

Solve the following two equations simultaneously:

$$6y - 8z = 20$$

$$y = -3z - 1$$

$$6(-3z - 1) - 8z = 20$$

$$-18z - 6 - 8z = 20$$

$$-26z = 26$$

$$z = -1$$

We already found the equation: $y = -3z - 1$

$$y = 3 - 1 = 2$$

We already found the equation: $2x + 3y + z = 7$

$$2x + 6 - 1 = 7$$

$$2x = 2$$

$$x = 1$$

$$x = 1, y = 2, z = -1$$

293. Answer: C

Number of shoes	Frequency	xf
1	4	4
2	x	$2x$
3	6	18
4	y	$4y$
5	10	50
Total	$20 + x + y$	$72 + 2x + 4y$

The formula for the mean is $\frac{\Sigma xf}{n}$

The mean of the students with $1 - 4$ pairs of shoes (inclusive) is 3:

$$\frac{4 + 2x + 18 + 4y}{4 + x + 6 + y} = 3$$

$$\frac{22 + 2x + 4y}{10 + x + y} = 3$$

$$22 + 2x + 4y = 30 + 3x + 3y$$

$$x - y = -8$$

The mean of the students with $2 - 5$ pairs of shoes (inclusive) is 4:

$$\frac{2x + 18 + 4y + 50}{10 + 6 + x + y} = 4$$

$$\frac{2x + 4y + 68}{16 + x + y} = 4$$

$$2x + 4y + 68 = 64 + 4x + 4y$$

$$2x = 4$$

$$x = 2$$

Equation 1 tells us that:

$$y = x + 8$$

$$y = 10$$

Therefore,

$$x = 2 \ and \ y = 10$$

294. Answer: F

The question asks for the number of students who like both red **and** yellow. No information in the question will tell us the split between students who like red only, yellow only or red and yellow both. The question also does not state anywhere that each student can only like one colour.

There is insufficient information to answer this question.

295. Answer: B

The formulae to consider for a histogram:

Assuming that the total area is equal to the total frequency, then:

$$frequency = frequency\ density \times class\ width$$

$$42 = 10 \times x$$

$$x = 4.2$$

Therefore, going 7 units up in the y axis gives a value of 4.2, which means that one unit up is 0.6.

For a height above 195, the class width is 10 and the height is 0.6, which means the frequency is:

$$0.6 \times 10 = 6$$

296. Answer: C

Height	Frequency
$10 < h \leq 20$	8
$20 < h \leq 30$	22
$30 < h \leq 40$	52
$40 < h \leq 50$	118
$50 < h \leq 60$	152
$60 < h \leq 70$	160
Total	512

Using all the information given, the table above is derived.

We can now spot that 3 categories have frequencies between 30 and 155.

297. Answer: A

As the radius is $4cm$, $BD = 8$

The area of a single sector is found using the formula (in radians)

$$\frac{1}{2}r^2\theta = \frac{1}{2}(4)^2\left(\frac{\pi}{2}\right) = 4\pi$$

The area of any of the triangles, for example, OBC is found using the formula:

$$\frac{1}{2}absin(c)$$

$$\frac{1}{2}(4)(4)sin\left(\frac{\pi}{2}\right)$$

$$8$$

The area of one black segment is $4\pi - 8$

The area of the whole shaded section is $3(4\pi - 8) = 12\pi - 24$

264

298. Answer: C

The area of the sector OBC is found using the formula (use it in radians):

$$area = \frac{1}{2}r^2\theta$$

$$= \frac{1}{2}(8)^2\left(\frac{\pi}{3}\right)$$

$$= \frac{32}{3}\pi$$

The area of the triangle, OAD is found using the formula (use it in radians): $\frac{1}{2}absin(c) = \frac{1}{2}(4)(4)\sin\left(\frac{\pi}{3}\right)$

$\sin\left(\frac{\pi}{3}\right) = \frac{\sqrt{3}}{2}$, which is a value that you need to know.

$$= 8 \times \frac{\sqrt{3}}{2}$$

$$= 4\sqrt{3}$$

The area of the shaded section, is the area of the sector minus the area of the triangle:

$$\frac{32}{3}\pi - 4\sqrt{3}$$

299. Answer: B

$OC = OB$ as they are both radii of the circle sector.

Therefore, $OA = \frac{1}{3}(12) = 4$ and $OB = \frac{2}{3}(12) = 8$

The area of the shaded region is equal to the area of the circle sector minus the area of the triangle OAC.

The area of the sector is OBC is found using the formula (use it in radians):

$$area = \frac{1}{2}r^2\theta$$

$$= \frac{1}{2}(12)^2(\frac{\pi}{4}) = 18\pi$$

The area of the triangle, OAC is found using the formula (use it in radians):

$$\frac{1}{2}absin(c)$$

$$= \frac{1}{2}(4)(12)\sin\left(\frac{\pi}{4}\right)$$

$$= 24 \times \frac{\sqrt{2}}{2} = 12\sqrt{2}$$

The area of the shaded section, is the area of the sector minus the area of the triangle:

$18\pi - 12\sqrt{2}$

300. Answer: F

We can split the area into two section through the line BG. We can call the shaded area to the left of the line BG (closer to A) x and the shaded area to the right of the line BG (closer to H), y.

The area of x is equal to the area of the circle sector BHG minus the area of the triangle BHG.

$BC = 4$ and $CH = 3$. Use Pythagoras theorem to find BH:

$$BC^2 + CH^2 = BH^2$$

$$BH = \sqrt{4^2 + 3^2}$$

$$BH = 5$$

The area of the sector, where the radius is $BH = GH = 5$, is found using the formula (use it in radians):

$$area = \frac{1}{2}r^2\theta$$

$$= \frac{1}{2}(5)^2\left(\frac{\pi}{3}\right)$$

$$= \frac{25}{6}\pi$$

The area of the triangle, GHB is found using the formula (use it in radians):

$$\frac{1}{2}ab\sin(c)$$

$$= \frac{1}{2}(5)(5)\sin\left(\frac{\pi}{3}\right)$$

$\sin\left(\frac{\pi}{3}\right) = \frac{\sqrt{3}}{2}$, which is a value that you need to know.

$$= \frac{25}{2} \times \frac{\sqrt{3}}{2}$$

$$\frac{25\sqrt{3}}{4}$$

Therefore, $x = \frac{25}{6}\pi - \frac{25\sqrt{3}}{4}$

The area of y is equal to the area of the circle sector ABG minus the area of the triangle ABG.

The area of the sector, where the radius is $AB = AG = 6$, is found using the formula (use it in radians):

$$area = \frac{1}{2}r^2\theta$$

$$= \frac{1}{2}(6)^2\left(\frac{2\pi}{3}\right)$$

$$= 12\pi$$

The area of the triangle, ABG is found using the formula (use it in radians):

$$\frac{1}{2}ab\sin(c)$$

266

$$= \frac{1}{2}(6)(6)\sin\left(\frac{2\pi}{3}\right)$$

$\sin\left(\frac{2\pi}{3}\right) = \frac{\sqrt{3}}{2}$, which is a value that you need to know.

$$= 18 \times \frac{\sqrt{3}}{2}$$

$$9\sqrt{3}$$

Therefore, $y = 12\pi - 9\sqrt{3}$

$$x + y = \frac{25}{6}\pi - \frac{25\sqrt{3}}{4} + 12\pi - 9\sqrt{3}$$

$$x + y = \frac{97}{6}\pi - \frac{61}{4}\sqrt{3}$$

The Essay Section

ECAA Essay Guide

20 Extracts

20 Essay Questions

The ECAA Essay

How do you read the question?

The question will ask you to demonstrate that you have immersed yourself within the extract and that you have conducted some level of thinking by yourself, perhaps building from your current knowledge of world affairs or economics.

A mistake many candidates make is straying from the question. If the extract is discussing free trade, and the question is about the exploration of trade barriers, you should focus on trade barriers not components of free trade. This is especially important as you read your extract, think about how the extract ties into the question, not the other way around. Using what the extract gives you and your knowledge answer the question, the common mistake here is using your knowledge on the extract's topic rather than the question topic, be aware that there may be a distinction between the two. Overall, ensure you are answering the question and do not wind up following a garden of forking paths and ending up thoroughly lost.

Where do you start?

Even the ablest and learned candidate may be intimidated by an extract, particularly the original works of famous economists such as Adam Smith and David Ricardo whose work may not be as accessible. A writer's block may develop such that you are stumped as to what to write and given the 60-minute time frame you simply cannot waste any time. The process of academic writing involves a series of manageable steps, which you can use if you find yourself clueless.

  a. Identify the topic
  b. Break down the extract, use the question to help guide your thinking.
  c. Enter the conversation, with the aim to frame your thinking for the reader
  d. Explore the topic from the viewpoint which you most agree with
  e. Explore the other side of the topic, the counterargument
  f. Evaluate the counterargument and present your viewpoint as the stronger thesis

How should you break down an extract?

Close reading is where you thoroughly analyse and interpret a short extract, essentially what you should aim to do with the ECAA essay extract. How to close read:

  1. Read with a pencil in hand and mark the text.
     - Underline or highlight keywords and phrases which strike you as surprising, significant, or that raise questions based on the question given.
  2. Take notes
     - Use the margins and surrounding free area in the paper as you go along, this not only helps develop a deeper understanding of the text but also keeps information accessible.
  3. Plan
     - Using the annotations and notes you have made, as well as incorporating your knowledge start informally structuring your essay while close reading.

Planning the essay

The first step is to have a rough sense of what you will be arguing in the essay, so from your close reading notes, you should have a good idea of this. Your goal is to arrange your ideas, notes, and the overall raw material of your essay into a coherent guide for yourself, that too in the space of a few minutes at maximum. A general structure for an essay may include 2-4 points for and 2-4 points against with a short introduction, conclusion and/or evaluation.

What should an introduction include?

It should introduce the essay, more specifically the topic, your specific approach (especially for open-ended questions), and orient readers to locate them in your discussion. The entirety of your thinking will only emerge as the reader approaches the end of your essay, but indicate the direction in which you want to steer the reader, you should convince them of your arguments while also including detailed economic thinking.

How should I structure my paragraphs?

Each paragraph whether it is contributing to the argument or the counterargument should be signposted by a topic sentence, this provides clarity of understanding to the reader. You should use clear logical chains of analysis throughout your essay, it is essential to remember that the reader is looking at your thinking process and your application of the given material rather than anything else.

The counterargument structure is also essential, you should explore what are the flaws with your argument and you should not undermine the counterargument simply to further your argument. The counterargument consists of two stages, you turn against your argument to challenge it and then you turn back to your argument to re-affirm it, this can be done evaluatively or in the conclusion or within the same paragraph. Do not be flippant or dismissive of the counterargument instead explain with strong logical chains of analysis why and how your argument is superior.

Within each paragraph, you should set the stage, provide context, and provide evidence. There are two types of paragraph structure you can follow: the deductive and the inductive argumentative structures. The most common is deductive in which you start with an assertation or generalisation and then provide support. Alternatively, you can work within an inductive framework in which you provide facts and then present your argument. We generally recommend following the deductive structure as this is the most common in English prose and is the one most often seen within modern economic writing.

How should I structure my conclusions?

A conclusion should concisely recap the main points and reaffirm your position on the matter at hand. Many students find it helpful to introduce their assumptions for their thinking here, although this is entirely down to personal preference. A conclusion should be succinct and informative.

How is the essay marked?

The essay is graded by the individual admissions tutors at the respective college you applied for or (were assigned to in the case of an open application), they will mark the essay and from the range of marks a modified Rasch distribution would be used outputting values in the range of 1.0 to 9.0 with the average score being 4.0, generally stronger candidates receive higher scores but by no means is a bad essay the end of the line. Further ECAA information is found as part of our general ECAA guide.

There is no specific marking rubric which is released by the University of Cambridge, nor any of its constituent colleges. However, a good framework to use is the A-Level or IB HL economics grading rubrics. Overall they are looking for logical chains of analysis and to see how you go about tasks, they want to see how potential you have, rather than how much economics you have learnt.

General tips on Grammar and Punctuation

1. Commas and semi-colons

When you read your sentences, see where you natural pause, for a short pause a comma is likely necessary and for a longer pause a semi-colon would be necessary (given it is not a full stop length of pause quite yet). One key rule to remember is that on either side of a semi-colon there must a be a fully coherent sentence.

2. Always identify abbreviations

While there is an element of judgement to be employed here, the general rule is before introducing an abbreviation such as QE, IMF, EBRD etc. one should identify it in the following manner, 'Quantitative Easing (QE)'. The element of judgement comes into play when discussing items such as NATO or CEO, but if you are unsure opt for identification.

3. Avoid split infinitives

While this rule does not always hold, it should be used as a rule of thumb. An example is 'to not be' rather than 'to be not'.

4. Ensure referents are clear

Whenever the words 'this', 'that', 'they', 'it' etc. are used to ensure that it is evident to the reader of your essay what you are referring to. An essay which is clearer is easier to follow and easier to appreciate for its intricacy of thought.

5. Avoid the passive voice

Using the passive voice draws impact from your prose and leaves it relatively unsatisfying for a reader. It is better to say, 'The College's land' versus 'The land of the College'.

6. Try to avoid using repetitive sentence structure

Try to vary the length of your sentences, varying the rhythm to avoid a monotonous reading. If your prose is difficult to focus on reading it will not be beneficial.

7. Avoid clichés

This simply draws away from your focus of answering the question at hand, although at times cliché may be the aim when quoting directly from economists etc.

8. Avoid imprecise language

Imprecise language such as 'almost', 'could', 'maybe' should be avoided, they detract from the statement of your argument and only sow seeds of support for the counterargument of the point you are attempting to justify. You should address the counterargument but separately and should focus on each side of the argument one at a time.

9. Avoid words and phrases that are stilted, jargon or pompous

Justify your argument, the use of inappropriately elevated language is often referred to; this simply subtracts from your argument rather than adding.

10. Read through your essay

A point you have undoubtedly heard from educators throughout your strong academic careers, however, it is one of the utmost importance especially when the stakes are as high as that of the ECAA. Read through your essay correcting grammar, content, and any other mistakes you come across. We recommend leaving 3-4 minutes of your allocated time specifically for this.

Essay Questions

Essay Questions

This section has 20 practice essay questions.

We have split the essay questions into 3 levels of difficultly:

- **Level 1**: a straightforward essay covering a simple topic with many possible points. The extract will be easier to understand and this question should not be too challenging.
- **Level 2**: a medium difficulty essay question. The extract may take a while to understand and the key points may not jump out. It will take careful planning and critical thinking to answer the question
- **Level 3**: a particularly challenging essay question, with a difficult to understand extract and an equally challenging question. It will take a detailed plan and perhaps more than one read of the extract to grasp the true meaning. The key points may be obscure, and the essay will push the boundaries of your essay writing, critical thinking, and economic analysis skills.

Here are a few tips we suggest for the essay section:
- Work at a clear desk, with no clutter and ideally work on your own without any help from friends or family
- Do not answer the essay in "chunks", where you write one paragraph in one sitting, then leave and return later to finish the essay. Always write the essay in strict time conditions, of 60 minutes, including planning and writing. The 60-minute essay should be written in one sitting.
- Do not use Google or other online sources to write your essay, try and complete it without any help from other sources for ideas, to mimic the real exam situation
- These questions are meant to be challenging! Do not be disheartened if you cannot understand or answer the question on the first attempt. Some questions include the works of some of the greatest economists ever, hence, they are not simple by any means.
- To have the most accurate practice, handwrite every essay question you practise, typing on the laptop and handwriting an essay is simply not the same, in speed nor in feel.
- We have based a number of the extracts on the US economy, which you may be less familiar with than the United Kingdom, to increase the challenge in answering the question and reduce the support you have on pre-existing knowledge

We suggest a series of steps to answer these questions:
1. In a single sitting, set a timer for 1 hour and answer the essay question. Spend a reasonable amount of time planning your answer (around 5-10 minutes) and then write it out fully
2. Read over your essay and critique it, what points may have been better to include, were there too many SPAG mistakes and did you manage to finish in time?
3. Compare your essay to the "Essay Writing Guide" included in this book. Did you follow the suggested structure or any other sensible structure? Did you consider the view of different stakeholders and consider various trade-offs? Did your answer have enough depth?
4. Go through the recommended points in the guide, step by step, and try and ascertain where and how you could have improved your answer. Perhaps re-write a weak paragraph without any time conditions.
5. Annotate your essay with extra points you missed when you first answered it, economic diagrams, and theories that you could have mentioned, trade-offs you could have considered etc.
6. Encourage your fellow Cambridge Economics applicant friends to purchase this book and compare answers you both wrote. If possible, ask a teacher or a family member to read your essay and provide their constructive feedback.

Essay Question 1 (Level 2)

Read the extract below and then answer the question:

Analyse the strengths and weaknesses of the Kotlikoff plan in mitigating climate change

Your answer will be assessed taking into account your ability to construct a reasoned, insightful and logically consistent argument with clarity and precision.

A recent NBER working paper by a distinguished team of economists argues that a properly designed carbon tax can be a generational win-win.

By a generational win-win, Kotlikoff et al. mean a policy that would benefit not only future generations, who would reap the benefits of reduced warming, but also those of us who would begin paying the costs of mitigation now but would live to see only small, initial, climate improvements. The perception of a long lag between investments in climate mitigation and their full benefits has been a serious impediment to effective climate action. That is true both for democratic governments and for more authoritarian regimes, to the extent they are sensitive to public opinion. Although the paper discusses only carbon taxes, similar issues are raised by cap-and-trade, public investment, direct regulation, and other mitigation strategies.

The Kotlikoff plan:

The difficulty of getting to an intergenerational win-win on climate policy arises from the fact that both climate change itself and mitigation measures operate over a long time-horizon. To simplify only a little, the adverse effects of global warming are an increasing function of the total amount of greenhouse gases (GHGs) emitted into the atmosphere, while carbon taxes affect only the rate of emissions. Since GHGs, especially carbon dioxide, persist for long periods, even a big change in the rate of emissions affects climate damages only partially and over a long time period. Consequently, the ratio of the benefits of a carbon tax to its costs is less obvious in the short run than the long.

If no carbon tax is imposed ("business as usual"), global temperatures would rise by about 4 degrees by the end of the century. Global GDP in 2100 would be about 4.7 times higher than it is now—but that would make it about 6 percent smaller than it would be with no climate damages. The acceptable degree of warming is higher and the resulting economic damages lower than those for the scenarios considered by other researchers—a point we will return to shortly.

Based on the assumptions of the baseline scenario, Kotlikoff et al. recommend a carbon tax that begins at $30 per ton of CO2 and increases at a rate of 1.5 percent per year. According to their model, if such a tax were imposed in 2020, only people born in 2057 or later would experience net benefits over their lifetimes. As Robert P. Murphy has pointed out, the decision to impose the tax in 2020 would have to be made by voters and their representatives born in the 20th century, but the benefits would accrue not to themselves or their children, or even, in most cases, to their grandchildren, but only to their great-grandchildren and even later generations.

To make the carbon tax into a win-win, Kotlikoff et al. recommend rewarding early generations with a lump-sum cut in net taxes that would allow them to increase their consumption during the years after the carbon tax is first imposed. By a lump-sum tax cut, they mean one that is distributed equally to all citizens without regard to their level or source of income. In that regard, their tax cut would resemble the "citizens' dividends" proposed, for example, by the Citizens' Climate Lobby and the Climate Leadership Council. However, unlike those proposals, which are tax-neutral in the sense that total dividends equal total revenues from the carbon tax, the net lump-sum tax cut envisioned by the Kotlikoff model would require a "super dividend" in the form of a distribution or tax cut that would give more back to households than the revenues of the carbon tax itself.

The super dividend would be financed by issuing debt that would be retired by a tax increase scheduled for later years, after the reduction in climate damages was sufficient to produce net benefits. For example, Kotlikoff et al. calculate that in their baseline case, the net tax cut would give people born in 2020 a boost of 1.17 percent in their lifetime consumption, while those born in 2075 would be asked to pay extra taxes equal to 1.36 percent of their lifetime consumption. Even so, the scheme would produce a generational win-win since the burden of higher future taxes would be more than offset by the benefits of reduced climate damages. Importantly, the model assumes that utility is a function only of lifetime consumption. No allowance is made for utility received from direct enjoyment of environmental amenities.

…

The Kotlikoff plan aims to achieve a win-win using a carbon tax, a debt-financed net tax cut for early generations, and higher taxes on future generations to retire the debt. I have argued that such a plan is best understood as a Pareto-improving bargain in which "altruistic" members of the current generation offer higher immediate consumption to "selfish" members in return for their support for a carbon tax. Although future generations do not participate in the original bargain, they gain to the extent they inherit a capital stock that is smaller, but more heavily skewed toward clean energy, in line with their presumed interest in mitigating climate damages.

If our own generation did not have a mixture of selfish and altruistic members, the whole issue addressed by Kotlikoff et al. would disappear. If we were all selfish, and if a carbon tax would not produce net benefits in our own lifetimes, we would just leave future generations to deal with their own problems. On the other hand, if we were all altruistic, we would have enacted effective mitigation policies long since.

The fact that some of us are more altruistic toward future generations than others is the whole driving force behind the debate over climate policy. The altruists want an effective climate policy, but they can't get a majority on board. Properly understood, then, what the Kotlikoff plan proposes is a Pareto-improving bargain within the present generation, with altruistic members offering a payoff to selfish members in return for their support for climate action. The payoff is not delivered through a wormhole from the future, but rather, through a tax cut that diverts present-day resources from saving to consumption. The desired climate effects are then achieved by focusing a greater share of the smaller amount of saving on investments in decarbonization.

Extract adapted from the article "How Can We Ensure That a Carbon Tax is a Generational Win-Win?" By Ed Dolan. January 2020

https://dolanecon.blogspot.com/2020/01/how-can-we-ensure-that-carbon-tax-is.html

Essay Question 2 (Level 3)

Read the extract below taken from "The Wealth of Nations" and then answer the question:

Explain what you understand by the process of specialisation, the benefits of it and its significance in the field of economics.

Your answer will be assessed taking into account your ability to construct a reasoned, insightful and logically consistent argument with clarity and precision.

To take an example, therefore, from a very trifling (trivial) manufacture; but one in which the division of labour has been very often taken notice of, the trade of the pin-maker; a workman not educated to this business (which the division of labour has rendered a distinct trade), nor acquainted with the use of the machinery employed in it, could scarce, perhaps, with his utmost industry, make one pin in a day, and certainly could not make twenty. But in the way in which this business is now carried on, not only the whole work is a peculiar trade, but it is divided into a number of branches, of which the greater part are likewise peculiar trades. One man draws out the wire, another straights it, a third cuts it, a fourth points it, a fifth grinds it at the top for receiving the head; to make the head requires two or three distinct operations; to put it on, is a peculiar business, to whiten the pins is another; it is even a trade by itself to put them into the paper; and the important business of making a pin is, in this manner, divided into about eighteen distinct operations, which, in some manufactories, are all performed by distinct hands, though in others the same man will sometimes perform two or three of them.

I have seen a small manufactory of this kind where ten men only were employed, and where some of them consequently performed two or three distinct operations. But though they were very poor, and therefore but indifferently accommodated with the necessary machinery, they could, when they exerted themselves, make among them about twelve pounds of pins in a day. There are in a pound upwards of four thousand pins of a middling size. Those ten persons, therefore, could make among them upwards of forty-eight thousand pins in a day. Each person, therefore, making a tenth part of forty-eight thousand pins, might be considered as making four thousand eight hundred pins in a day. But if they had all wrought separately and independently, and without any of them having been educated to this peculiar business, they certainly could not each of them have made twenty, perhaps not one pin in a day; that is, certainly, not the two hundred and fortieth, perhaps not the four thousand eight hundredth part of what they are at present capable of performing, in consequence of a proper division and combination of their different operations.

... *(Reasons why specialisation increases efficiency)*

First, the improvement of the dexterity of the workman necessarily increases the quantity of the work he can perform; and the division of labour, by reducing every man's business to some one simple operation, and by making this operation the sole employment of his life, necessarily increases very much the dexterity of the workman. A common smith, who, though accustomed to handle the hammer, has never been used to make nails, if upon some particular occasion he is obliged to attempt it, will scarce, I am assured, be able to make above two or three hundred nails in a day, and those too very bad ones.

A smith who has been accustomed to make nails, but whose sole or principal business has not been that of a nailer, can seldom with his utmost diligence make more than eight hundred or a thousand nails in a day. I have seen several boys under twenty years of age who had never exercised any other trade but that of making nails, and who, when they exerted themselves, could make, each of them, upwards of two thousand three hundred nails in a day. The making of a nail, however, is by no means one of the simplest operations. The same person blows the bellows, stirs or mends the fire as there is occasion, heats the iron, and forges every part of the nail: In forging the head too he is obliged to change his tools. The different operations into which the making of a pin, or of a metal button, is subdivided, are all of them much simpler, and the dexterity of the person, of whose life it has been the sole business to perform them, is usually much greater. The rapidity with which some of the operations of those manufactures are performed, exceeds what the human hand could, by those who had never seen them, be supposed capable of acquiring.

Extract adapted from "An Inquiry into the Nature and Causes of the Wealth of Nations" By Adam Smith. March 1776

Essay Question 3 (Level 1)

Read the extract below and then answer the question:

Should the United States adopt a system of congestion pricing, as the United Kingdom have done?

Your answer will be assessed taking into account your ability to construct a reasoned, insightful and logically consistent argument with clarity and precision.

The Highway Trust Fund (*in the United States*) will soon be broke. Gasoline tax revenues haven't kept up with spending, and it's likely that demands for new highway infrastructure will grow in the future.

Joseph Kile, head of the microeconomics studies division at the Congressional Budget Office, discussed various policy options to deal with this funding gap in his testimony to the Senate Finance Committee on Tuesday. Most news coverage of Joe's testimony emphasised his suggestion that taxes based on miles travelled, rather than gasoline consumption, might be a better way to finance America's highways. After all, miles travelled is, along with weight, the primary driver of wear and tear on the roads. And it's a decent proxy for the benefit that drivers get from having functioning roads.

That's an interesting idea, but I'd like to highlight another important point that Joe made: the amount of infrastructure America should build depends very much on how we price it. If a six-lane highway gets congested, that doesn't necessarily mean that we need to build new lanes or lay out parallel roads. We could charge congestion fees instead. That would discourage driving at peak times and thus speed traffic without new construction. That's what London and Singapore famously do to limit traffic in their downtowns. And it's something we should more here in the United States.

Joe reports estimates from the Federal Highway Administration (FHWA) that congestion pricing could decrease highway spending needs by 25 to 33 percent: The federal government spent about $43 billion on highway investment in 2010. To maintain the same quality of highway performance would require an average of $57 billion in annual federal spending in coming years, according to the FHWA. That price tag drops to only $38 billion, however, if we make good use of congestion pricing.

Congestion pricing would thus save federal taxpayers almost $20 billion per year; state and local governments would save even more, since they pay for more than half the costs of these projects.

Congestion pricing can make our roadways work better, save Americans precious time, and reduce federal, state, and local budget pressures. That a great combination in this time of growing infrastructure needs and tightening budgets.

Extract adapted from the article "Congestion Pricing Saves Time and Money" By Donald Marron. May 2011

https://dmarron.com/2011/05/18/congestion-pricing-saves-time-and-money/

Essay Question 4 (Level 3)

Read the extract below taken from the book "Capitalism, Socialism and Democracy" by Joseph Schumpeter and then answer the question:

"Capitalism should be studied as a dynamic process, and failing to do so obscures the true behaviour of a capitalist firm"

By considering the theory of Creative Destruction, to what extent do you agree with the statement above.

Your answer will be assessed taking into account your ability to construct a reasoned, insightful and logically consistent argument with clarity and precision.

Capitalism is by nature a form or method of economic change and not only never is but never can be stationary. And this evolutionary character of the capitalist process is not merely due to the fact that economic life goes on in a social and natural environment which changes and by its change alters the data of economic action; this fact is important and these changes (wars, revolutions and so on) often condition industrial change, but they are not its prime movers. Nor is this evolutionary character due to a quasi-automatic increase in population and capital or to the vagaries of monetary systems of which exactly the same thing holds true. The fundamental impulse that sets and keeps the capitalist engine in motion comes from the new consumers' goods, the new methods of production or transportation, the new markets, the new forms of industrial organization that capitalist enterprise creates.

Similarly, the history of the productive apparatus of a typical farm, from the beginnings of the rationalization of crop rotation, ploughing and fattening to the mechanized thing of today—linking up with elevators and railroads—is a history of revolutions. So is the history of the productive apparatus of the iron and steel industry from the charcoal furnace to our own type of furnace, or the history of the apparatus of power production from the overshot water wheel to the modern power plant, or the history of transportation from the mail coach to the airplane. The opening up of new markets, foreign or domestic, and the organizational development from the craft shop and factory to such concerns as U.S. Steel illustrate the same process of industrial mutation—if I may use that biological term—that incessantly revolutionizes the economic structure from within, incessantly destroying the old one, incessantly creating a new one. The process as a whole works incessantly, in the sense that there always is either revolution or absorption of the results of revolution, both together forming what are known as business cycles. This process of Creative Destruction is the essential fact about capitalism. It is what capitalism consists in and what every capitalist concern has got to live in. This fact bears upon our problem in two ways.

First, since we are dealing with a process whose every element takes considerable time in revealing its true features and ultimate effects, there is no point in appraising the performance of that process ex visu *(from a person's writing)* of a given point of time; we must judge its performance over time, as it unfolds through decades or centuries. A system—any system, economic or other—that at every given point of time fully utilizes its possibilities to the best advantage may yet in the long run be inferior to a system that does so at no given point of time, because the latter's failure to do so may be a condition for the level or speed of long-run performance.

Second, since we are dealing with an organic process, analysis of what happens in any particular part of it—say, in an individual concern or industry—may indeed clarify details of mechanism but is inconclusive beyond that. Every piece of business strategy acquires its true significance only against the background of that process and within the situation created by it. It must be seen in its role in the perennial gale of creative destruction; it cannot be understood irrespective of it or, in fact, on the hypothesis that there is a perennial lull.

But economists who, ex visu of a point of time, look for example at the behaviour of an oligopolist industry—an industry which consists of a few big firms—and observe the well-known moves and countermoves within it that seem to aim at nothing but high prices and restrictions of output are making precisely that hypothesis. They accept the data of the momentary situation as if there were no past or future to it and think that they have understood what there is to understand if they interpret the behaviour of those firms by means of the principle of maximizing profits with reference to those data. The usual theorist's paper and the usual government commission's report practically never try to see that behaviour, on the one hand, as a result of a piece of past history and, on the other hand, as an attempt to deal with a situation that is sure to change presently—as an attempt by those firms to keep on their feet, on ground that is slipping away from under them. In other words, the problem that is usually being visualized is how capitalism administers existing structures, whereas the relevant problem is how it creates and destroys them. As long as this is not recognized, the investigator does a meaningless job. As soon as it is recognized, his outlook on capitalist practice and its social results changes considerably.

Extract adapted from "Capitalism, Socialism and Democracy" By Joseph Schumpeter. 1942

Essay Question 5 (Level 2)

Read the extract below taken from "Principles of Economics" and then answer the question:

Analyse the role of incentives (monetary and non-monetary) in shaping the field of economics and wider society

Your answer will be assessed taking into account your ability to construct a reasoned, insightful and logically consistent argument with clarity and precision.

Economics is a study of men as they live and move and think in the ordinary business of life. But it concerns itself chiefly with those motives which affect, most powerfully and most steadily, man's conduct in the business part of his life. Everyone who is worth anything carries his higher nature with him into business; and, there as elsewhere, he is influenced by his personal affections, by his conceptions of duty and his reverence for high ideals. And it is true that the best energies of the ablest inventors and organizers of improved methods and appliances are stimulated by a noble emulation more than by any love of wealth for its own sake. But, for all that, the steadiest motive to ordinary business work is the desire for the pay which is the material reward of work. The pay may be on its way to be spent selfishly or unselfishly, for noble or base ends; and here the variety of human nature comes into play. But the motive is supplied by a definite amount of money: and it is this definite and exact money measurement of the steadiest motives in business life, which has enabled economics far to outrun every other branch of the study of man. Just as the chemist's fine balance has made chemistry more exact than most other physical sciences; so, this economist's balance, rough and imperfect as it is, has made economics more exact than any other branch of social science. But of course, economics cannot be compared with the exact physical sciences: for it deals with the ever changing and subtle forces of human nature. The advantage which economics has over other branches of social science appears then to arise from the fact that its special field of work gives rather larger opportunities for exact methods than any other branch. It concerns itself chiefly with those desires, aspirations and other affections of human nature, the outward manifestations of which appear as incentives to action in such a form that the force or quantity of the incentives can be estimated and measured with some approach to accuracy; and which therefore are in some degree amenable to treatment by scientific machinery. An opening is made for the methods and the tests of science as soon as the force of a person's motives—not the motives themselves—can be approximately measured by the sum of money, which he will just give up in order to secure a desired satisfaction; or again by the sum which is just required to induce him to undergo a certain fatigue.

...

Thus though it is true that "money" or "general purchasing power" or "command over material wealth," is the centre around which economic science clusters; this is so, not because money or material wealth is regarded as the main aim of human effort, nor even as affording the main subject-matter for the study of the economist, but because in this world of ours it is the one convenient means of measuring human motive on a large scale. If the older economists had made this clear, they would have escaped many grievous misrepresentations; and the splendid teachings of Carlyle and Ruskin as to the right aims of human endeavour and the right uses of wealth, would not then have been marred by bitter attacks on economics, based on the mistaken belief that that science had no concern with any motive except the selfish desire for wealth, or even that it inculcated a policy of sordid selfishness9 . Again, when the motive to a man's action is spoken of as supplied by the money which he will earn, it is not meant that his mind is closed to all other considerations save those of gain. For even the most purely business relations of life assume honesty and good faith; while many of them take for granted, if not generosity, yet at least the absence of meanness, and the pride which every honest man takes in acquitting himself well. Again, much of the work by which people earn their living is pleasurable in itself; and there is truth in the contention of socialists that more of it might be made so. Indeed, even business work, that seems at first sight unattractive, often yields a great pleasure by offering scope for the exercise of men's faculties, and for their instincts of emulation and of power. For just as a racehorse or an athlete strains every nerve to get in advance of his competitors, and delights in the strain; so, a manufacturer or a trader is often stimulated much more by the hope of victory over his rivals than by the desire to add something to his fortune

Extract adapted from "Principles of Economics" By Alfred Marshall. 1890

Essay Question 6 (Level 2)

Read the extract below and then answer the question:

To what extent is global trading based on the system of comparative advantage better than absolute advantage.

Your answer will be assessed taking into account your ability to construct a reasoned, insightful and logically consistent argument with clarity and precision.

Two centuries ago in 1817, the great economist David Ricardo published his most prominent work: "On the Principles of Political Economy and Taxation." Among many other insights, it's the book that introduced the idea of "comparative advantage" (especially in Chapter 7) and thus offered a way of thinking about the potential for gains from trade - both between countries and within areas of a single country - that has been central to economic thinking on these topics ever since.

Most people have no difficulty with the idea that two countries can at least potentially benefit from trade if each one has a productivity advantage in a certain good. There are places in the Middle East where finding oil doesn't seem to involve a lot more than jamming a sharp stick into the ground. Those places should produce and export oil. The United States has vast areas of fertile soil. Those places should produce and export corn and wheat.

But an immediate issue arises. What about areas that don't seem to have a productivity advantage in any area? How can they possibly benefit from trade? Ricardo's theory establishes the point that the key factor in what areas or nations will choose to export or import is not whether there is an overall productivity advantage (*absolute advantage*), but instead where that productivity advantage is greatest--or where the productivity disadvantage is smallest. It is the "comparative" advantage that matters.

"Consider the situation of a group of friends who decide to go camping together. The friends have a wide range of skills and experiences, but one person in particular, Jethro, has done lots of camping before and is a great athlete, too. Jethro has an absolute advantage in all aspects of camping: carrying more weight in a backpack, gathering firewood, paddling a canoe, setting up tents, making a meal, and washing up. So, here's the question: Because Jethro has an absolute productivity advantage in everything, should he do all the work?

"Of course not. Even if Jethro is willing to work like a mule while everyone else sits around, he still has only 24 hours in a day. If everyone sits around and waits for Jethro to do everything, not only will Jethro be an unhappy camper, but there won't be much output for his group of six friends to consume. The theory of comparative advantage suggests that everyone will benefit if they figure out their areas of comparative advantage; that is, the area of camping where their productivity disadvantage is least, compared to Jethro. For example, perhaps Jethro is 80% faster at building fires and cooking meals than anyone else, but only 20% faster at gathering firewood and 10% faster at setting up tents. In that case, Jethro should focus on building fires and making meals, and others should attend to the other tasks, each according to where their productivity disadvantage is smallest. If the campers coordinate their efforts according to comparative advantage, they can all gain."

This way of phrasing the situation clarifies the essential economic issue: not who is most productive at various tasks, but how to allocate all of the available productive power across a range of tasks in the most efficient way. In that problem, everyone has a role to play. Even a party with productivity advantages in every area will have areas where their advantage is smallest; conversely, a party who is least productive at every single task will have an area in which the productivity disadvantage is least. Focusing on those areas will provide gains from trade.

Although Ricardo's theory of comparative advantage never disappeared, and has been a mainstay of basic principles of economics for 200 years, there was a period of some decades when it seemed less relevant to the facts of international trade. As Jonathan Eaton explores in his contribution to this volume, Ricardo's basic example of comparative advantage involved one factor of production (labour) and different technology across countries linked to differences in productivity of labour. By the middle of the 20th century, the focus was on models that had a number of different factors of production, and thus chose different methods of production, although they shared access to the same technology. By the 1980s, emphasis had shifted to models of how large firms would trade similar but not identical goods across countries: for example, international trade in cars or airplanes or machine tools.

Indeed, there is a long-standing argument in economics over whether trade leads to economic growth, or whether economic growth leads to more trade, or whether other external factors (like improved technology and transportation) affect both.

Extract adapted from the article "Ricardo's Comparative Advantage After Two Centuries" By Timothy Taylor. December 2017

https://conversableeconomist.blogspot.com/2017/12/ricardos-comparative-advantage-after.html

Essay Question 7 (Level 2)

Read the extract below and then answer the question:

"A universal basic income can be a successful tool to increase income security, whilst remaining economically plausible and maintaining efficiency"

To what extent do you agree with the statement above?

Your answer will be assessed taking into account your ability to construct a reasoned, insightful and logically consistent argument with clarity and precision.

The idea that cash is what people need most when adversity strikes is far from new. Decades ago, Milton Friedman argued for programs that give help "in the form most useful to the individual, namely cash." More recently, Charles Kenny cites examples from around the world in support of a simple policy recipe: "Give poor people cash without conditions attached, and it turns out they use it to buy goods and services that improve their lives and increase their future earnings potential."

A universal basic income

The simplest cash assistance policy is a universal basic income (UBI) that gives everyone an equal basic grant regardless of earnings or work status.

Income security:
The primary goal of cash assistance is income security. Income security is not just a matter of one's average level of income, but also of its reliability and of the availability of reserves to meet emergencies. For the sake of discussion, I will use a benchmark based on an average income at least equal to the federal poverty level (FPL).

A UBI would be fully effective in providing income security, so defined, only if the basic grant itself were above the FPL for every recipient. (The FPL for an unrelated individual is $12,760 in 2020, and $26,200 for a family of four.) However, even a considerably smaller basic grant would improve on the present situation.

Work incentives:
The preceding calculations for income security are "static" in that they assume a UBI would have no effect on work activity. Many critics worry that a UBI, even at a sub poverty level, would discourage work. They warn of loafers living in yurts in the woods, spending their handouts on drugs. However, a more serious evaluation suggests that only a small minority would choose a lay-about lifestyle.

There is, in fact, a large empirical literature on the ways that increases in income affect work behaviour. Some studies are based on how people react to windfalls such as lottery winnings, inheritance, and tribal casino dividends. Others use structural data on wages, salaries, and work behaviour.

Typically, such studies do find that, other things being equal, people tend to work less and take more leisure as their incomes increase, but the effect is small. Studies of the income effect, as economists call it, suggest that other things being equal, a 10 percent increase in income tends to induce a zero to 1 percent decrease in hours worked. For some people, that could mean abandoning employment altogether, but more often, it would just mean taking a vacation or a day off now and then.

Furthermore, in real life, "other things" are not equal. While windfall income has a negative effect on work, an increase in take-home pay from an added hour of work has a stronger and positive substitution effect that increases work effort. The term comes from the incentive to substitute income-producing work for leisure when wages rise. Estimates are that the substitution effect of a 10 percent increase in take-home pay tends to cause a 1 to 4 percent increase in hours worked.

A UBI that aimed to maximize work incentives could take advantage of the tendency for the stronger substitution effect to outweigh the weaker income effect. For that to happen, the UBI would have to replace the current system of means-tested welfare (a replacement UBI), not be added on top of it (an add-on UBI).

Affordability:

Any UBI would be costly, in that it would pay benefits not only to the needy, but to everyone. Taxing people with higher incomes and then returning a part of the revenue to them in the form of a cash grant might appear to be a wash, but in fact, taxes are inevitably a "leaky bucket." Taxes and transfers not only entail administrative costs; they can also distort economic behaviour in ways that undermine growth and efficiency.

The leaky-bucket problem could be lessened if a replacement UBI replaced not only existing poverty programs, but also middle-class income benefits like the tax-deductibility of mortgage payments, charitable contributions, and retirement savings. Since the benefits of those tax preferences are strongly skewed toward upper-middle and wealthy households, a majority of middle-class households would still come out ahead. The affordability of a replacement UBI could be further enhanced by a "double-dipping" rule that would allow Social Security recipients to take either their current benefits or the UBI, but not both. Restricting the UBI to resident citizens only would further stretch available funding.

However, even with these measures included, I estimate that a replacement UBI could offer a grant of no more than $2,800 to $3,200 per person per year without new taxes. That is only about half of the deep poverty level. Based on static estimates alone, without accounting for enhanced work incentives, such a UBI might well raise a smaller percentage of families out of poverty than current programs.

The safety-net trilemma:

Taken as a whole, our discussion of income security, work incentives, and affordability reveals a problem that a UBI shares with other proposed reforms of the safety net – a safety-net trilemma, as we can call it.

For a UBI, the trilemma looks like this: A replacement UBI with a benefit set at half or more of the FPL would arguably outperform the existing welfare system in terms of income security and work incentives, but it would not be affordable without significant new funding. An add-on UBI with a much lower benefit would be more affordable and could improve income security, but it would do nothing to mitigate the work disincentives of the current system. And a replacement UBI that drew only on existing funding would be affordable and would improve work incentives, but would have a benefit too low to improve income security, and might even reduce it.

Extract adapted from the article "A Social Safety Net For an Age of Uncertainty" By Ed Dolan. April 2020

https://dolanecon.blogspot.com/2020/04/a-social-safety-net-for-age-of.html

Essay Question 8 (Level 3)

Read the extract below taken from "Capitalism, Socialism and Democracy" and then answer the question:

- To what extent do you agree that the success of capitalism will also be its downfall and lead it into socialism.
- What is the social function of entrepreneurs, and is their role in society becoming less impactful?

Your answer will be assessed taking into account your ability to construct a reasoned, insightful and logically consistent argument with clarity and precision.

In our discussion of the theory of vanishing investment opportunity, a reservation was made in favour of the possibility that the economic wants of humanity might someday be so completely satisfied that little motive would be left to push productive effort still further ahead. Such a state of satiety is no doubt very far off even if we keep within the present scheme of wants; and if we take account of the fact that, as higher standards of life are attained, these wants automatically expand and new wants emerge or are created, satiety becomes a flying goal, particularly if we include leisure among consumers' goods.

However, let us glance at that possibility, assuming, still more unrealistically, that methods of production have reached a state of perfection which does not admit of further improvement. A more or less stationary state would ensue. Capitalism, being essentially an evolutionary process, would become atrophic (*waste away*). There would be nothing left for entrepreneurs to do. They would find themselves in much the same situation as generals would in a society perfectly sure of permanent peace. Profits and along with profits the rate of interest would converge toward zero. The bourgeois (*middle class*) strata that live on profits and interest would tend to disappear. The management of industry and trade would become a matter of current administration, and the personnel would unavoidably acquire the characteristics of a bureaucracy. Socialism of a very sober type would almost automatically come into being. Human energy would turn away from business. Other than economic pursuits would attract the brains and provide the adventure. For the calculable future this vision is of no importance. But all the greater importance attaches to the fact that many of the effects on the structure of society and on the organization of the productive process that we might expect from an approximately complete satisfaction of wants or from absolute technological perfection can also be expected from a development that is clearly observable already. Progress itself may be mechanized as well as the management of a stationary economy, and this mechanization of progress may affect entrepreneurship and capitalist society nearly as much as the cessation of economic progress would.

In order to see this, it is only necessary to restate, first, what the entrepreneurial function consists in and, secondly, what it means for bourgeois society and the survival of the capitalist order. We have seen that the function of entrepreneurs is to reform or revolutionize the pattern of production by exploiting an invention or, more generally, an untried technological possibility for producing a new commodity or producing an old one in a new way, by opening up a new source of supply of materials or a new outlet for products, by reorganizing an industry and so on. Railroad construction in its earlier stages, electrical power production before the First World War, steam and steel, the motorcar, colonial ventures afford spectacular instances of a large genus (*group*) which comprises innumerable humbler ones—down to such things as making a success of a particular kind of sausage or toothbrush. This kind of activity is primarily responsible for the recurrent "prosperities" that revolutionize the economic organism and the recurrent "recessions" that are due to the dis-equilibrating impact of the new products or methods. To undertake such new things is difficult and constitutes a distinct economic function, first, because they lie outside of the routine tasks which everybody understands and, secondly, because the environment resists in many ways that vary, according to social conditions, from simple refusal either to finance or to buy a new thing, to physical attack on the man who tries to produce it.

...

This function does not essentially consist in either inventing anything or otherwise creating the conditions which the enterprise exploits. It consists in getting things done. This social function is already losing importance and is bound to lose it at an accelerating rate in the future even if the economic process itself of which entrepreneurship was the prime mover went on unabated. For, on the one hand, it is much easier now than it has been in the past to do things that lie outside familiar routine—innovation itself is being reduced to routine.

Extract adapted from "Capitalism, Socialism and Democracy" By Joseph Schumpeter. 1942

Essay Question 9 (Level 1)

Read the extract below taken and then answer the question:

- Explain the role of a social safety net in a modern economy, and the key features it must possess
- Compare the efficacy of UBI, UBI-PO and a NIT system as a social safety net in the USA

Your answer will be assessed taking into account your ability to construct a reasoned, insightful and logically consistent argument with clarity and precision.

Article based on the US Economy

Social safety nets

Above all, if there is one thing, we have learned from the COVID-19 crisis, it is that our current social safety net is not as resilient as it should be.

The common hazards of life caused by business cycles, natural disasters, or events that strike individuals at random are the known-knowns of social policy — things we are aware of and understand how to deal with. Our safety net is not even capable of dealing with those. Millions find themselves ineligible for unemployment insurance because they work in the gig economy, or have not been at their present job long enough, or for other reasons. Half the population gets health insurance through their jobs, and when those jobs disappear, health coverage goes, too. Even moving from state to state to care for a family member can cause loss of unemployment- or health-benefits. We know these gaps exist, but year after year, we do nothing about them.

A truly resilient social safety net should also be capable of dealing with the known-unknowns of life — things we are aware of but do not fully understand. The effects of automation and technological change are an example. There are many indications that these forces are hollowing out the labour market, with middle-skilled and middle-income jobs disappearing while openings proliferate in low-skill, low-paid sectors, such as home health assistance. Maybe this trend will become a true job apocalypse, as some warn it will, or maybe it won't. In either case, a better social safety net would help us cope with whatever technological change throws at us. Wage subsidies to encourage people to fill essential but low-skilled jobs are one idea that could help.

Most important of all, we need a social safety net that is capable of dealing with unknown-unknowns — things that we do not anticipate and do not understand. The COVID-19 pandemic fits that pattern. Not the disease itself — pandemics were a known risk long before this one arrived. The unknown-unknowns in this case concern the follow-on effects of using social distancing as almost the sole means of controlling spread of the virus. We don't have a playbook for a sudden, deep recession with this combination of supply shocks and demand shocks.

Phaseouts and negative income taxes

Milton Friedman's negative income tax (NIT) is the best-known example. Friedman's original NIT featured a basic grant for those with no earnings, subject to a benefit-reduction rate of 50 cents per dollar of earned income. Another possibility is a hybrid of a UBI and NIT, which would pay a fixed basic grant to everyone up to an earned-income threshold, after which benefits would be gradually phased out. I will call such a plan a UBI with phaseout, or UBI-PO.

Affordability vs. income security:

Adding a phaseout to a UBI decreases total expenditures for any given basic grant. If the basic grant were set at or above the FPL, an NIT or UBI-PO could eliminate all measured poverty. Even if the basic grant were less than the FPL, the UBI-PO does as well in terms of income security as a simple UBI. Alternatively, we could hold the total cost of benefits constant when comparing a UBI and a UBI-PO. Using a phase-out to reduce the number of beneficiaries and focusing benefits on those most in need would allow the UBI-PO would to award a higher basic grant than a simple UBI. It would therefore have a stronger impact on income security.

Affordability vs. work incentives:

The downside of a UBI-PO or NIT, compared with a simple UBI, is that people subject to the phaseout would face reduced work incentives. At best, the phaseout range could be shifted to people whose incomes were already higher and whose attachment to the labour market was stronger, in the hope that the disincentives would be less damaging.

While on the subject of work incentives, it is often noted that a simple UBI financed by a flat-rate income tax would be mathematically identical to an NIT or UBI-PO having the same basic grant and a phaseout with the same rate as the tax.

The contention is true as far as it goes, but it implies a rather limited view of public finance. First, there is no reason either in law or economics that a UBI would have to be fully financed by a single, dedicated revenue source. Second, even if the UBI were tied to a specific revenue stream, there is no reason it would have to be a tax that was directly a function of income. For example, the UBI could draw on revenues from a wealth tax, an inheritance tax, a capital gains tax, a consumption tax, a carbon tax, or some combination of the above. Third, as noted earlier, the cost of the UBI could be offset, in whole or in part, by cutting existing means-tested welfare for the poor or by reducing middle-class tax preferences.

It is a valid point to say that the full effects of any safety-net program should be evaluated in terms of its impact on the government budget as a whole, not on the expenditure side alone. Ideally, government budgeting should evaluate expenditures on their own merit while optimizing the tax system to minimize deadweight losses. Having done that, broad budget rules should be invoked to establish a sustainable relationship between revenues and expenditures. But those considerations are not specific to income support policies. They should apply to all categories of government spending.

Extract adapted from the article "A Social Safety Net For an Age of Uncertainty" By Ed Dolan. April 2020

https://dolanecon.blogspot.com/2020/04/a-social-safety-net-for-age-of.html

Essay Question 10 (Level 1)

Read the extract below and then answer the question:

"Is it possible to have an economy where everyone is in work"

Answer the question above, by considering the 4 schemes explained in the extract given.

Your answer will be assessed taking into account your ability to construct a reasoned, insightful and logically consistent argument with clarity and precision.

Can we put everyone to work? [Based on the US economy]

In what follows I will discuss four proposals. The first two – guaranteed jobs, from the left, and work requirements, from the right – I view sceptically. The other two are wage subsidies and basic income. I see those as more promising, and more promising still if combined.

Guaranteed Jobs

A job guarantee (JG) is one of the three main pillars of the Green New Deal, along with clean energy and universal health care. Under a JG, anyone who wanted could get a full- or part-time job just by showing up. They would be directly employed by state or local governments and non-profit organizations, while the cost would be borne by the federal government. The jobs would pay a living wage of something like $15 per hour, plus full benefits. Jobs would be created to match workers' skills and places of residence, so they could start immediately without retraining or relocation.

According to two detailed descriptions, guaranteed jobs would be taken up by some 10 to 15 million workers, even with the job market as tight as it is now. Including wages, benefits, payroll taxes, and supplies, the total cost per job would be something like $45,000 to $56,000. The gross cost to the federal budget would be $409 billion to $543 billion per year, some 9 to 11 percent of current federal spending. The net cost could be substantially lower because of taxes paid by workers and budget savings on existing welfare programs, however.

Nevertheless, although the cost of a full job guarantee, even with offsets, would make such a program a hard sell in Congress, cost is not the biggest reason I am sceptical. Three things particularly concern me.

First, even though guaranteed jobs would be designed not to compete directly with the private sector, a JG would still be disruptive. Private employers would lose workers if they did not match a job-and-benefit package worth some $20 per hour. JG advocates are confident that private employers have enough slack to raise wages without cutting employment, but I am not so sure. JG jobs would not only offer good wages and benefits, but also, as advocates promise, they would be more accommodating than many private sector jobs to workers' personal schedules, family needs, and disabilities. A large outflow from private employment to guaranteed jobs could raise the cost of the program sharply.

Second, I think advocates overstate the ease of creating 10 to 15 million meaningful new public service jobs. To avoid competing with the private sector, they could not be jobs in hotels or factories. They could not require advanced skills or investments in heavy equipment, which would mean JG workers could play a limited role in projects like replacing aging bridges or building green energy infrastructure. When we read advocates' descriptions of JG jobs, they talk about things like teachers' aides, recycling, and planting trees on vacant lots. How many workers could be absorbed in such jobs before they became mere make-work?

Third, many of those who remain out of work in today's booming economy are, almost by definition, among the "hard to employ." Those include people with criminal records, unstable housing, substance abuse issues, family situations that interfere with regular work schedules, and borderline mental and physical conditions that fall short of full disability but still create problems on the job. Programs that try to find work for the hard-to-employ are not a new idea. Many existing programs are well run. Still, their experience shows that lasting success requires intensive, one-on-one casework to help with things like soft job skills and support with personal issues. Even then, success rates are far from 100 percent. The leading JG proposals do not, in my view, come close to budgeting enough for administration, counselling, and support services.

Work Requirements

Although the issues just discussed make me sceptical of guaranteed jobs, I am no less sceptical of the leading conservative alternative – work requirements on welfare recipients. Welfare reforms of the 1990s already imposed work requirements on most recipients of cash welfare. The current administration now wants to extend work requirements to noncash programs such as SNAP, Medicaid, and housing assistance.

A recent report from the Council of Economic Advisers claims that the welfare reforms of the 1990s prove that work requirements can increase employment and reduce dependence. I see two reasons to doubt such confidence.

For one thing, backers of work requirements assume there are many nondisabled welfare recipients who are able to work, but who choose not to. The data show otherwise. They show that a majority of nondisabled welfare recipients already work or face serious barriers to work.

A second problem is that the kind of work requirements that conservative's favour is not, in practice, very work-friendly. They often place unrealistic burdens on beneficiaries, such as detailed record keeping, frequent verifications, and unrealistic allowances for family needs or irregular work schedules. Administrative lapses are often punished with extended lockouts from benefits. Furthermore, these programs – like some JG proposals – offer inadequate personal assistance to the hard-to-employ, leaving it up to them to find work or training and to deal with personal barriers to work.

In the end, then, many people who ought to qualify for assistance fail to do so. Many who are pushed off welfare rolls do not find work. On balance, work requirements trim welfare rolls but increase poverty. Cynics say that is the intended outcome.

Wage Subsidies

Progressives promise jobs in the public sector. Conservatives propose using the stick of work requirements to push people into private-sector jobs. Wage subsidies fall somewhere between these alternatives. They focus on private- rather than public-sector jobs, but they use a carrot rather than a stick to encourage employment.

By far the largest wage subsidy program is the Earned Income Tax Credit (EITC). In existence since 1975, it has earned wide bipartisan support. Liberals like it because it raises 6 million families out of poverty each year. Conservatives like it because it encourages work and self-sufficiency. Ronald Reagan called it "the best anti-poverty, the best pro-family, the best job creation measure to come out of Congress."

The amount of wage subsidy offered under the EITC varies both with income and the number of dependent children. For the lowest-paid workers, it provides a bonus of 35 to 45 cents for each dollar earned. Once earnings approach the official poverty level, the subsidy is gradually phased out. Benefits are paid in a lump sum, once a year, as a refundable tax credit.

Basic Income

Successful though it is, the EITC has its critics. Some point out that the once-yearly payment makes budgeting difficult for low-income families and dilutes the program's incentive value. Others note that it does little to help people with no children and nothing to help those who cannot work or cannot find work.

One way to meet those criticisms would be to pay a Universal Basic Income (UBI) to everyone regardless of whether they worked or not, and regardless of the number of dependent children. For example, the Freedom Dividend proposed by Democratic presidential candidate Andrew Yang would give every adult citizen a payment of $1,000 per month. Many other UBI variants have been discussed, including some with conservative backing.

How would a basic income affect work incentives? It might at first seem that a UBI would discourage work. After all, you might think, if you give people money whether they work or not, why would they work? In reality, though, the effect on work incentives depends on what a UBI would replace. Current means-tested welfare programs like TANF, SNAP, and housing vouchers, which reduce benefits for each dollar a person earns, have a strong negative effect on work incentives. If a UBI replaced those, as Yang's Freedom Dividend and many other versions do, the net effect would be to encourage work. The spending saved on those other forms of welfare could go a long way toward paying for the UBI itself.

Extract adapted from the article "Can We Put Everyone to Work? Four Ideas Compared." By Ed Dolan. January 2020.

https://dolanecon.blogspot.com/2020/01/can-we-put-everyone-to-work-four-ideas.html

Essay Question 11 (Level 1)

Read the extract below and then answer the question:

Should governments tax products that are fun but harmful?

Your answer will be assessed taking into account your ability to construct a reasoned, insightful and logically consistent argument with clarity and precision.

Should you face an extra tax if you drink soda? Eat potato chips? Uncork some wine? Light up a cigarette or joint? Toast yourself in a tanning booth?

Many governments think so. Mexico taxes junk food. Berkeley taxes sugary soft drinks. Countless governments tax alcohol and tobacco. Several states tax marijuana. And thanks to health reform, the U.S. government taxes indoor tanning.

One rationale for these taxes is that some personal choices impose costs on other people, what economists call externalities. Your drinking threatens bystanders if you get behind the wheel. Tanning-induced skin cancer drives up health insurance costs.

Another rationale is that people sometimes overlook costs they themselves face, known as internalities. Limited self-control, inattention, or poor information can cause people to eat too many sweets, drink too much alcohol, or take up smoking only to later regret the harm.

In a new paper, Should We Tax Internalities Like Externalities?, I examine whether the internality rationale is as strong as the externality one. Economists have long argued that taxes can be a good way to put a price on externalities like the pollutants causing climate change, but does the same logic apply to internalities?

People who look down on certain activities sometimes think so, with taxes being a way to discourage "sinful" conduct. People who prioritize public health often favour such taxes as a way to encourage healthier behaviour. Those who emphasize personal responsibility, by contrast, often oppose such taxes as infringing on individual autonomy—the overreaching "nanny state."

Economists don't have much to say about sin. But we do have ideas about balancing health and consumer autonomy. One approach is to focus on efficiency: How do the benefits of a tax compare to its costs? Internalities and externalities both involve people consuming too much because they overlook some costs. Taxes can serve as a proxy for those overlooked costs and reduce consumption to a more beneficial level. In that way, the logic of taxing internalities is identical to that for taxing externalities.

But that equivalence comes with a caveat. Internality taxes should be targeted only at harms we overlook. If people recognize the health risks of eating bacon but still choose to do so, there is no efficiency rationale for a tax. Informed consumers have decided the pleasure is worth the risk. Efficiency thus differs sharply from sin and public health views that would tax harmful products regardless of whether consumers appreciate the risks.

Economists often temper cost-benefit comparisons with concerns about the distribution of gains and losses. At first glance, taxes on internalities and externalities generate similar equity concerns. Both target consumption, so both may fall more heavily on poor families, which tend to spend larger shares of their incomes.

But there's another caveat. Internality taxes do not target consumption in general. Instead, they target products whose future costs consumers often overlook. Nearly everyone does that, but it may be more of a problem for people with low incomes. The stress of poverty, for example, can make it more difficult to evaluate the long-term costs of decisions today. As a result, taxes aimed at internalities are more likely to hit low-income families than are those aimed at externalities.

A third, paternalistic perspective focuses on people who overlook harms. Do internality taxes help them? To meet that standard, the benefit consumers get from reducing purchases must exceed their new tax burden. That can be a high hurdle. If consumers only buy a little less, they may end up with small health gains but a large tax bill. That might be a success from

293

an efficiency perspective since the tax revenue ultimately helps someone. But it's a loss from the perspective of affected consumers.

The economic case for taxing internalities is thus weaker than for taxing externalities. Internality taxes raise greater distributional concerns, and they place a new burden on the people they are intended to help. Internality taxes can still make sense if consumers find it easy to cut back on taxed products (so health gains are large relative to the new tax burden), if overlooked health risks are very large (as with smoking), or if governments rebate revenues to affected consumers. But when those conditions do not hold, we should be sceptical.

Extract "Should governments tax products that are fun but harmful?" By Donald Marron at the Urban-Brookings Tax Policy Center. November, 2015

https://www.taxpolicycenter.org/taxvox/should-governments-tax-products-are-fun-harmful

Essay Question 12 (Level 2)

Read the extract below taken from "Essays in Persuasion" and then answer the question:

Examine the role of price level changes in an economy and the effects it can have

Your answer will be assessed taking into account your ability to construct a reasoned, insightful and logically consistent argument with clarity and precision.

Money is only important for what it will procure. Thus, a change in the monetary unit, which is uniform in its operation and affects all transactions equally, has no consequences. If, by a change in the established standard of value, a man received and owned twice as much money as he did before in payment for all rights and for all efforts, and if he also paid out twice as much money for all acquisitions and for all satisfactions, he would be wholly unaffected.

It follows, therefore, that a change in the value of money, that is to say in the level of prices, is important to Society only in so far as its incidence is unequal. Such changes have produced in the past, and are producing now, the vastest social consequences, because, as we all know, when the value of money changes, it does not change equally for all persons or for all purposes. A man's receipts and his outgoings are not all modified in one uniform proportion. Thus, a change in prices and rewards, as measured in money, generally affects different classes unequally, transfers wealth from one to another, bestows affluence here and embarrassment there, and redistributes Fortune's favours so as to frustrate design and disappoint expectation.

The fluctuations in the value of money since 1914 have been on a scale so great as to constitute, with all that they involve, one of the most significant events in the economic history of the modern world. The fluctuation of the standard, whether gold, silver, or paper, has not only been of unprecedented violence, but has been visited on a society of which the economic organisation is more dependent than that of any earlier epoch on the assumption that the standard of value would be moderately stable.

During the Napoleonic Wars and the period immediately succeeding them the extreme fluctuation of English prices within a single year was 22 per cent; and the highest price level reached during the first quarter of the nineteenth century, which we used to reckon the most disturbed period of our currency history, was less than double the lowest and with an interval of thirteen years. Compare with this the extraordinary movements of the past nine years. From 1914 to 1920 all countries experienced an expansion in the supply of money to spend relatively to the supply of things to purchase, that is to say Inflation. Since 1920 those countries which have regained control of their financial situation, not content with bringing the Inflation to an end, have contracted their supply of money and have experienced the fruits of Deflation. Others have followed inflationary courses more riotously [resembling a riot] than before.

Each process, Inflation and Deflation alike, has inflicted great injuries. Each has an effect in altering the distribution of wealth between different classes, Inflation in this respect being the worse of the two. Each has also an effect in overstimulating or retarding the production of wealth, though here Deflation is the more injurious. The division of our subject thus indicated is the most convenient for us to follow,—examining first the effect of changes in the value of money on the distribution of wealth with most of our attention on Inflation, and next their effect on the production of wealth with most of our attention on Deflation.

Extract adapted from "Essays in Persuasion" By John Maynard Keynes. 1931

Essay Question 13 (Level 2)

Read the extract below and then answer the questions:

- **What has been the driving force of China's economic growth since the 1970s?**
- **To what extent is China's economic growth sustainable?**

Your answer will be assessed taking into account your ability to construct a reasoned, insightful and logically consistent argument with clarity and precision.

When I chat with people about China's economic growth, I often hear a story that goes like this: The main driver's behind China's growth is that it uses a combination of cheap labour and an undervalued exchange rate to create huge trade surpluses. The most recent issue of my own Journal of Economic Perspectives includes a five-paper symposium on China's growth, and they make a compelling case that this received wisdom about China's growth is more wrong than right.

For example, start with the claim that China's economic growth has been driven by huge trade surpluses. China's major economic reforms started around 1978, and rapid growth took off not long after that. But China's balance of trade was essentially in balance until the early 2000s, and only then did it take off.

How does China's pattern of trade balances line up with argument about China's undervalued exchange rate? The yuan does indeed get weaker relative to the U.S. dollar for much of the 1980s and first half of the 1990s--but this is the time period when China's trade balance is near-zero. China's exchange rate is pretty much unchanging for the five years or so before China's trade surplus takes off. Since 2006, the yuan has indeed been strengthening. Last week the yuan hit a record high against the dollar since 1994.

What about China's purportedly cheap wages? China's wages were fairly during much of the 1980 and 1990s, which is the time when China's trade was nearly in-balance. But whether the conversion is done using yuan/dollar exchange rates or by inflation in China (measured by the producer price index), wages in China have been rising at double-digit annual rates since the late 1990s. In other words, China's big trade surpluses of the last decade have co-existed with sharply rising wages.

Clearly, China's pattern of economic growth since the start of its reforms needs a different storyline than the basic tale of low wages, a cheap currency, and big trade surpluses. After working with these authors, my own view is that it's useful to think of China's economy since about 1978 in two main stages--although there isn't a clean-and-clear break between them.

The first stage of China's growth that went through the 1980s and a bit into the early 1990s was really about rural areas. Yasheng Huang makes this argument strongly in his JEP article "How Did China Take Off?" Huang writes:

"China's take-off in economic growth starting in the late 1970s and its poverty reduction for the next couple of decades was completely a function of its rural developments and its internal reforms in general. During the golden era of rural industry in the 1980s, China had none of what are often thought of as the requisite features of the China growth model, like massive state-controlled infrastructural investments and mercantilism." This was the time period when the agricultural sector was allowed to operate under a market framework, and as agricultural output exploded, rural workers moved to employment in the "township and village enterprises." Huang makes a strong argument that these enterprises should be thought of a privately owned firms, operating with what was in many ways a private-sector financial market.

But in the 1990s, the emphasis of China's economy began to change. New leaders favoured urban development over rural development, and they cut the township and village enterprises down to size by re-nationalizing their sources of finance They began to reform the money-losing state-owned enterprises that still dominated China's urban economy as of the early 1990s. They moved China toward joining the World Trade Organization, which happened in 2001.

But this process of change brought an unexpected macroeconomic imbalance. As Dennis Tao Yang point out in his JEP paper, "Aggregate Savings and External Imbalances in China," China's 11th Five-Year Plan for the years from 2006-2010 called for trade to be in balance overall--clearly an expectation that was not close to being met. Yang looks at a variety of reasons why savings rates took off in China: for example, after China joined the WTO in 2001, exports took off, but firms lacked useful ways in China's underdeveloped financial system to pass these savings to the household sector; as exports took off, China's government received an unexpectedly huge surplus, with budget surpluses upward of 8% of GDP; and households, concerned about retirement and health costs for themselves and their families, and with little access to loans for mortgages or consumer durables, continued to save at very high rates. Yang notes that in China, this combination of outcomes is sometimes criticized as the "Nation Rich, People Poor" policy.

Thus, although China's economy continues to grow rapidly, it is faced with many challenges. Along with the macroeconomic imbalances emphasized by Yang, Xin Meng raises another cluster of issues in her paper, "Labour Market Outcomes and Reforms in China": the extraordinary back-and-forth migration from rural to urban areas, now at well over 100 million people per year, and perhaps headed much higher; the growing inequalities in wages as labour markets move away from the administratively determined wages that were so common even just 20 years ago; the inequalities being created by the spread of education; and China's coming demographic bulge with many elderly and few young workers--a hangover of the one-child rules to limit population growth.

With little effort, one can compile quite a list of economic difficulties facing China: macroeconomic imbalances, an underdeveloped financial sector, inequalities in wages and across rural and urban areas, the demographic bulge, corruption, environmental problems, and more. Still, with all that said, it's worth remembering that China's economy still has enormous potential upside. China started from such a low per capita GDP back in 1978 that even now, productivity levels are only about 20% of the U.S. level. In yet another JEP paper, "Understanding China's Growth: Past, Present, and Future," Xiaodong Zhu points out that when Japan and Korea and Taiwan had their rapid spurts of economic growth int he 1950s and 1960s and 1970s, they were essentially raising their productivity levels from 40-50% of the U.S. level up to 70-80% of the U.S. level. In other words, China is still far below the level that was the take-off point of rapid growth for countries like Japan, Korea and Taiwan. As Zhu points out, China is making enormous investments in education, physical capital investment, and research and development. In many ways, it is laying a framework for continued growth.

Surely, many things could go wrong for China's economy. For continued growth, it will need to transform its economy again and again. But it also seems to me that hundreds of millions of people in China have developed a sense of possibility, and of what their economic lives could hold for them. China's future growth is sure to have fits and starts, like every country, but its economy continues to have enormous momentum toward a much higher standard of living.

Extract adapted from "China's Economic Growth: A Different Storyline" By Timothy Taylor. November, 2012

https://conversableeconomist.blogspot.com/2012/11/chinas-economic-growth-different.html

Essay Question 14 (Level 1)

Read the extract below and then answer the question:

- **Analyse the importance of statistics in shaping policy decisions**
- **To what extent is a carbon tax a mutually agreeable policy to both climate change stakeholders and lower income households?**

Your answer will be assessed taking into account your ability to construct a reasoned, insightful and logically consistent argument with clarity and precision.

How to Slow Climate Change Without Hurting the Poor

"Energy is the lifeblood of any economy," writes H. Sterling Burnett, a fellow at the Heartland Institute. "A carbon tax would increase energy prices and thus cost jobs, making it difficult U.S. companies to compete with foreign rivals and punishing the poor."

The Manhattan Institute's Robert Bryce agrees. In an article for the National Review, he tells us that a carbon tax would "disproportionately hurt low-income consumers," especially those who "live in rural areas and must drive long distances to get to and from their job sites."

The American Energy Alliance echoes that sentiment, placing the "it will hurt the poor" argument in the third spot on a list of 10 reasons to oppose carbon taxes:

The carbon tax is by nature regressive, because it will raise the prices of gasoline, electricity, and other goods by the same dollar amount for all consumers, regardless of their incomes. This disproportionately affects the poor, because energy costs are a bigger portion of their overall budgets. A carbon tax will therefore hurt low-income families and seniors more than it will hurt middle- and upper-class households.

It is true, as we will see, that poor households do devote larger shares of their incomes to energy than do those with higher incomes, but there is more to the story than that. If we properly measure the impacts of carbon pricing and look at the full range of policy alternatives, there is no reason why concern for the poor should block policies to protect the environment.

The wrong way to help the poor

Let's begin with the conventional wisdom, which holds that low-income households would be disproportionately impacted by a carbon tax since they devote a relatively high share of their incomes to energy.

…

In other words, as you move up the income ladder, a smaller portion of your budget goes to energy, but you still emit more. As a result, the top income quintile is responsible for almost 35 percent of total emissions, compared to just under 10 percent for the lowest quintile.

Even if we take these numbers at face value, it is clear that forgoing a carbon tax in order to keep energy prices low is an absurdly inefficient way to help the poor. Based on their share of national emissions, the top two income quintiles would capture 58 percent of the benefits of such a policy, compared to just 24 percent for the bottom two quintiles. The very richest households would gain three-and-a-half times more than the very poorest.

Furthermore, looking only at incomes and energy use gives a misleading picture of the degree to which the effects of a carbon tax would be concentrated on the poor. A more recent study by Julie Anne Cronin, Don Fullerton, and Steven E. Sexton took a different approach. Cronin et al. considered not only the direct impact of a carbon tax on household energy prices, but also indirect impacts on the prices of goods like housing, food, and clothing. In addition to income, they also looked at the impact of carbon taxes in proportion to household consumption expenditures, which are more stable from year to year than incomes. They also accounted for the fact that transfer payments to low-income households are indexed to rise automatically when prices increase, whether because of general inflation or due to a policy change like a carbon tax.

When all of those factors are considered, Cronin et al. found that the impact of a carbon tax is more equally distributed in proportion to household income and consumption than the conventional wisdom assumes. The burden of a carbon tax as a percentage of household income varies only slightly, from 0.54 percent of income for the poorest income decile to 0.46 percent of income for the wealthiest decile. If the calculation is done as a percentage of consumption rather than a percentage of income, the impact of a carbon tax on wealthy households is actually proportionally greater than on poor households.

If we judge by the Cronin method rather than the earlier Grainger method, the idea of helping the poor by keeping carbon prices low is even more suspect. According to the Cronin data, the top two income quintiles would capture 77 percent of the benefit of forgoing a carbon tax, rather than the 58 percent they would capture based on the older data. Meanwhile, the poorest two income quintiles would receive only 10 percent of the benefit of a low-price policy, rather than the 24 percent they would get based on the older data.

Still, though, a carbon tax would have some adverse effect on the poor, even if its impact would not be as regressive as the conventional wisdom suggests. If forgoing a carbon tax is the wrong way to help the poor, what is the right way?

How to help the poor and the planet

The right way to assist low-income families would be to give them extra income to pay the higher prices that a carbon tax would bring. Every serious carbon pricing proposal that I have seen includes some such compensation scheme.

For example, the Citizens' Climate Lobby, one of the leading backers of a carbon tax, proposes distributing the tax revenue equally among the entire population as a "citizen's dividend." A group of 45 prominent economists recently wrote an open letter in support of a carbon tax that would take the same approach.

Alternatively, some favour a revenue-neutral tax swap that would offset carbon tax revenues by reducing the rates of other taxes. If enough of the rate reductions were focused on payroll taxes or other taxes that are disproportionately burdensome for low-wage households, the net impacts of a revenue-neutral tax swap could be made neutral with respect to income, or even moderately progressive. Still other carbon tax backers propose distributing all or part of the compensation in the form of increased benefits for existing income-support programs, such as food stamps, Social Security, and the earned income tax credit.

Finally, some backers favour spending carbon tax revenues to address climate change directly, for example, by investing in clean-energy infrastructure or adaptation. If the benefits of slowing climate change are enjoyed equally by everyone, regardless of income, the distributional effects of such a policy would be similar to those of a tax-and-dividend scheme. If, as is sometimes claimed, climate change hurts the poor disproportionately, using carbon tax revenue for climate mitigation would could be even more progressive than a citizens' dividend.

These are not either-or options. Carbon tax revenue could be divided in some way among all of them. In a report for the Brookings Institution, Aparna Mathur and Adele Morris calculate that compensating low-income households for the impact of a carbon tax could take as little as 11 percent of the tax revenues. In an analysis of the 2018 Market Choice Act, researchers from Columbia University and Rice University found that allocating 10 percent of carbon tax revenue to transfers to the lowest 20 percent of income earners increased household wealth and especially benefited younger workers.

However, Cronin et al. add a big caveat. They point out that not all families in a given income bracket are equally affected. Those who live in temperate climates use less energy for heating and cooling than do those in more severe climates. People who commute to jobs use more energy than retirees with equal incomes, and so on. The impacts from family to family within an income bracket can vary more than the average effect of the tax across income brackets. The implication is that to be sure that most in the poorest quintile were not hurt, it would be necessary to spend more on compensation than Mathur and Morris's 11 percent, or to target compensation to regions or activities with high carbon consumption.

One final point regarding compensation: The basic point of carbon pricing is to incentivize conservation of energy, investments in low-carbon technology, and other behaviours that reduce emissions. There is a trade-off between compensation and incentives. On the one hand, to make compensation more effective, it makes sense to tailor it to the specific circumstances of beneficiaries, so that fewer are undercompensated or overcompensated. On the other hand, it is important not to allow the compensation plan itself to undermine incentives.

For example, low-wage workers who have to drive a long way to their jobs will be more severely impacted by a carbon tax than those who have access to public transportation or can work from home. It would be a mistake, though, to automatically offer extra compensation in proportion to miles driven, or to provide vouchers to allow purchase of gasoline at pre-tax prices. Any such forms of compensation would remove incentives to move closer to work, use public transportation, or buy a more efficient car. Similarly, fully compensating people who live in hot or cold climates for their extra home heating costs could erode incentives to make their homes more energy efficient or even to move to more temperate areas.

Extract adapted from "How to Slow Climate Change Without Hurting the Poor" By Ed Dolan. March, 2019.

https://dolanecon.blogspot.com/2019/03/how-to-slow-climate-change-without.html

Essay Question 15 (Level 3)

Read the extract below taken from "On the Principles of Political Economy and Taxation" and then answer the question:

Analyse the relation between the immobility of capital between nations and the theory of comparative advantage?

Your answer will be assessed taking into account your ability to construct a reasoned, insightful and logically consistent argument with clarity and precision.

Under a system of perfectly free commerce, each country naturally devotes its capital and labour to such employments as are most beneficial to each. This pursuit of individual advantage is admirably connected with the universal good of the whole. By stimulating industry, by rewarding ingenuity, and by using most efficaciously the peculiar powers bestowed by nature, it distributes labour most effectively and most economically: while, by increasing the general mass of productions, it diffuses general benefit, and binds together, by one common tie of interest and intercourse, the universal society of nations throughout the civilized world. It is this principle which determines that wine shall be made in France and Portugal, that corn shall be grown in America and Poland, and that hardware and other goods shall be manufactured in England.

In one and the same country, profits are, generally speaking, always on the same level; or differ only as the employment of capital may be more or less secure and agreeable. It is not so between different countries. If the profits of capital employed in Yorkshire, should exceed those of capital employed in London, capital would speedily move from London to Yorkshire, and an equality of profits would be effected; but if in consequence of the diminished rate of production in the lands of England, from the increase of capital and population, wages should rise, and profits fall, it would not follow that capital and population would necessarily move from England to Holland, or Spain, or Russia, where profits might be higher.

If Portugal had no commercial connexion with other countries, instead of employing a great part of her capital and industry in the production of wines, with which she purchases for her own use the cloth and hardware of other countries, she would be obliged to devote a part of that capital to the manufacture of those commodities, which she would thus obtain probably inferior in quality as well as quantity.

The quantity of wine which she shall give in exchange for the cloth of England, is not determined by the respective quantities of labour devoted to the production of each, as it would be, if both commodities were manufactured in England, or both in Portugal.

England may be so circumstanced, that to produce the cloth may require the labour of 100 men for one year; and if she attempted to make the wine, it might require the labour of 120 men for the same time. England would therefore find it her interest to import wine, and to purchase it by the exportation of cloth.

To produce the wine in Portugal, might require only the labour of 80 men for one year, and to produce the cloth in the same country, might require the labour of 90 men for the same time. It would therefore be advantageous for her to export wine in exchange for cloth. This exchange might even take place, notwithstanding that the commodity imported by Portugal could be produced there with less labour than in England. Though she could make the cloth with the labour of 90 men, she would import it from a country where it required the labour of 100 men to produce it, because it would be advantageous to her rather to employ her capital in the production of wine, for which she would obtain more cloth from England, than she could produce by diverting a portion of her capital from the cultivation of vines to the manufacture of cloth.

Thus, England would give the produce of the labour of 100 men, for the produce of the labour of 80. Such an exchange could not take place between the individuals of the same country. The labour of 100 Englishmen cannot be given for that of 80 Englishmen, but the produce of the labour of 100 Englishmen may be given for the produce of the labour of 80 Portuguese, 60 Russians, or 120 East Indians. The difference in this respect, between a single country and many, is easily accounted for, by considering the difficulty with which capital moves from one country to another, to seek a more profitable employment, and the activity with which it invariably passes from one province to another in the same country.

It would undoubtedly be advantageous to the capitalists of England, and to the consumers in both countries, that under such circumstances, the wine and the cloth should both be made in Portugal, and therefore that the capital and labour of

England employed in making cloth, should be removed to Portugal for that purpose. In that case, the relative value of these commodities would be regulated by the same principle, as if one were the produce of Yorkshire, and the other of London: and in every other case, if capital freely flowed towards those countries where it could be most profitably employed, there could be no difference in the rate of profit, and no other difference in the real or labour price of commodities, than the additional quantity of labour required to convey them to the various markets where they were to be sold.

Extract adapted from "On the Principles of Political Economy and Taxation" By David Ricardo. 1817

Essay Question 16 (Level 3)

Read the extract below taken from "Das Kapital, Volume 1" and then answer the question:

Analyse the relationship between the value of a commodity and the labour used to produce it.

Your answer will be assessed taking into account your ability to construct a reasoned, insightful and logically consistent argument with clarity and precision.

Some people might think that if the value of a commodity is determined by the quantity of labour spent on it, the more idle and unskilful the labourer, the more valuable would his commodity be, because more time would be required in its production. The labour, however, that forms the substance of value, is homogeneous human labour, expenditure of one uniform labour power. The total labour power of society, which is embodied in the sum total of the values of all commodities produced by that society, counts here as one homogeneous mass of human labour power, composed though it be of innumerable individual units. Each of these units is the same as any other, so far as it has the character of the average labour power of society, and takes effect as such; that is, so far as it requires for producing a commodity, no more time than is needed on an average, no more than is socially necessary. The labour time socially necessary is that required to produce an article under the normal conditions of production, and with the average degree of skill and intensity prevalent at the time. The introduction of power-looms into England probably reduced by one-half the labour required to weave a given quantity of yarn into cloth. The handloom weavers, as a matter of fact, continued to require the same time as before; but for all that, the product of one hour of their labour represented after the change only half an hour's social labour, and consequently fell to one-half its former value.

We see then that that which determines the magnitude of the value of any article is the amount of labour socially necessary, or the labour time socially necessary for its production. Each individual commodity, in this connexion, is to be considered as an average sample of its class. Commodities, therefore, in which equal quantities of labour are embodied, or which can be produced in the same time, have the same value. The value of one commodity is to the value of any other, as the labour time necessary for the production of the one is to that necessary for the production of the other. "As values, all commodities are only definite masses of congealed labour time."

The value of a commodity would therefore remain constant, if the labour time required for its production also remained constant. But the latter changes with every variation in the productiveness of labour. This productiveness is determined by various circumstances, amongst others, by the average amount of skill of the workmen, the state of science, and the degree of its practical application, the social organisation of production, the extent and capabilities of the means of production, and by physical conditions. For example, the same amount of labour in favourable seasons is embodied in 8 bushels of corn, and in unfavourable, only in four. The same labour extracts from rich mines more metal than from poor mines. Diamonds are of very rare occurrence on the earth's surface, and hence their discovery costs, on an average, a great deal of labour time. Consequently, much labour is represented in a small compass. Jacob doubts whether gold has ever been paid for at its full value. This applies still more to diamonds. According to Eschwege, the total produce of the Brazilian diamond mines for the eighty years, ending in 1823, had not realised the price of one-and-a-half years' average produce of the sugar and coffee plantations of the same country, although the diamonds cost much more labour, and therefore represented more value. With richer mines, the same quantity of labour would embody itself in more diamonds, and their value would fall. If we could succeed at a small expenditure of labour, in converting carbon into diamonds, their value might fall below that of bricks. In general, the greater the productiveness of labour, the less is the labour time required for the production of an article, the less is the amount of labour crystallised in that article, and the less is its value; and vice versa, the less the productiveness of labour, the greater is the labour time required for the production of an article, and the greater is its value. The value of a commodity, therefore, varies directly as the quantity, and inversely as the productiveness, of the labour incorporated in it.

A thing can be a use value, without having value. This is the case whenever its utility to man is not due to labour. Such are air, virgin soil, natural meadows. A thing can be useful, and the product of human labour, without being a commodity. Whoever directly satisfies his wants with the produce of his own labour, creates, indeed, use values, but not commodities.

In order to produce the latter, he must not only produce use values, but use values for others, social use values. (And not only for others, without more. The mediaeval peasant produced quit-rent-corn for his feudal lord and tithe-corn for his parson. But neither the quit-rent-corn nor the tithe-corn became commodities by reason of the fact that they had been produced for others. To become a commodity a product must be transferred to another, whom it will serve as a use value, by means of an exchange.) Lastly nothing can have value, without being an object of utility. If the thing is useless, so is the labour contained in it; the labour does not count as labour, and therefore creates no value.

Extract adapted from "Das Kapital, Volume 1 (1867)" By Karl Marx

Essay Question 17 (Level 2)

Read the extract below and then answer the question:

"Rising inequality hampers economic growth "

By considering the extract given, to what extent is the statement above supported by evidence and economic theory?

Your answer will be assessed taking into account your ability to construct a reasoned, insightful and logically consistent argument with clarity and precision.

Those who find the rise in income inequality over the last few decades to be concerning, like me, can find themselves facing the "so what?" question. Is my concern over rising inequality an ethical or perhaps an aesthetic judgement, and thus a personal preference where economics really doesn't have much guidance to offer? Faced with this possibility, the temptation arises to claim the following syllogism: 1) We have experienced greater inequality, which is undesirable. 2) We have experiences slower economic growth, which is undesirable. 3) Therefore, greater inequality causes slower economic growth.

A variety of studies have undertaken to prove a connection from inequality to slower growth, but a full reading of the available evidence is that the evidence on this connection is inconclusive. For example, the OECD has recently published a report called "In It Together: Why Less Inequality Benefits All," and Chapter 3, titled "The Effect of Income Inequality on Economic Growth," offers an OECD analysis seeking to connect the two. But before presenting the new study, the OECD report has the honesty and forthrightness to point out that the full body of literature on this subject is inconclusive as whether such a relationship even exists--and if so, in what direction the relationship goes.

The report first points out (pp. 60-61) that as a matter of theory, one can think up arguments why greater inequality might be associated with less growth, or might be associated with more growth. For example, inequality could result less growth if: 1) People become upset about rising inequality and react by demanding regulations and redistributions that slow down the ability of an economy to produce growth; 2) A high degree of persistent inequality will limit the ability and incentives of those in the lower part of the income distribution to obtain more education and job experience; or 3) It may be that development and widespread adoption of new technologies requires demand from a broad middle class, and greater inequality could limit the extent of the middle class.

In passing, it's worth noting that the first reason falls into the category of "frustrated people killing the goose that lays the golden eggs." In other words, finding a correlation between rising inequality and slower growth could be a sign of dysfunctional responses to the rise in inequality.

On the other side, inequality could in theory be associated with faster economic growth if: 1) Higher inequality provides greater incentives for people to get educated, work harder, and take risks, which could lead to innovations that boost growth; 2) Those with high incomes tend to save more, and so an unequal distribution of income will tend to have more high savers, which in turn spurs capital accumulation in the economy. The report doesn't mention a third hypothesis that seems relevant in a number of developing economies, which is that fast growth may first emerge in certain regions or industries, leading to greater inequality for a time, before the gains from that growth diffuse more widely across the economy.

Given the competing theoretical explanations, what does the actual evidence say? The OECD writes (pp. 61-62):

The large empirical literature attempting to summarize the direction in which inequality affects growth is summarised in the literature review in Cingano (2014, Annex II). That survey highlights that there is no consensus on the sign and strength of the relationship; furthermore, few works seek to identify which of the possible theoretical effects is at work. This is partly tradeable to the multiple empirical challenges facing this literature.

The report then goes on to discuss issues like: 1) variations in estimation methods, including whether the analyst looks at one country over time, multiple countries at a point in time, or multiple countries over time, along with the statistical tools used; 2) in many countries around the world, the data on income distribution is not measured well, not measured consistently over time, and not measured in ways that are easily comparable to other countries; 3) in empirical studies the already-weak data on inequality is often boiled down into a single number, like a Gini coefficient or a ratio between those in the 90th and 10th income percentiles, a simplification that might miss what is happening; 4) the connections between income inequality and growth might differ across groups of countries (like high-income and low-income countries), and looking at all countries together averages out these various effects; and 5) whether (and how) the researcher should take into account factors like the extent of progressive taxation and redistribution, the extent of financial markets, or the degree of economic and social mobility over time.

There's an old saying that "absence of evidence is not evidence of absence," in other words, the fact that the existing evidence doesn't firmly show a connection from greater inequality to slower growth is not proof that such a connection doesn't exist. But anyone who has looked at economic studies on the determinants of economic growth knows that the problem of finding out what influences growth is very difficult, and the solutions aren't always obvious. For example, the OECD study argues that inequality leads to less investment in human capital at the bottom part of the income distribution. If this result holds up in further study, an obvious answer is not to focus on inequality directly, but instead to focus on additional support for human capital accumulation for those most in need.

There are a few common patterns in economic growth. All high-income countries have near-universal K-12 public education to build up human capital, along with encouragement of higher education. All high-income countries have economies where most jobs are interrelated with private and public capital investment, thus leading to higher productivity and wages. All high-income economies are relatively open to foreign trade. In addition, high-growth economies are societies that are willing to allow and even encourage a reasonable amount of disruption to existing patterns of jobs, consumption, and ownership. After all, economic growth means change.

On the other hand, it's also true that fast-growing countries around the world, either now or in the past, show a wide range of levels and trends of inequality, as well as considerable variation in the extent of government regulation and control, patterns of taxation and redistribution, structure of financial sector, and much more. Consider the pattern of China's fast economic growth in recent decades, with rising inequality and an evolving mixture of private initiative and government control. At least to me, China looks like a situation where growth is causing inequality, not where inequality is slowing growth. It may be that the question of "does inequality slow down economic growth" is too broad and diffuse to be useful. Instead, those of us who care about both the rise in inequality and the slowdown in economic growth should be looking for policies to address both goals, without presuming that substantial overlap will always occur between them.

Extract adapted from "Does Inequality Reduce Economic Growth: A Skeptical View" By Timothy Taylor. May, 2015

https://conversableeconomist.blogspot.com/search?q=inequality+

Essay Question 18 (Level 1)

Read the extract below and then answer the question:

Critically evaluate the importance of behavioural nudges in driving effective public policies

Your answer will be assessed taking into account your ability to construct a reasoned, insightful and logically consistent argument with clarity and precision.

A considerable body of evidence suggests that people's decisions are affected by how a choice is presented, or what the default option looks like. There's a reason that grocery stores put some products at eye-level and some near the floor, or why the staples like milk and eggs are often far from the door (so you have to walk through the store to grab them), or why the checkout counters have nearby racks of candy. There's a reason that gas stations sometimes advertise that gas is 5 cents a gallon less if you pay cash, but never advertise that gas is 5 cents more per gallon if you don't pay cash. There's a reason that many people have their employer automatically deduct money from pay checks for their retirement accounts, rather than trying to make their own monthly or annual payments to that same account.

Once you have admitted that people's decisions are affected by these kinds of factors, an obvious question is whether public policy might make use of how decisions are presented to influence behavior. A decade ago, in 2007, Richard H. Thaler and Cass R. Sunstein brought this possibility to public attention in their book Nudge: Improving Decisions About Health, Wealth, and Happiness.

As one example of a "nudge" policy, consider organ donation. In opinion polls, people overwhelmingly support being an organ donor. But in practice, fewer than half of adults are actually signed up. A nudge policy might suggest that all driver be automatically enrolled as organ donors--with a choice to opt out if they wish to do so. In other words, instead of framing the choice as "do you want to sign up to be an organ donor?", the choice would become "do you want to opt out of being an organ donor?" As long as the choice is presented clearly, it's hard to argue that anyone's personal autonomy is being violated by the alternative phrasing of the question. But the alternative phrasing would lead to more organ donors--and the United States alone currently has about 100,000 people on waiting lists for organ transplants.

Perhaps the best-known example is that employers can either offer workers the option to enrol in a retirement savings plan, or they can automatically enrol workers in a retirement savings plans, with a choice to opt out. Phrasing the choice differently has a big effect on behavior. And a lot of people who never quite got around to signing up for the retirement plan end up regretting that choice when it's too late in life to do much about it.

Once you start thinking about nudging, possibilities blossom. Along with applications to organ donation and saving, Holmes discusses nudges related to home energy use, willingness to use generic drugs, choice of when to start receiving Social Security, requiring a common and simpler format for information about mortgages or phone contracts to make them easier to comprehend and compare,

Holmes reports: "At last count, more than 60 government departments and international agencies have established "nudge units" tasked with finding and pulling the right behavioural levers to accomplish everything from increasing retirement savings to boosting diversity in military recruits to encouraging people to get vaccinated against flu. The United Kingdom's Behavioural Insights Team, one of the first and largest such units, has expanded from a handful of people in 2010 to about 100 today, with global reach. Clearly, nudging has moved into the mainstream."

Three broad concerns discussed by Holmes seem worth noting. First, nudges can often be very specific to context and detail. For example, when people in the UK got a letter saying that most people pay their taxes on time, the number of tax delinquents fell sharply, but the same nudge in Ireland had no effect. Sometimes small details of a government notification--like whether the letter includes a smiley face or not--seem to have a substantial effect.

Second, the total effect of nudge policies may be only moderate. But saying that a policy won't totally solve, say, poverty or obesity hardly seems like a reason to rule out the policy.

Finally, there is a legitimate concern over the line between "nudge" policies and government paternalism. The notion that government is purposely acting in subtle ways to shift our choices is mildly disturbing. What if you just sort of forget to opt out of being an organ donor--but you actually have genuine personal objections to doing so? What if you just sort of forget to opt out of the retirement savings account, but you know that you have a health condition that is extremely likely to give you a shortened life expectancy? A nudge policy can be beneficial on average, but still lead to less desirable choices in specific cases.

Moreover, what if the goals of a nudge policy start to reach beyond goals like adequate retirement saving or use of generic drugs, and start edging into more controversial settings? One can imagine nudge policies to affect choices about abortion, or gun ownership, or joining the military, or enrolling your child in a charter school. No matter which direction these nudges are pushing, they would certainly be controversial.

In the Annual Review of Psychology for 2016, Cass Sunstein contributed an essay titled, "The Council of Psychological Advisers." It begins: "Many nations have some kind of council of economic advisers. Should they also have a council of psychological advisers? Perhaps some already do." For many people, the idea of a government council of psychological advisers seeking to set up your choices in such a way as to influence the outcome, in ways you don't even know are happening, will sound fairly creepy.

Like many people, I like to think of myself as someone who considers options and makes choices. But the reality of nudge policies calls this perception into doubt. For many real-world life choices, a truly neutral presentation of the options does not exist. There will always be a choice about the order in which options are presented, how the options are phrased, what background information is presented, what choice serves as the default option. Even when no official nudge policy exists, and all of these choices have been made for other reasons, the setting of the choice will often influence the choice that is made. It will influence me, and it will influence you, too. Thus, there isn't any escape from nudge policies. There is only a choice as to what kinds of nudges will happen--and a need for all of us to be aware of how we are being nudged and when we want to shove back by making other choices.

Extract adapted from "Nudge Policies" By Timothy Taylor. February, 2018

https://conversableeconomist.blogspot.com/search?q=nudges

Essay Question 19 (Level 2)

Read the extract below and then answer the questions:

- How has the increased use of randomised trials impacted the field of economics
- How has the new-style approach to development economics changed the way we perceive poverty, and what policy prescriptions do you think it favours?

Your answer will be assessed taking into account your ability to construct a reasoned, insightful and logically consistent argument with clarity and precision.

Several decades ago, the most common ways of thinking about problems of poor people in low-income countries involved ideas like the "poverty trap" and the "dual economy." The "poverty trap" was the idea low-income countries were close to subsistence, so it was hard for them to save and make the investments that would lead to long-term growth. The "dual economy" idea was that low-income countries had both traditional and a modern part of their economy, but the traditional part had large numbers of subsistence-level workers. Thus, if or when the modern part of the economy expanded, it could draw on this large pool of subsistence level workers and so there was no economic pressure for subsistence wages to rise. In either case, a common policy prescription was that low-income countries needed a big infusion of capital, probably from a source like the World Bank, to jump-start their economies into growth.

These older theories of economic development captured some elements of global poverty, but in many of their details and implications have proved unsatisfactory for the modern world. For example, it turns out that low-income countries often do have sufficient saving to make investments in the future. Also, in a globalizing economy, flows of private investment capital along with remittances sent back home from emigrants far outstrip official development assistance. Moreover, there have clearly been success stories in which some low-income countries have escaped the poverty trap and the dual economy and moved to rapid growth, including China, India, other nations of east Asia, Botswana, and so on.

Of course, it remains important that low-income countries avoid strangling their own economies with macroeconomic mismanagement, overregulation, or corruption. But a main focus of thinking about economic development shifted from how to funnel more resources to these countries to what kind of assistance would be most effective for the lives of the poor. The 2019 Nobel prize in economics was awarded "for their experimental approach to alleviating global poverty" to Abhijit Banerjee, Esther Duflo, and Michael Kremer. To understand the work, the Nobel committee publishes two useful starting points: a "Popular Science" easy-to-read overview called "Research to help the world's poor," and a longer and more detailed "Scientific Background" essay on "Understanding Development and Poverty Alleviation."

In thinking about the power of their research, it's perhaps useful to hearken back to long-ago discussions of basic science experiments. For example, back in 1881 Louis Pasteur wanted to test his vaccine for sheep anthrax. He exposed 50 sheep to anthrax. Of those 50, half chosen at random had been vaccinated. The vaccinated sheep lived and others died.

Social scientists have in some cases been able to use randomized trials in the past. As one recent example, the state of Oregon wanted to expand Medicaid coverage back in 2008, but it only had funding to cover an additional 10,000 people. It chose those people through a lottery, and thus set up an experiment about how having health insurance affected the health and finances of the working poor. In other cases, when certain charter high schools are oversubscribed and use a lottery to choose students, it sets up a random experiment for comparing students who gained admission to those schools with those who did not.

The 2019 laureates took this idea of social science experiments and brought it to issues of poverty and economic development. They went to India and Kenya and low-income countries around the world. They arranged with state and local governments to carry out experiments where, say, 200 villages would be selected, and then 100 of those villages at random would receive a certain policy intervention. Just dealing with the logistics of making this happen--for different interventions, in different places--would deserve a Nobel prize by itself.

Many of the individual experiments focus on quite specific policies. However, as a number of these experimental results accumulate, broader lessons become clear. For example, consider the question of how to improve educational outcomes in low-income countries. Is the problem a lack of textbooks? A lack of lunches? Absent teachers? Low-quality teachers? Irregular student attendance? An overly rigid curriculum? A lack of lights at home that make it hard for students to study?

Once you start thinking along these lines, you can think about randomized experiments that address each of these factors and others, separately and in various combinations. From the Nobel committee's "Popular Science Background":

Kremer and his colleagues took a large number of schools that needed considerable support and randomly divided them into different groups. The schools in these groups all received extra resources, but in different forms and at different times. In one study, one group was given more textbooks, while another study examined free school meals. Because chance determined which school got what, there were no average differences between the different groups at the start of the experiment. The researchers could thus credibly link later differences in learning outcomes to the various forms of support. The experiments showed that neither more textbooks nor free school meals made any difference to learning outcomes. If the textbooks had any positive effect, it only applied to the very best pupils.

Later field experiments have shown that the primary problem in many low-income countries is not a lack of resources. Instead, the biggest problem is that teaching is not sufficiently adapted to the pupils' needs. In the first of these experiments, Banerjee, Duflo et al. studied remedial tutoring programmes for pupils in two Indian cities. Schools in Mumbai and Vadodara were given access to new teaching assistants who would support children with special needs. These schools were ingeniously and randomly placed in different groups, allowing the researchers to credibly measure the effects of teaching assistants. The experiment clearly showed that help targeting the weakest pupils was an effective measure in the short and medium term.

Such experiments have been done in a wide range of contexts. For example, what about issues of improving health?

One important issue is whether medicine and healthcare should be charged for and, if so, what they should cost. A field experiment by Kremer and co-author investigated how the demand for deworming pills for parasitic infections was affected by price. They found that 75 per cent of parents gave their children these pills when the medicine was free, compared to 18 per cent when they cost less than a US dollar, which is still heavily subsidised. Subsequently, many similar experiments have found the same thing: poor people are extremely price-sensitive regarding investments in preventive healthcare....

Low service quality is another explanation why poor families invest so little in preventive measures. One example is that staff at the health centres that are responsible for vaccinations are often absent from work. Banerjee, Duflo et al. investigated whether mobile vaccination clinics – where the care staff were always on site – could fix this problem. Vaccination rates tripled in the villages that were randomly selected to have access to these clinics, at 18 per cent compared to 6 per cent. This increased further, to 39 per cent, if families received a bag of lentils as a bonus when they vaccinated their children. Because the mobile clinic had a high level of fixed costs, the total cost per vaccination actually halved, despite the additional expense of the lentils.

How much do the lives of low-income people change from receiving access to credit? For example, does it change their consumption, or encourage them to start a business? If farmers had access to credit, would they be more likely to invest in fertilizer and expand their output?

As the body of experimental evidence accumulates, it begins to open windows on the lives of people in low-income countries, on issues of how they are actually making decisions and what constraints matter most to them. The old-style approach to development economics of sending money to low-income countries is replaced by policies aimed at specific outcomes: education, health, credit, use of technology. When it's fairly clear what really matters or what really helps, and the policies are expanded broadly, they can still be rolled out over a few years in a randomized way, which allows researchers to compare effects of those who experience the policies sooner to those who experienced them later. This approach to economic development has a deeply evidence-based practicality.

Extract adapted from "A Nobel for the Experimental Approach to Global Poverty for Banerjee, Duflo, and Kremer" By Timothy Taylor. October, 2019

https://conversableeconomist.blogspot.com/2019/10/a-nobel-for-experimental-approach-to.html

Essay Question 20 (Level 2)

Read the extract below and then answer the questions:

Should the UK adopt a wealth tax and if they should, then what factors should they consider for the design of the tax?

Your answer will be assessed taking into account your ability to construct a reasoned, insightful and logically consistent argument with clarity and precision.

A wealth tax is what it sounds like: a tax imposed not on income, but on wealth. The standard economic definition of wealth includes both nonfinancial assets like real estate and financial assets like stocks and bonds. Thus, a wealth tax doesn't care if the value of someone's wealth went up or down in the last year It is not a tax on the transfer of wealth to others, like an inheritance tax or a gift tax. It is just imposed on the amount of wealth.

In the US, property taxes are a cousin of a part of a broader wealth tax, in the sense that they are imposed annually on the value of a property, whether the value rises or falls. But they are not at true wealth tax in the sense that they don't differentiate between someone who own their home debt-free--and thus all the value of the home is wealth--and someone who is still paying off the mortgage, where only the equity you have in your home is wealth. The inheritance tax is also a form of a wealth tax.

Back in 1990, 12 high-income countries had wealth taxes. By 2017, that had dropped to four: France, Norway, Spain, and Switzerland (In 2018, France changed its wealth tax so that it applied only to real estate, not to financial assets.) The OECD describes the reasons why other countries have been dropping wealth taxes, along with providing a balanced pro-and-con of the arguments over wealth taxes, in its report The Role and Design of Net Wealth Taxes in the OECD (April 2018).

For the OECD, the bottom line is that it is reasonable for policymakers to be concerned about the rising inequality of wealth and large concentrations of wealth. But it also points out that if a country has reasonable methods of taxing capital gains, inheritances, intergenerational gifts, and property, a combination of these approaches are typically preferable to a wealth tax. Here, I want to use the OECD report to dig a little deeper into what wealth taxes mean, and some of the practical problems they present.

The most prominent proposals for a US wealth tax would apply only to those with extreme wealth, like those with more than $50 million in wealth. However, European countries typically imposed wealth taxes at much lower levels of wealth.

It's interesting, then, that in these European countries the wealth tax generally accounted for only a small amount of government revenue. The OECD writes: "In 2016, tax revenues from individual net wealth taxes ranged from 0.2% of GDP in Spain to 1.0% of GDP in Switzerland."

The fact that wealth taxes collect relatively little is part of the reason that a number of countries decided that they weren't worth the bother. In addition, it suggests that a US wealth tax which doesn't kick in until $50 million in wealth or more will not raise meaningfully large amounts of revenue.

Why do wealth taxes imposed on what seem to be quite low levels of wealth collect so little revenue in various European countries, especially during the last few decades when high-wealth individuals as a group have done pretty well? The answer seems to be that when countries impose a wealth tax, they often typically create a lot of exemptions for certain kind of wealth that aren't covered by the tax. Each of these exemptions has a reasonable-sounding basis. But every exception also creates a potential loophole.

For example, a number of common exemptions are based on "liquidity" problems, which in this context refers to the idea that we don't want people to have to sell their homes to pay the wealth tax, and we don't want family businesses or farms that are maybe hitting a tough patch to have to be sold off because of the wealth tax. Thus, many European countries exempt a primary residence from the wealth tax (and instead apply a property tax).

Countries also often exempt the value of a business in which you are actively working, which of course means a potentially voluminous set of rules for what "actually working" means.

Another common exemption is that wealth tax is usually not applied to the value of pensions and retirement savings. One can sympathize with this, but also recognize that it leads to potential issues. As the OECD notes: "Pension assets typically get full relief under net wealth taxes. ... However, this creates inequities between different taxpayers, raises fairness concerns, and creates tax planning opportunities. .... "

What other incentives does a wealth tax create? Here are some examples that often are not included in the discussion:

While we often think of a wealth tax as being applied to those who have already "made it" and accumulated a fortune, it's worth remembering that when a small- or medium-sized business is trying to get established, or going through hard times, it may lead to a situation where the overall value of the asset is substantial, but profits may be near-zero or even negative for a time. But at least in theory, a wealth tax would still be owed.

A wealth tax will tend to encourage borrowing. Total wealth is equal to the value of assets minus the value of debts. Thus, one way to avoid a wealth tax is to borrow a lot of money, in ways that may or may not be socially beneficial.

To get a fair picture of a wealth tax, one needs to look at it in the context of all the other taxes that exist, along with different situations that arise. It's quite possible for there to be situations where when the wealth tax is added, someone who saves more will actually reduce their wealth. The OECD notes: "In France and Spain, METRs [marginal effective tax rates] reached values above 100%, which means that the entire real return is taxed away and that by saving people actually reduce the real value of their wealth." Indeed, France recently decided to apply its wealth tax just to certain kinds of property wealth, not financial wealth, for this reason. Indeed, many wealth taxes have provisions that if the combined tax burden gets too high, then the wealth tax gets scaled back.

A wealth tax is typically at a fairly low rate, like 1-2%, in recognition of the fact that it will be imposed every year. But if a wealthy person is investing in a way that has low risk and low returns, this wealth tax could completely swallow up low return, while having no effect on higher returns. In general, setting up a situation where people receive no gain from saving is not usually regarded as a good set of incentives.

On the other side, it is sometimes argued that a wealth tax will encourage the wealthy to make more productive use of their wealth:

"For instance, if a household owns land which is not being used and therefore does not generate income, no income tax will be payable on it. However, if a wealth tax is levied, the household will have an incentive to make a more productive use of their land or to sell it to someone who will ... The argument here is that wealth taxes do not discourage investment per se but discourage investments in low-yielding assets and reinforce the incentives to invest in higher-yielding assets because there is an additional cost to holding assets, which is not linked to the return they generate."

A wealth tax may not seem especially fair if applied across people who started in similar circumstances. As one example, imagine two adults who split a large inheritance. One heir spends the money. The other heir tries to invest, with some success, in creating new technology and businesses and jobs. The spender depletes the inheritance and thus avoids the wealth tax. More broadly, consider wealth from a variety of sources: inherited financial wealth, inheriting a family business, inheriting a family-owned piece of property, starting and running a business, investing in businesses run by others, investing in property that increases in value over time, wealth from having a patent on an invention, wealth from producing a book or music or movie with high sales. A wealth tax treats all of these the same.

The practicalities of imposing a wealth tax can be nontrivial. It means updating the value of assets and debts every year. If the assets are something that is bought and sold in financial markets, like shares of stock, then updating the value is easy. But updating the value of an expensive house or piece of property on an annual basis isn't easy. Updating the value of art or jewellery owned by a wealthy person isn't easy. Updating the value of a privately owned business isn't easy. Updating the current value of assets held in other countries can be hard, too. In general, it's a lot easier to track flows of income than it is to measure changes in asset values.

Extract adapted from "Why Have Other Countries Been Dropping Their Wealth Taxes?" By Timothy Taylor. February, 2019

https://conversableeconomist.blogspot.com/search?q=wealth+tax

Concluding Remarks

Congratulations!

You have finished The Complete ECAA Guide, which hopefully has guided you through all the content needed to score highly in the exam. If you did find this guide beneficial in your preparation, we would greatly appreciate it if you could leave a review for us on Amazon.

If you have any queries or suggestions or would like to get in touch with us, please feel free to drop us an email at contact@sapienteducation.co.uk

You may also be interested in the other products that Sapient Education offers, such as an expert personal statement editing service. For more information, please visit our website: www.sapienteducation.co.uk

Best of luck for the ECAA and your university application!

The Sapient Education Team